Praise for *The Art of Conversation*:

"In this handy guide to civilized banter, Blyth reintroduces the craft of modern discourse."   —*Elle*

"*The Art of Conversation* will make your next foray into a bar or business reception much more entertaining. . . . It will help both wallflowers and those lost in cyberspace achieve conversational connections."   —*Los Angeles Times*

"Blyth makes a spirited pitch for old-fashioned talk."

—Salon.com

"Witty, eloquent and insightful, Blyth's book is a delightful encouragement to rediscover conversation as the best communication technology."   —*Publishers Weekly*

"Finally, a bit of fun by a young genius. *The Art of Conversation* is a witty meditation upon all aspects of talk. If you give it to a friend it will itself provoke hours of amusing chat as you read out her jokes and her wisdom."   —*Reader's Digest (*UK)

"A witty and thoroughly entertaining guide to the noble art of conversation."   —Katie Hickman, author of *The Aviary Gate*

"Modern men—and women—have forgotten how to engage larynx and ears. Catherine Blyth teaches the lost art with wit and charm."   —Harry Mount, author of *Carpe Diem: Put a Little Latin in Your Life*

"Get off that bloody computer and read this bloody great book. Reclaim the orgasmic pleasures of a bloody good conversation. Don't let modern technology turn you into an uncommunicative ninny: ingest this book and start conversing . . . and then start living."   —Simon Doonan, author of *Eccentric Glamour*

"Take the wittiest, most spellbinding dinner companion and put her between book covers; that's *The Art of Conversation*. . . .By turns arch, humane, historical, and hysterically funny, [Blyth] is a person you hope you'll find at the next cocktail party—or the person you'd like to be. With this book you too can skewer the bores, deliver gift-wrapped insults the victims are grateful to receive, cultivate the shrinking violets, and listen intelligently until you're the most charming person in the room."
                              —Margaret Shepherd, author of *The Art of Civilized Conversation*

© HENRYKH.COM

Catherine Blyth is a writer and editor. Her work has appeared in numerous British publications, including the *Times* and the *Daily Telegraph*. Despite her marriage to a mischievous gossip columnist, she still manages to enjoy a thriving social life

The Art of
CONVERSATION

A GUIDED TOUR OF A
NEGLECTED PLEASURE

CATHERINE BLYTH

GOTHAM
BOOKS

GOTHAM BOOKS
Published by Penguin Group (USA) Inc.
375 Hudson Street, New York, New York 10014, U.S.A.

Penguin Group (Canada), 90 Eglinton Avenue East, Suite 700, Toronto, Ontario M4P 2Y3, Canada (a
division of Pearson Penguin Canada Inc.); Penguin Books Ltd, 80 Strand, London WC2R 0RL, England;
Penguin Ireland, 25 St Stephen's Green, Dublin 2, Ireland (a division of Penguin Books Ltd); Penguin
Group (Australia), 250 Camberwell Road, Camberwell, Victoria 3124, Australia (a division of Pearson
Australia Group Pty Ltd); Penguin Books India Pvt Ltd, 11 Community Centre, Panchsheel Park,
New Delhi–110 017, India; Penguin Group (NZ), 67 Apollo Drive, Rosedale, North Shore 0632, New
Zealand (a division of Pearson New Zealand Ltd); Penguin Books (South Africa) (Pty) Ltd, 24 Sturdee
Avenue, Rosebank, Johannesburg 2196, South Africa

Penguin Books Ltd, Registered Offices: 80 Strand, London WC2R 0RL, England

Published by Gotham Books, a member of Penguin Group (USA) Inc.

Previously published as a Gotham Books hardcover edition

First trade paperback printing, January 2010

1   3   5   7   9   10   8   6   4   2

Gotham Books and the skyscraper logo are trademarks of Penguin Group (USA) Inc.

Copyright © 2009 by Catherine Blyth
All rights reserved

The Library of Congress has catalogued the hardcover edition of this book as follows:
Blyth, Catherine.
The art of conversation : a guided tour of a neglected pleasure /
by Catherine Blyth. — 1st ed.
p. cm.
ISBN 978-1-592-40419-3 (hardcover)   ISBN 978-1-592-40497-1 (paperback)
1. Conversation. I Title.
BJ2121.B59 2009
395.5'9—dc22   2008024276

Printed in the United States of America
Set in Adobe Garamond   Designed by Ginger Legato

While the author has made every effort to provide accurate telephone numbers and Internet addresses at
the time of publication, neither the publisher nor the author assumes any responsibility for errors, or for
changes that occur after publication. Further, the publisher does not have any control over and does not
assume any responsibility for author or third-party Web sites or their content.

FOR VIVIAN AND STEPHEN

CONTENTS

The Art of
CONVERSATION

INTRODUCTION

We Need to Talk

We need to talk.

When did this become a threat rather than a statement of fact? Is it a fact?

Walk into an Internet café and you might think speech obsolete. Visit a bar with wide-screen sports, eat in a Planet Hollywood, see if you can sneak a word through the Dolby Stereo barrier. On a bus, you might have no choice but to hear conversation, in babel-like halves, but would you strike one up with a stranger? Go on, I dare you.

Some say this is the age of information; others, the communication age. There is no question that our ever growing means of keeping in touch have unleashed intelligence, creativity, passion, and fun, offering countless new directions in which to stretch our hours. Yet these riches leave many of us feeling not so much lucky as time-poor, as if life were hurtling by in a fuzzy stream of images glimpsed from an accelerating car.

Fewer of us complain that conversation, especially face-to-face—for thousands of years the core of human interaction—is being pushed to the sidelines. But we should. We are losing out on one of life's greatest, certainly most useful, pleasures. One that has the power to slow and enrich the passage of time, rooting us in a shared moment as no other pastime can. Potentially.

Yet have you never sat at a dinner, waited for someone to speak, watched a glittering frost of smiles seal the silence, and wondered how innocent cutlery can sound so very like the theme from *Psycho*? What about Christmas with the family? Lunch with the boss? The mute couples who garnish restaurants, pre-cocktails, on Valentine's Day?

Surely someone had something to say. Each had a life, and a pulse, presumably. It's tempting to assume that they couldn't be bothered. A more worrying possibility is that they hadn't a clue where to begin.

If you haven't toiled in such deserts, lucky you. In my experience conversation breakdown is increasingly common, and other people are bewilderingly tolerant of it. I have seen otherwise savvy professionals struck dumb at supposed celebrations; been interviewed by Trappists posing as publishers; witnessed parties lurch from awkward chat to addled oblivion, while hosts revolve the room like circus plate spinners, frantic to keep it moving, their efforts drowned out by the crashing of bores.

Extreme measures are being taken. A friend's annual office jamboree, a fancy, candles-and-cleavage affair, was ruined by rude waiters. Until it was revealed that they were actors: the entertainment.

"But hey," said my friend, "at least it gave us something to talk about."

Fear is understandable. If great conversation enhances any situation, when it flounders, it can be hell. I love to hate my screw-ups because friends laugh at the retelling; however, alone, at night, ancient cringes still awaken spasms of shame.

So I feel for the man whom Samuel Johnson's friend, Mrs. Thrale, mocked for having the ill-breeding to complain:

*"I am invited to conversations, I go to conversations, but, alas!
I have no conversation."*

(He had acquired a fortune in—whisper it—trade.)

In his era conversation was a status symbol. Thankfully we
needn't take it so seriously, at least, not so formally. Still, even casual
chat requires a confidence that seems to be waning, and I'm sure
that in many blue-chip companies the con artist unmasked in G. K.
Chesterton's *The Club of Queer Trades* could, with discreet marketing, coin it:

*"A new trade," repeated [the detective] Grant, with a strange
exultation, "a new profession! What a pity it is immoral."*

*"But what the deuce is it?" cried Drummond and I in a
breath of blasphemy.*

*"It is," said Grant calmly, "the great new trade of the Organ-
iser of Repartee . . . a swindler of a perfectly delightful and novel
kind. He hires himself out at dinner parties to lead up to other
people's repartees. According to a preconcerted scheme (which
you may find on that piece of paper), he says the stupid things
he has arranged for himself, and his client says the clever things
arranged for him. In short, he allows himself to be scored off for
a guinea a night."*

Winning witty points may be old hat, but conversation remains
an art as well as a social duty. Somewhere along the way too many
of us seem to have dropped the idea that it is something worth striving to be good at—as if we are either born great conversationalists
or not. If only.

Conversation works in ways infinitely more various, and devi-
ous, than you might suspect. Take a closer look and you find an en-
tertainingly candid portrait of the human animal, as well as a means
to almost everything that you could wish for in life.

THE MULTITASKING MIRACLE

When it works, conversation can come close to heaven. Be it sharing a laugh with a stranger, transforming a contact into a friend; that joyful moment when you click, share a joke, or spark a new idea; or just letting off steam with someone who knows how to listen—there are countless adventures between minds out there, waiting to happen, in each encounter, each day of our lives.

Networking is part of conversation's value, although the word sounds chilly and strategic. Conversation is something bigger: It is the spontaneous business of making connections, whether for work, friendship, or pure, fleeting pleasure.

Some writers have argued that it's where the raw stuff of life is spun into art. Speech—the gift of provoking thoughts in others' minds by rapidly modulated outtakes of breath—is certainly a wonder, and conversation a miracle upon that miracle. Indeed, if evolutionary psychologists are right, it fathered language, out of grooming, the conversation of apes, when our ancestors sat about picking off fleas, flirting, working out who was boss.

But I find simpler reasons to treasure it. Get on with others, you will get on in life, and enjoy it more. Good talkers get dates, win contracts. They make job interviews fun, whichever side of the desk they are on. Furthermore, the qualities of a satisfying chat—vitality, clarity, wit, relish, tact, a light touch—are the same as we want of the people around us. Respect the rules of artful conversation and not only are you on your way to being a better person, but learn to steer discussion, to entertain not dominate, and you're on the road to power.

Conversation is brilliant at both polishing thoughts and frothing up new ones, and although professionalism encourages us to wring the maximum from meetings in minimum time, serendipity produces many of the best ideas. Since information flows better through stories than through year-end reports, censoring gossip—whether at the water cooler or on email—can dull a business's cutting edge.

Just as monarchs had their favorites and Arab rulers their salaried *nadim* ("cup companions") with whom to trade jokes and keep track of the court's mood, not to mention boost their own, so productivity and morale shot up when a Puerto Rican tobacco company started paying a cigar roller the same hourly rate to down tools, sit in the middle of the work area, read papers aloud, chatter, and clown.

There are other benefits. Paul McCartney loves talking as well as crooning to audiences because "I remember stuff that I'd forgotten for thirty years in explaining it." Holocaust survivor Alice Herz-Sommer, a 103-year-old concert pianist, would agree. Asked about her fizzing social life, she confided she wasn't avid to hear about "lives and problems" purely out of altruism or curiosity: "This is good for the brain ... better than a hundred pills."

How come she was so skilled at conversation? "Chamber music is a discussion with your partner. You have to listen."

More than words, conversation is music: Its harmony, rhythm, and flow transcend communication, flexing mind and heart, tuning us for companionship.

It doesn't have to be grave to supply life's turning points. When a young worker at Mother Teresa's Home for the Dying in Calcutta, novelist Jeffrey Eugenides was toying with taking up holy orders. But he couldn't work out why he lacked the spirit of his nice, somewhat oatmeally fellow volunteers. Until one day, strolling with a non-volunteer, he rediscovered something they had not: humor.

A beggar approached and Eugenides spurted a piety:

I said, "Jesus said that whoever asks of you, you should give something." And my friend said, "Well, obviously Jesus has never been in Calcutta."

Eugenides laughed, then quit.

At around six I had the most important conversation of my life, with a social worker who wanted to know how my sister and I would feel about another sibling. In the excitement beforehand, planning what to say, fantasizing about being a mini-Mum—painting an alphabet frieze in this new child's bedroom, reading her stories, teaching her words—on some level, I realized that just talking could change a life, all our lives—or not, if this conversation didn't work out. But it did, and we adopted Heidi.

And random collisions mean the world. A drunken chat with a writer transformed my love of books—although this matters less to me than our friendship. A crack about the predigested look of the canteen slop for which we were queuing began another; a journey on a minibus, yet another—one that led, in time, to meeting my future husband.

Most thrillingly, conversation awakens us to one another, as in this rare happy tale from the wards of the Royal Hospital for Neuro-disability:

Young man with motorbike head injury in a coma. His mum, a keen evangelical, comes every day with friends to sing "Onward, Christian Soldiers" by his bedside. She's hoping to stimulate his brain into action. It works: he comes round, but he can't speak. So they fit him up with one of those Stephen Hawking–type laptops, and the first words he speaks are: "For God's sake, Mum, shut it!"

Two minds striking can kindle something magical. In his memoir, *The Diving Bell and the Butterfly*, Jean-Dominique Bauby, condemned to speak in eye blinks after a paralyzing stroke, snared it:

My communication system disqualifies repartee: the keenest rapier grows dull and falls flat when it takes several minutes to thrust it home. By the time you strike, even you no longer understand what had seemed so witty before you started to dictate it, letter by letter ... I count this forced lack of humour one of the great drawbacks of my condition.

In short, conversation is second only to sex, a lot less hassle, and it really matters.

Perhaps your meals are a respectful communion with a television set and perhaps you like that just fine. Still, in the frame of human evolution, you're a novelty, even a weirdo. Companionship ("the sharing of bread") has ever been, if not the bread of existence, then the spirit that refreshed it, and conversation, once a broad term for "being together," used to be considered so delicious as to be a sin. Monasteries and convents forbade it and totalitarian states monitored it, because it is unruly, fun, and seems utterly instinctive.

Casanova, visiting Louis XV's palace, could hardly contain his laughter at the spectacle of the queen, dining alone at "a table that could have seated twelve," while a dozen courtiers stood watch in a silence ruptured only by this solemn exchange, when she hailed a Monsieur de Lowendal:

"Madame."
"I believe that chicken fricassee is the best of all stews."
"I am of the same opinion, madame."

But solitary dining, and living, no longer appear so unnatural.

WHY MODERN LIFE IS BAD
FOR CONVERSATION

The irony of this communication age is that we communicate less meaningfully. Not despite but because of our dizzying means of being in touch. So many exchanges are conducted via electronic go-betweens that, what with the buzz, bleeps, and blinking lights, it is easy to overlook the super-responsive information technology that is live-action; up-close-and-personal; snap, crackle, and pop talk—one that has been in research and development for thousands of years.

Communication tools may bring us together, but equally they keep us apart, not least from the here and now. Laptops, Black-Berries, and three billion mobile phones have perforated the division between public and private, and we're growing used to toting about portals of availability as if they were vital electronic organs. Men, women, and children stride about, bellowing unself-consciously into mouthpieces like deranged town criers, and entertainment permeates: Children watch films in the backs of car seats; on buses, TV screens assail passengers with cod-celebrity news; motion picture ad boards entice the riders of London underground escalators.

Today's gizmogemony alters human experience in a way that trains, planes, automobiles, even the wheel, did not—nibbling at the conditions in which we operate, confusing the real with the virtual. Inevitably, this changes us.

Compared to face-to-face, Internet communication is two-dimensional. Yet the emphasis on appearances is growing, redefining how we relate, and with it, ideas of what constitutes a relationship. Many young people happily swallow the notion that textual exchange is interaction. Avid social networker Henry Elliss claims:

> *It's only fuddy-duddies who think it'll kill socializing. Did they say that about the telephone, or faxes? It's building relationships.*

I wake up in a cold sweat sometimes—if Facebook disappeared, those friends would be gone.

If that's building, the foundations are weak. And where's the time or space to socialize, if like him, you have 453 friends to hold vigil over? You hire a barn? Or are these perhaps imaginary friends, pulses of light on a screen?

As distractions multiply, fewer receive our full attention, and nuances are neglected. We don't look at the man selling us coffee, never mind shoot the breeze; we're too busy fiddling with our iPod. I've witnessed wedding guests with more qualifications than they have chromosomes text-messaging during the vows.

Developments, yes, but progress? Although these innovations crowd out conversation, it isn't redundant; rather, like an ancient, still mighty beast, it is endangered unless we appreciate it, and carve out space for it. The nuances are no less valuable to us than they were to our forefathers, nor are the joys. Abandon them, and we miss out.

Admittedly, there are superficially sound commercial reasons why conversation should be whittled away. Business disdains it because, unless flogging goods by that unsteady Zeitgeist vehicle word of mouth, it is hard to monetarize (oh, woeful word). Worse, it guzzles airtime, face time, eye time; attention that could be consumed consuming or ogling ads. So fast-food joints have their fast-forward music, agitations of beats designed to drive you through your hapless meal and out the door as soon as possible. And J. D. Wetherspoon, owner of 691 British pubs, has announced that families will be served no more than two drinks:

Once they have finished the meal with the child, we would expect them to leave.

It is surprising formal restrictions should be necessary. Modern life may seem like a conspiracy against conversation, but we are complicit, and if we learned its skills by osmosis, this is less likely to be the case for our children. Psychologists fear that families are talking to each other less than ever, and there is plenty of evidence to support this.

Two trends pull us away from conversation: Either it is underappreciated or so highly rated that it seems daunting—as if, compared to email, it were a luxury, couture form of communication, requiring special training, perhaps at charm school (yes, these are back in vogue).

Technology plays a large part in this. We want our toys, but short-term pleasures too seldom serve long-term interests. Nobel laureate economist Gary S. Becker observed:

> *Individuals maximize welfare* as they conceive it, *whether they be selfish, altruistic, loyal, spiteful, or masochistic.*

Many twenty-first-century delights are individualistic, not to say onanistic; distractions that narrow horizons and, with them, social arteries. As Matthew Taylor of the Royal Society of Arts put it:

> *We have to ask ourselves why the internet is so good for wankers, gamblers and shoppers, and not so good for citizens and communities.*

If language was born of the evolutionary accident that our species thrived better in groups, then so, as we cease operating that way, conversation becomes less incidental. It cannot flourish in isolation. Nor can we.

A communication-fixated culture leads us to expect, by right, levels of understanding in our relationships that our grandparents would hoot at. Unfortunately, we're less practiced than they were at the conversational give-and-take that might enable such understanding, and feel—irrationally—crushed, even cheated, when our lofty aspirations aren't met. This is so prevalent as to seem almost banal, rather than what it is: sad.

Isolation magnifies disconnect and disenchantment. Many more of us live alone, frequently bombarded by images of lifestyles to dream of, all of which feeds a sense of existence as a performance that we're failing at. Television scarcely features sociable conversation, because disagreement, like horrifying news stories, makes better drama. So pundits joust with prefab sound bites, and too many talk shows are either bland publicity exercises fluffed up by a comic, or non-celebrity fistfights.

Understandably, we enjoy watching a good dustup of an evening when, by day, service-industry culture demands niceness to order. Shouting at reality TV's latest Punch and Judy is sort of fun. But is it any wonder we fear confrontation, or prefer to hide behind our screens?

We may be in touch, potentially, with anybody, anywhere on the planet. Nevertheless, what kind of existence is lived 24/7, ever on-call? Naturally, we offset our accessibility with portable solitudes and head-space expanders, first Walkmen, then iPods—to compensate for being packed cheek to butt in overcrowded trains. But while a soundtrack makes life seem more exciting, it also takes you out of it.

It's hardly surprising on-line activity should be addictive (and it is: in South Korea, the world's most plugged-in country, up to 30 percent of under-eighteens are thought to be at serious risk, with government-sponsored boot camps to wean them off). Like the Latin *utopia*, the Internet is a "nowhere," and, like all drugs, it is unsatisfying, whetting appetites that it cannot fulfill, stimulating the mind's eye as it starves our other senses. In so doing, it depletes users' sensibility and intuition, skills that may feel instinctive, but, like language, are acquired through being together. That is, in conversation.

Arguably, this saps social confidence. Certainly, unlike the pixellated peacocks that strut the cyber-playgrounds, out and about, face-to-face, even in innocuous situations, growing numbers of us seem so scared of saying the wrong thing that we say nothing. We think we're shy. We don't realize how arrogant, selfish, and idle we seem.

It is glib to blame media scaremongers, drugs, images of violence for rising antisocial behavior. Something deeper yet simpler is happening. Talk less and we understand each other less.

In 1958 philosopher Hannah Arendt pondered how bizarre it was that men could journey into space, yet few could discuss these Promethean powers sensibly, because science had leapt ahead of human intelligence, the spectrum of its possibilities beyond any single person's ken, let alone everyday conversation. For her, the fact that this development coincided with rising rudeness—complacent "thoughtlessness" being "among the outstanding characteristics of our time"—was no coincidence:

> It could be that we, who are earth-bound creatures and have begun to act as though we were dwellers of the universe, will forever be unable to understand, that is, to think and speak about the things which nevertheless we are able to do. In this case, it would be as though our brain, which constitutes the physical, material condition of our thoughts, were unable to follow what we do, so that from now on we would indeed need artificial machines to do our thinking and speaking.

Unable to discuss the machinery that manufactures our human conditions, we're forced into blindness, an innocence that she feared would brutalize us:

> If... knowledge (in the modern sense of know-how) and thought have parted company for good, then we would indeed become

the helpless slaves, not so much of our machines as of our know-how, thoughtless creatures at the mercy of every gadget which is technically possible, no matter how murderous it is.

An atomized society, returning humanity to a mental Eden, but in a world of atomic bombs?

What worried Arendt was that we'd lose the ability to question: Ethics, after all, derive from our feelings, and if we don't understand something, it is harder to sense whether it is right or wrong, let alone argue against it. How many of us can comprehend, never mind democratically vote on, nanotechnology, or genetically modified food, animals, embryos? Arendt may have been thinking nuclear. But how about brain death by iPod?

Actually, you're more likely to be flattened if you cross the road talking on your cell phone, according to studies of pedestrians at a busy Chicago junction. Why?

Conversation absorbs more of our senses than listening to music.

I don't hate technology: I used to thank Christmas I had television instead of a weekly gawk at stained-glass windows, or whatever passed for entertainment in Granny's day. (With TV, hell, who needed imaginary friends?) But I slightly fear it. Computers and their ancillaries are evolving exponentially faster than we human animals, supplanting our creature comforts, yet in no way altering our Stone Age emotional or social needs.

Are we serving tools made to free us, like the conscientious gym slaves who, rather than eat less, burn hours servicing the surplus calories of the low-input banquet that is the daily bread of the sedentary, developed world? Whatever else, like it, hate it, in and out of cyberspace, we're undergoing self-consciousness hyperinflation.

Social psychologist Sonia Livingstone said of today's image-conscious teenagers:

Celebrity is about people being interested in you when you fall over in the pub.... There's an element of them being their own self-production.

The change is as profound and spirit-pummeling as that brought by the mirror and the portrait, which in the seventeenth century heralded new levels of self-fashioning, guardedness, and melancholy—to historian Lionel Trilling, "a mutation in human nature." Just as the camera and the moving image, for all their inspiration, helped mass-produce self-awareness, alienation, and longing, making (with the aid of mechanized murder) depression the black dog of the twentieth century.

But while we may feel splintered, juggling ten roles a day where our parents had two or three, we need our distractions too: That is what other people are for. As social networking sites and three billion mobile phones testify, we still crave to meet new people, hear what they have to say. And the joke is, despite the loquacious pyrotechnics that passed for the conversational genius of Oscar Wilde, conversation isn't a performance. It takes two or more people and two things: attention and interest.

We can easily fold more of it into our life, and it's imperative that we try, not just for ourselves. The tide against conversation has a powerful undertow.

THE LOGIC OF RUDENESS

Manners are shaped by their times. At medieval revels communal dishes gave an incentive to greedy guts with sharp knives and elbows. In ritzy Renaissance Italy, however, the new-minted fashion for genteel meals, with individual place settings and multiplying forks and spoons, "reconfigured" pecking orders and definitions of good behavior. This created a niche, and conduct manuals, like Stefano Guazzo's 1574 best seller, *Civile Conversation,* the earliest treatise on the subject, sprang up to fill it, with advice on how to plug gaps between courses with suitably pitched chitchat.

Today, industrialization is on the march, social fragmentation litters its progress, and as manners thin to accommodate overstretched lifestyles, a time-paring, talk-sparing attitude is spreading, and it stinks. If you're watching the clock, awaiting a text, how easy is it to sit back, relax, and enjoy the present company? Think of the cannibalistic romantic scene parodied in *Sex and the City*, where dates are debated like commodity trades. Do you want to laugh or cry at the true story of Manhattan child Olivia Gopnik, whose imaginary friend, Charlie Ravioli, too busy "grabbing lunch" to play, eventually hired an "imaginary secretary" to keep Olivia at bay?

Yet some yearn for even fewer social niceties. Like Oscar-winner Halle Berry:

> *Being politically correct is bullshit. I want to know how some-one really feels, what I'm dealing with. I want to know who you really are, and then maybe we can have a conversation.*

Sadly, her dream of transparency belongs in la-la land, and is far from universal.

Generally speaking, the more individualist a society, the more direct its manners. While many Americans prefer an up-front approach, collectivist societies tend to favor indirectness. Such as urban southern China, where *laoshi* ("simple and honest") is a cussword for country bumpkins, and the highest term of praise is *congming*—"clever," in the Ancient Greeks' sense of *mētis* or "cunning" (think Odysseus, not Achilles). Why?

To respect the maxim at polite behavior's core: *Do not embarrass the other person.* Analyst Robin Lakoff explained the logic behind the three styles of being polite:

Don't impose (distance)—formal
Give options (deference)—hesitant, euphemistic
Be friendly (camaraderie)—direct

Being deferentially friendly is the definitely maybe of getting along, and entails contradictions, since manners are asymmetrical and often what is polite for speakers to imply would be rude for listeners to say. ("Won't you have some juice?" versus "I want some juice.") As a consequence, in super-polite company, the nuances can be a veritable merry-go-round of implication and suggestion, as my dad found when he was a relatively uncouth English child visiting well-drilled cousins in 1950s South Africa. After a month he worked out that the correct answer to "Would you like some salt?" was not "No, thank you" but "May I pass it to you?"

In varying degrees, such push-me-pull-you diplomacy underpins all conversational exchanges; it is how we broker relationships. Therefore local differences, however filigree, are worth mastering. Alas, cultural variations are complicated by a further factor: scale. Where openness is sensible in small communities, in larger ones it becomes a liability. It cannot pay to be on nodding acquaintance with everyone in town—you'd dislocate your neck—or to ask the whole street in for tea—how could you trust them not to filch the kettle?

And if cunning is useful in towns, ignoring seems to make more sense in large multicultural cities, because stealth requires expertise; however, when norms are so diverse that a smile can be a come-on to one person and a taunt to the next, reactions are impossible to predict. So people shut down, conversation shrinks, resulting in a net loss in skill at reading others and self-expression. In such crowds, individuals become isolated and grab what intimacy they can get. The result?

Rudeness (ignoring people) $\times$ Rudeness (being too direct) = Rudeness^2

Escalating rudeness is a logical outcome, but politeness is surely wiser, and safer.

Politicians extol tolerance, but what a chiseling aspiration this can be, so often freighted with hate. Rather than sympathize, it asks us to put up, shut up. This isn't sociable: It's antisocial. But if we don't socialize, don't master the reflexes of politic self-correction, we're stuck with clunking political correctness, which, as Halle Berry said, often seems not sensitive but imposed. And lip service is as unlike to virtue as a fig leaf is to innocence.

We need artful conversation. Cooperation is its operative principle, enthusiasm its divine breath, and its power to raise spirits is supernatural. It can make us not only less socially stupid, but also significantly brainier.

THE MIND MECHANIC

Some proclaim the Internet a great oom-pah-pah for literacy. Regardless of whether you see bloggers as scapegrace ego-casters or Samuel Pepys's worthy heirs, solo self-expression is feeble at training minds, the workhorses of communication. Linguist William Labov caused blushes when he analyzed recordings from different classes and settings:

> *The highest percentage of ungrammatical sentences [appeared] in the proceedings of learned academic conferences.*

It's no fluke that the monologue-asteries of lab and library nurture woolly jargon. Talking distills thoughts (we know they're unclear by the befuddled look on the other person's face) and book learning is harder to absorb than education through conversation.

What's less well known is that studying the craft of conversation improves thinking all round.

In the late 1990s sample groups of eight- to eleven-year-old British schoolchildren took a course of Talk Lessons. Afterward they accounted for thoughts as other classmates did not, more often using words like "because," "if," and "why." Tellingly, they outperformed in written intelligence tests too. Having learned to think aloud together, they were better equipped to reflect alone.

Conversation has been the engine of intelligence since *Homo* became *sapiens*. The species evolution rewarded those with conversational skills—social and political skills—and these continue to select social leaders and spur cultural development. But as those schoolchildren and grammar-mangling academics prove, this tradition means diddlysquat unless each of us incorporates conversation into our personal evolution.

After exhaustive exploration of the everyday conversations around and with babies in a cross section of American homes, researchers Todd Risley and Betty Hart found that:

> *The large differences in the language experience that had accumulated before the children were three years old accounted for most of the equally large differences in vocabulary growth and verbal intellectual outcomes by age three—and many years later.*

How does conversation exercise the intellect? Knowledge is defined by neuroscientist Ira Black as a "pattern of connectivity" between neurons, and learning as modifications of this pattern. Similarly, communication follows social grammar, as we make connections by guile and guesswork, extracting signals from face, tone, and gesture as much as words. As psychologist Nicholas Humphrey described, it's unbelievably artful; a dance, close to telepathy:

Like chess, a social interaction is typically a transaction between partners. One animal may, for instance, wish by his own behaviour to change the behaviour of another; but since the second animal is himself reactive and intelligent the interaction soon becomes a two-way argument where each "player" must be ready to change his tactics—and maybe his goals—as the game proceeds.

Conversation doesn't feel this hard, not if you practice it. But if you don't, as Stefano Guazzo wrote four and a half centuries ago:

He that useth not company hath no experience, he that hath no experience, hath no judgment, and he that hath no judgment is no better than a beast ... so the common saying is, that there is no other name meete for a solitarie person, but either of a beast, or a tyrant.

The word Guazzo used was *"humanitas"*—communal conversation. For anyone still unconvinced it can be learned or improved, I'm afraid it is how we all learn to learn. If we don't learn well, we limp through life.

"Goo-goo" is the most important word in the world, because when parents coo at babies, they're educating them in what behaviorists call "musical companionship." As babies goo-goo back, they absorb timing, taking turns, tone, coordination, gestures, facial expressions, storytelling—the orchestra of instruments by which emotions are transmitted and relationships formed.

No synthetic alternative will do, witnessed in a cruel experiment that showed an infant a video of its burbling mum (distressed, it withdrew). And babies who aren't talked to, or who are talked at abusively, grow into disruptive kids who can't express themselves. As do too many South Korean children, despite loving parents and the world's best education system. With little free time, some become socially malnourished, seeking solitary solace online, trading interaction's challenges for virtual games—short-circuit gratifications that foster ingrown personalities and make their lives hell.

Dr. Kim Hyun-soo, chair of the Association of Internet Addiction, explained: "These people are very frustrated inside and full of anger."

Any parent too busy to sit down for tea and ask about school should hear what teachers have to say about fading listening and learning abilities, or perhaps read the UNICEF report rating British kids' well-being the lowest in twenty developed countries, not least because Mum and Dad scarcely speak to them. Then have a weep, then think again.

Conversation can heal us. Children of talkative parents have higher IQs and know how to make connections, and friends. While we pay therapists to listen, in talking cultures depression remains a dictionary term. And the centenarian concert pianist's intuitions were confirmed by a study of geriatric nuns, which found that gunky brain cells don't equate with dementia, not if the nun keeps chatty, happy, and takes the odd toddle.

As Nicholas Humphrey demonstrated, good conversationalists see others' perspectives, so have less destructive arguments. They don't, unlike the last, word-cudgelling president of the United States, inhabit an either/or universe. To assert that "you're with us or against us" is to quash debate, leading to bad decisions.

In 1940, Sir Kinahan Cornwallis, the British diplomat who helped forge the kingdom of Iraq, wrote:

> The value of personal contacts and friendships has been proved over and over again in the Middle East, and the evil effects of aloofness and indifference are clear for all to see.

If only the lesson were learned. Not talking—failure to acknowledge the other point of view, never mind engage with it—polarizes, killing debate. In its absence, silence breeds suspicion, anger, and violence, creating further distance—distance that comes to seem unbridgeable, faced with the unspeakable.

My hell is not, as it was for Sartre, other people. It is a twenty-first century with six billion plus of us, on a shrinking planet, with dwindling resources, not talking. Lose the means to work out who we are, what we have in common, and we lose stories, the greatest consolation. Novelist John Steinbeck understood the creative balm of sympathy:

> *We are lonesome animals. We spend all of our life trying to be less lonesome. One of our ancient methods is to tell a story begging the listener to say—and to feel—"Yes, that is the way it is, or at least that is the way I feel it."*

Guazzo was right, conversation gives us humanity. Without it we're less than the sum of our parts, unable to improvise or be what roguish seventeenth-century philosopher Francis Bacon called a "ready man." And we need to be. Service industry is the future, and if not the cheapest workers, we'd better be smarter to beat the competition. In a sense many of us are already courtiers. Yet the decline in everyday courtesy—failure to meet the eye, switch off that phone—attests to an urgent need to reawaken nerve endings.

Historically, the periods when conversation was most revered have been among the most fruitful for reason, invention, and respect for the individual; times when people believed that their opinions could change the world. Think of the babbling coffee houses frequented by Samuel Johnson and enlightened chums; the great French salons, which brought together thinkers and artists and politicians, galvanizing mind-shifts and freedoms from which the

West continues to benefit. For Johnson and company, newspapers and print sped up talk. The Internet can do more for us if we're sane about it. This is an exciting time for conversation. Potentially.

Stand on each other's shoulders and we can, like acrobats, build pyramids. Just as Jimmy Connors raised John McEnroe's game, so Coleridge spurred Wordsworth, so the Almohad court propagated scientific and cultural advance. What would Shakespeare, Jonson, and chums have been had they not met in pullulating Elizabethan London and hung out at the Mermaid Tavern, where pub banter was:

> So nimble, and so full of subtle flame
> As if that every one from whence they came
> Had meant to put his whole wit in a jest,
> And had resolved to live a fool the rest
> Of his dull life—

Einstein appreciated this: He trundled to his office in Princeton's Institute for Advanced Study solely for "the privilege of walking home with Kurt Gödel." Three freewheeling years of chatter led Francis Crick and James Watson to their epochal discovery of the structure of DNA. Do I hear you ask, "But is it art?"

Were it not for mental and social workouts at a *tertulia*, a salon in Barcelona that he came to dominate like Barnum did his circus, seventeen-year-old Picasso might not have become a genius anecdote-teller, as well as a poet (little appreciated outside Spain), or won the renown and contacts that eased his scramble to the apex of the twentieth-century's artistic pyramid. Walter Sickert, a lesser painter, famously donned his "lying suit" to wow Mayfair dinner parties and butter the crumpets of rich admirers.

Conversation makes connections. For heaven's sake, it's a laugh.

THERE IS NO RIGHT WAY

On the other hand, if you want to kill a conversation, tell people you're writing a book on the subject. Either they feel like lab rats, or they turn nasty.

"Why you?" asked a doubting friend.

"Nice idea, but you can't make anyone better at it," said a tactful teacher.

"So what's it all about then?" demanded a scary novelist.

"Oh, well," I replied, "you know, being interested in people."

"Yeah?"

"But you don't want me to go on about that now, or I'll start reciting my manuscript," I blustered, hoping to shuffle to another topic.

"Right." But the look on the man's face said, "wrong."

"Sorry, I'm tired. My defense is that you don't have to be a grand master to discuss chess, so I needn't be a brilliant conversationalist."

"No," he said. "But you'd better be bloody good at it."

Who am I to tell you what to do?

I've been obsessed with words and reading since I can remember, and, though shy, I always loved talking, was often dragged to the front of the class for it. But that's not exactly conversation skill.

My parents valued conversation, and sent me and my middle sister to practice on a long-suffering blind man, Colonel Colbeck (complete with curlicue mustache and much-repeated tales of secreting whoopee cushions under bustles at Mama's Edwardian tea parties). Despite their efforts, I'm no Oscarina Wilde, and have often failed to keep the ball rolling. For work, I've navigated the challenges of interviewing celebrities, as well as publicized naked Russian poets and negotiated with wily agents—champion cud-chewers all. However, I also tend to interrupt, jump between thoughts, and on too many occasions have had cause to wish my foot didn't fit so snugly in my mouth. And I have suffered bores.

I'm not an expert, but an enthusiast, an interested party, and this isn't a script. There is no one great way to hold conversation. But certain approaches are more flexible, and there are plenty of avoidable errors as well as artful dodges. My ideal is to draw the best out of companions. Whatever yours is, appreciate conversation's finer points and your experience will be more rewarding.

Investigating this ancient art form, its great and its knee-grindingly dreadful exponents, has been like a mystery tour of what it means to be human; fascinating, and often hilarious. I'd never suspected that greetings were such important gatekeepers; or that small talk is hugely significant, if you trim it to advantage; or how creative listening is; or how easily dynamics tilt for or against you. You will be amazed.

I have explored what topics are fit for purpose; why bores drain our wits, and how they can be stopped; the gymnastic arts of humor, flattery, and seduction; the wisdom of lying; tactics for shop talk, getting your own way, and, if truly necessary (but deeply satisfying), shutting people up.

Two conversations convinced me this book was necessary. The first took place on a train. I sat near a beautiful young man who was wearing a white cap. As the train rolled out of the station, he took a small leather book from his jacket. When he began chanting, I noticed he had no luggage except a couple of bags containing large, sloshing containers of fluid.

After the London bombings, I was paranoid, and ashamed: Who was I to judge him? Ridiculous! Part of me wanted to change cars. Instead, I asked if he was praying. We talked for half an hour about the Koran.

The second happened at a dinner. For two hours I sat by a self-styled publicity guru who regaled me with his zip code's wonders

("I love Notting Hill; all the same, I have the pleasure of being the most brilliant man in Battersea"—and this dinner was in Battersea), recommended his forthcoming book on self-promotion skills, but, apart from where I lived, asked me almost nothing.

If his is the direction of civilization, it is in reverse gear.

In 427 B.C. the orator Gorgias of Leontini conquered Athens with his defense of runaway bride Helen of Troy. It wasn't her fault, he said, but words': They "stop fear, remove sorrow, create joy and increase pity," but they also "poison and bewitch the mind."

Two-and-a-half millennia on, nothing has changed. There is no greater power, no pleasure so serious.

Can conversation save lives? It certainly saves marriages, and few would dispute it builds self-esteem. Shouldn't it be obvious it can also raise social esteem, generating the goodwill that funds the best in life and business? Neglecting it graffitis cultural DNA, muddles minds, and helps granulate us into extremists. But using it can rebuild our crumbling common ground. As researching this book has taught me, we are more complicated and magnificent than we realize: Far from behind technology, we're beyond it.

Close your eyes a moment. Imagine saying hi to the strangers on your street. Imagine everyone saying it. Imagine it is the start of a conversation.

Is that so preposterous? It never used to be.

Let's wage war on shyness. With a friendlier environment, we have a better chance of making it into the next century. And enjoying it.

As Alexander Pope nearly wrote:

> *True ease in talking comes from art, not chance,*
> *As those move easiest who have learned to dance.*

Understand the steps, you will hear the music.

We need to talk.

THE CONCISE MANIFESTO

Attention $\times$ Interest $=$ Conversation $=$ Joy

WHAT CONVERSATION ISN'T
Performance art
Competition
Scripted

WHAT IT IS
Mutual appreciation
Cooperation
Spontaneous

THREE PRINCIPLES
Generosity
Openness
Clarity

FIVE MAXIMS
Think before you speak
Listen more than speak
Find the incentive for talking
Never assume you know what they mean or that they
    understand you
Take turns

I

HELLO

On Conversation's Casting Couch

D on't talk to strangers? Don't speak until spoken to?
    Forget it. Inhibition is useless. How do you start a conversation? Simple: Say hi.

It's easy to say. But as with flying, the critical phase of conversation is takeoff, and greetings don't follow straight lines, but vary from place to place. Even chimpanzees have a host of hand clasps. Some grip, some press wrists, some grab and groom, and all respect one rule: The dominant chimp's hand goes on top.

By contrast, many humans bungle customary overtures. Some dive in, so keen to have an impact, they're blind to the impression they make. Other, shy souls stumble, mumble, or say nothing. What does it matter?

The chimps get it: Greetings announce who we are. They reveal plenty about a relationship:

"Hello, reptile," she said. "You're here, are you?"

"Here I am," I responded, "with my hair in a braid and ready to the last button. A very merry pip-pip to you, aged relative."

"The same to you, fathead. I suppose you forgot to bring that necklace?"

(It is abundantly clear Aunt Dahlia adores her reptile nephew, Bertie Wooster, the beloved P.G. Wodehouse character.)

And they can shape relationships. When the Earl of Oxford was presented to Elizabeth I, he bowed, issued a loud burst of flatus, and fled England in shame. After seven years' self-imposed exile, he returned to court. Her Majesty greeted him: "My lord, I had forgott the fart."

→ Rule one: Greetings spark connections

Initial impressions are indelible. Compare the shopkeeper who asks how you are with the one who snorts, her eyes glued on your down-at-heel shoes.

She may not mean to be rude, but she might as well turn her back. Yet in most towns, would this surprise you?

No word costs less or counts more in a conversation than hello. Even in a megalopolis such as London there's something unsettling about a person who won't return it, like the man on my street whose liveliest response to "Hi" is a grunt (usually he looks away). I'm not sure what I, or life, have done to him, but the sense of a person stranded in his own bleak world is strong. It crystallizes the importance of greetings for making contact and wiring conversation for sound.

HOW GREETINGS CONNECT

If conversation is music, then the start, the strike of a tuning fork, sets the tone and reveals others' key.

Greetings' exchange betokens a pact that people's attention is, for now, each other's. Not only does a casual "Hi" or formally begged "How do you do?" announce where you're coming from, but, like a diplomatic gift, the way you present it sends a message. However relaxed, it is a mark of respect, not an excuse to grab attention. (Which may shock U2's Bono. A friend's party was silenced when a bagpiper burst in, piped ten long minutes, then announced that the rock singer couldn't make it, but had sent him to say "Hi" instead.)

Not greeting emits a message too. Indeed, in Colette's novella *Gigi*, the heroine, her mother, and her grandmother (the last two both retired courtesans) use it to dent the ego of an ageing roué and coax him into proposing marriage:

> *"Good afternoon, Mamita. Good afternoon, Gigi," he said airily. "Please don't move, I've come to retrieve my straw hat."*
>
> *None of the three women replied, and his assurance left him. "Well, you might at least say a word to me, even if it's only How-d'you-do?"*

→ **Rule two: Greetings are charms to open minds and doors**
Getting greetings right means hitting the same register as the other person—whether formal, friendly, or intimate. Getting them wrong signals that you're uninterested, not on his wavelength, or an outsider; bad news in dangerous places. For instance, Tuareg nomads crossing paths in the Sahara desert will reveal names only after trading set phrases like undercover spies.

The lower status person (usually the younger) begins:

Younger: *Peace be on you.*
Elder: *What do you look like?*
Younger: *Only peace.*
Elder: *What has gone wrong?*
Younger: *Nothing. Only peace.*
Elder: *What is new?*
Younger: *Nothing. Only peace.*
Elder: *Where are you going?*

Such rituals reflect that manners are not universal but sprout up to serve regional circumstance. Nothing if not conventional, refined over millennia, they broker relationships, playing out social assumptions embedded in our cultural software, and so, by their nature, transcend finer feeling.

So Nigeria's Ibo, who believe the first person they greet dictates their day's fortune, happily ignore their own granny if there is a whiff of illness about her. So, to a Western Apache, introducing yourself is presumptuous (a keepsake of justified suspicion against men bearing gifts). Whereas in most urban societies not to do so— even if out of shyness—is rude, a bit like asking "Don't you know who I am?" To which the reply must be "No, thank goodness."

In complicated settings, negotiating the right to say hi can be a gorgeous dance. Intrepid Rory Stewart learned the worth of due respects hiking across Afghanistan—over mountains, in winter, shortly after tumultuous war. Initially he found the forms funny:

> *Finally a soldier marched in and, holding his right hand to his chest, said,* "Salaam aleikum. Chetor hastid? Jan-e-shoma jur ast? Khum hastid? Sahat-e-shoma khub ast? Be khair hastid? Jur hastid? Khane kheirat ast? Zinde bashi." *Which in Dari, the Afghan dialect of Persian, means,* "Peace be with you. How are you? Is your soul healthy? Are you well? Are you well? Are you healthy? Are you fine? Is your household flourishing? Long life to you." *Or:* "Hello."

But passing through shattered communities, Stewart soon mastered how to hail by lushly barnacled local custom, if need be invoking the forefathers of well-connected warlords who had guaranteed his passage. Time and again this, rather than gold, saved his life.

If seldom a question of life and death, like a letter of introduction clasped to the bosom of a Brontë heroine, greetings remain passports as well as the embodiment of the style by which you will be expected to behave. So if others bow, go ahead, and when in Rome, best do as they do, because respecting native customs is the first sign you can give someone that he should respect you.

THE ORIGINS OF CONFUSION

I'm exaggerating? Of course, most of us pay greetings scant attention, precisely because they are conventional. But given the whirligig nature of globalized life, attending to their finer details is arguably more important than ever.

Thanks to globalization, a vast array of options beckons, with a profusion of gestures, from high-fives to Continental high society's hovering *Handkuss* (uh-uh—no lips on Her Serenity's glove). Yet on closer inspection, amazingly few fit general use. Recall the nose-clash as you misjudge which cheek to kiss. The pause as you open a door, the other person hesitates, then you both walk into each other.

Confusion reigns because social codes are fading, and etiquette increasingly resembles a branch of astrology. Change is nothing new, but the information age has scrambled the software that programs how we behave, multiplying distortions. We don't just copy our parents; we cut and paste from Web, film, and TV. And although each walk of life looks increasingly the same, nuances proliferate and instincts are less instructive—fashion shifts too fast. (Try high-fiving a teenager and watch him sneer.)

Nevertheless, we form assumptions about personalities from the briefest encounter. I was utterly thrown when a business contact shook hands with her left paw (not coincidentally, she is a demon negotiator). Even with people we see all the time, jarring notes magnify into signs. Aren't you disconcerted by your Andalusian pal's earsplitting air-smackeroos? The weirdo who winks when you buy milk at his shop? The aunt who still pinches cheeks? The tennis partner whose grip is like a drowning man's?

↪ **Rule three: The first notes you strike should be on a general frequency**

Common sense ceases to exist when the pool of local certainties is awash with every other drop in the ocean. On the other hand, as your parents might have indicated, common sense has always been a thing of the past.

One answer to the dilemma is to ditch greetings. Another is to get arty and improvise. Sure, you could twirl someone instead of shaking her hand (it happened to me). But why heap confusion upon confusion?

Trusty product of countless exchanges, the standard-issue gestures—the smile, the handshake—are already an amazing collective work of art, and evolved as they have for good reason. What is more, your opening—"Hi" or "Howdie?"—is already a bold tick in the social register, enough information for now, surely. This should be the easy bit.

↪ **Rule four: Smiling is a confidence trick**

It is apt that the first self-help guide, imaginatively titled *Self-Help*, should have been written by Samuel Smiles. Far from meek, anthropologists reckon baring teeth is as much designed to show yourself as an adversary with bite as to express warm feelings.

Our cousin the chimpanzee peels back his lips to warn of danger—suggesting that, as well as gently intimidating, the smile helpfully muzzles its wearer's fear; a confidence-boosting reflex, like giggling at splatter movies. Certainly, it is an assertion, bold, hardly modest, and some cultures prefer ladies to titter, a demure hand over lowered mouth. Admittedly, Tudor aristocrats had a brief grinning craze, when on-trend dames showed off blackened teeth to prove they were rich enough to rot them on costly sugar (and some resorted to fake blacking). But don't be put off. As Horace observed,

Smiling faces are turned on those who smile.

If you smile, the other person, unless very odd or hostile, will feel compelled to return it, for no other reason than that the mimicry instinct is so entrenched that smiles and laughter are contagious. (A 1962 hysteria epidemic in Tanganyika took two years' quarantine to stamp out.)

➔ Rule five: Eyes make contacts

The Zulu have an elegant phrase for hello and good-bye: *Sawu bona*—"I see you." This encapsulates the power of greeting: It gives recognition. Not looking at the other person while doing it renders him invisible, implicitly declaring that either you're afraid to meet his eye or he is beneath your contempt. Either way, it's bad manners, making you seem weak or pompous—a worse weakness still for making conversation.

Faces reveal useful information too. Your smile should reach your eyes because if the orbicularis oculi muscles don't contract, smocking your crow's feet, it will be read as false. Moreover, your eyes should reach into the other person's. True, not long ago debutantes embarking on the husband-fishing trip that was "The Season" were advised, "Never look a man straight in the eye." Such a gaze, counseled M. Dono Edmond, adviser to Queen Marie of Romania no less, informs its object that "you are trying to probe his mind." Heaven forfend....

But for artful conversation between equals, inattention tenders disaster. Take Ronald Reagan, never one to overlook niceties. At his adopted son's graduation, after he was famous but years before he was the U.S. president, he ambled around, extending his hand, saying, "My name is Ronald Reagan. What's yours?"

Eventually he bumped into his son. Out went the mitt.

"My name is Ronald Reagan. What's yours?"

Isn't it tempting to read intimations of senility in his faux pas? Friendly as can be, yet so far, far away....

Missteps during greetings not only put people on guard instead of persuading them to lower it, but also prime them to expect that the blunderer isn't worth talking to. Charm can't work on autocue, and as somebody should tell Bono, the truly charismatic don't show off; they're too busy, having eyes only for you.

MAPPING BOUNDARIES

The passive-aggressive grin makes a poetically fitting start to conversation, since it recalls that human relations have always been unequal parts antagonism and cooperation. Although smiling is an ancient primate inheritance, we hang on to it, because at root, conversation is our species' miraculous innovation (catalytic converter?) for managing the tension between our desire to connect and our need for independence; a tension that has been nothing if not creative. As conversation developed, it allowed us to turn thoughts to words to collaborative deeds that led Homo sapiens out of the woods, and on to run the planet—more or less.

Civility enabled this evolution. The word's meaning has been diluted, but to have a civil tongue in your head was once the prized asset of a privileged social group; like "citizen," "civility" spoke of a world that favored discussion over violence or despotism (both derive from *civitas*, "self-governing community"). For Ancient Roman Cicero, the first thinker to explore the grammar of conversation, civility safeguarded "community" by "assigning to each individual his due" and making a "habit of affability." This remains true today.

➺ Rule six: Respect territorial claims

We soon dread the kind woman we meet twice daily at the school gate, if each time she hugs us like a long-lost child, because little civilities remain important protocols for calibrating intimacy. They pace out the distance between us at the same time as draw us together. And if conversation's primary aim is to map common ground, greetings demarcate personal space.

What contact is too intimate? The territory is fluid. Although air kisses are bubbling up outside luvviedom, most Britons still shake hands then draw back, and don't hug strangers. However, five centuries ago Italian visitors to England were aghast not at stiff upper lips, but at having to smack them:

> *If a foreigner enters a house and does not first of all kiss the mistress on the mouth, they think him badly brought up.*

France currently favors two-way kiss trades, yet in 1831 Alexis de Tocqueville, new to America, made a shattering discovery: "Everyone shakes hands." To a post-Revolutionary Frenchman, such manifest egalitarianism was wildly touchy-feely. Then again, unlike his predecessor Reagan, George W. Bush considered handshakes highrisk. On first meeting freshman senator Barack Obama, Bush offered a squirt of the antiseptic with which he had been anointing the presidential palm:

> *"Want some? Good stuff. Keeps you from getting colds."*

In general an unlikely weapon for biological attack, a handshake remains the safest gesture for greeting someone new. In fact, it came into use in more violent times, to show that one did not wield a sword. Cicero would approve.

→ **Rule seven: Pay attention and already you have a connection**
The bonus of conventionality is that while performing your hand-shake, saying "Hi" or "Howdie," your mind, if not quite on Reagan energy-saving mode, has space to take in the other person. So approach a new face like the start of a novel, magnetized for clues to an unfamiliar world.

Even handshakes reveal character, if only what a person wishes to project. Take note. Does he grip or squeeze? Lock eyes? Flick away? I tremble before knuckle-crunchers, and those pushy deal-closer types, who place a second hand on top, trapping me, then pump away, as if to draw deep on the well of fast-drying friendship.

As for secret signalers, Freemasons and so on, their clinches are no affair of mine.

CENTRAL CASTING

Ignore a person at the fringe of a conversation and he'll soon go. Etiquette expert John Morgan explained:

> *In a curious way, until someone is introduced ... socially they only half exist.*

He didn't mean this in a derogatory sense; rather, that recognition is all. It can create an advantage. In Ancient Rome senators hired *nomenclators*, who shadowed them around town, ready to whisper the correct form of address for approaching dignitaries, thereby enabling the senators to greet first, putting them in charge of the conversation. The same tactic is deployed by the internal editor in *The Devil Wears Prada*.

Such power play illuminates the dark game of greetings and introductions. If the first business is trading names, a close second is establishing terms of engagement, offering enough information about each other for talk to crack on apace. But don't forget prestige is at stake: Little status signals flash away, so the art of introducing someone else is to cast them in their preferred light, then bathe in the reflected glory.

In the past deference codes were overt. You could tell how to treat someone by how he dressed, and caps were doffed according to what, or not, sat on another's head (hatlessness being near to godlessness in times of epidemic head lice). In our socially mobile era, status is customized, making it harder to scan egos. At the corporate do, that unshaven, chain-smoking bum growling at all who graze his pungent biosphere will be the billionaire boss—his lack of grace, something for the "little people," as effective a social barrier as a VIP's velvet rope.

But although manners alter, the human needs they exist to service—especially pride—remain. And of all social injuries, most avoidable is bungling a name.

The Name Game

Can't afford a *nomenclator*? Remembering is easier with the antique style of introduction—"Zebedee, I'd like you to meet Aphra Jones. Aphra, allow me to introduce Zebedee Taylor." But if this is de trop, why not repeat a name after it's told to you?

And be generous with your own. When introduced, if you detect the slightest pause, say it. Say it introducing yourself, even if you've met before, especially if the other person's name escapes you. In return, he should give you his. If not, prompt: remind him where you met. Equally, if it's your job to introduce other people, start with someone whose name you know, pause, then smile; hopefully, others will take the cue.

But if they're socially tone-deaf, own up. This can be positive: "I couldn't forget you, but I'm afraid I'm hopeless at names."
Never, ever guess. (Sheila/Eileen, forgive me.)

Perhaps your memory is impeccable. Still, have a care how
you show it. Some salesmen repeat clients' names to fast-track
rapport, creating a faint yet oddly powerful sense of obligation to
be nice back. Personally, I loathe it. And while it's good to drop
a child's name into a bedtime story if you feel her attention wan-
der, would you do the same talking to an adult? Many do. But I
know my name—why remind me?

Because someone else does not. To bring a fresh person into
conversation, without breaking momentum, try a slick lateral
introduction: "Zebedee Taylor, there you are. Aphra here was
about to tell us about her windmill."

TO "HI" OR "HOW DO YOU DO?"

So how to acknowledge status in introductions?

At a corporate event, I once watched the chief executive of a
multinational media conglomerate being introduced as the chief
executive of a multinational media conglomerate to—*be still your
beating heart*—Don Johnson.

The CEO's TV-wide shades could not hide her perplexity.
She smiled, extended a lizard hand, and rotated her head ninety
degrees.

"And what," she asked her host through unparted teeth, like a
ventriloquist addressing a dummy, "does Don do?"

The unfortunate host may have thought he was paying the CEO
a great compliment in giving her such fanfare to the *Miami Vice*
veteran. He can't have been aware that, although greeting first means

you lead an encounter, conversely, in introductions, the lower status person is traditionally introduced first—equivalent to the diplomatic gift being offered the pasha. Not nice, but that's status games for you.

➥ Rule eight: Introduce the higher status person (older, female) second

Remember the playground chant? First the worst, second the best ...

In a pub or bar, with close friends, who cares? But if in any doubt about the level of formality, pay attention; there are endless clues. (One grande dame used to prejudge a function by the aerodynamics of the invitation: The stiffer the card, the farther it flew when frisbeed across her dressing room, the smarter the togs she wore.)

➥ Rule nine: Don't try to regrade the social register in greetings

I've been in starchy situations where people act as if their personalities are in corsets, and most give the impression they'd rather not be (the alcohol intake usually confirms this). Even so, if you want to loosen up, it is the job of small talk, not introductions, to ascend the stair of friendship. Presuming intimacy from the off won't get you there. Old hands such as Princess Anne defy coercion. When she met the former premier's wife, Cherie Blair, the other said, "Call me Cherie."

"I'd rather not, Mrs. Blair," said the princess.

13 Unlucky Gambits for Opening Conversation with Strangers

1. A funny voice
2. Batting eyelids, twitching, itching, winking, etc.
3. The clothes inspection (radiates ill-will, regardless of whether you like the other person's look)
4. Touching, except the hand, cheek kiss, or clasping an elbow (for a power shake)
5. Refusing a hand
6. Holding on after its owner begins to withdraw
7. Wiping yours before or after shaking
8. Looking away during introductions
9. Laughing unprompted
10. That joke about the comedy surname
11. Rejecting a compliment
12. Saying, "Oh yes, I've heard about you" without further elaboration
13. Silence

→ **Rule ten: Introductions present the first thread for discussion**
Meeting a potential contact/employer/lover may feel to you like stepping under a Broadway hot-spot, but the other person may be equally intimidated, or thinking about what to buy for dinner. At this point it's impossible to know. So if you feel self-conscious, invert it: Be conscious of others, let your enthusiasm show, and focus on introductions, the primer for what you two might have to talk about.

An effective introduction is small-ad brief, splicing in only two ingredients per person:

A (who they are) + B (why they are relevant)

The salient information is not so much formal title (royals, snobs, and servicemen excepted) as how you relate to one another or the event (housemate, client, mother-in-law, single male drafted in for ladies like you). Identify points of contact, charge people up, and you have a connection.

So put your best hand forward, smile, and remember the virtue of *Sawu bona*: "I see you." It says the other person matters.

Now conversation can begin.

TYPOLOGY OF BORES, CHORES, AND
OTHER CONVERSATIONAL BEASTS

THE CROWD OF STRANGERS   *Tyrannoborus rex*

You arrive late, as planned. The joint is jumping. There is your host, and there is everybody else you have never met.

Before a virgin expanse of unfamiliar faces, the prospect of mingling may feel little more alluring than staging a burglary. Simply saying hello can induce instant lockjaw. As can overfamiliar faces, as at office parties, where, with shop-talk taboo, in nonwork clothes and gauche mental mufti, colleagues may suddenly act like aliens without phrase books.

It's tempting to stay in the revolving door, as I once saw the actor Robert De Niro do, coming and going at a dog-eared film awards extravaganza. But for pity's sake, you've come this far. So think like a criminal: Roam around, case the joint, and find its weak points.

Best are fringe areas where groups break and re-form. Stand near food and drink and you've a ready-made topic, plus something to do. If this is a house party, offer to help serve. (Hold the honeypot: bees will swarm.) And if you see a new group forming, stand by with an attentive expression; they may invite you in.

Someone nice is waiting to meet you; he just doesn't know it yet. He is the person not talking much who smiles, meets your eye. Or she is on her own, looking about hopefully like you, or he is studying the distant progress of a waitress, his glass as empty as yours. So join forces and catch her. Or you could hotwire talk with mild provocation, such as this shameless flattery I overheard: "Magnificent skirt. Are you a ballerina?" She pirouetted.

Once you've jimmied an opening, be ready to make small talk.

2

SMALL TALK, BIG DEAL

On Striking Up a Tune

There was my target, deep in discussion with the museum curator. "One Hundred Years of Cinema" was being opened by one bona fide British star. Just one hundred rooms to chase him through, as I sought my chance to strike.

At least, it felt like one hundred, and I felt like an assassin. In fact this was my first assignment for a gossip column. All afternoon I had read brown press cuttings on the antics and tepid shames of Jeremy Irons. Twenty questions? I had two hundred.

Until I started stalking and fear took over. Story—what story?

"ACTOR VISITS MUSEUM SHOCK"?

Finally, boredom slew fear: How bad could it be?

I went up, said my name and place of work. Irons smiled. I gulped. My throat and mind congealed. He smiled some more. Then came the melt, starting in my nose, pores welling springs of treacherous sweat. At last he spoke.

"Good to meet you, Catherine Blyth of the *Evening Standard*. Have you met my wife?" He wafted a Hollywood-white hand. "Sinead, Catherine Blyth, *Evening Standard*."

"Hello," I said, and fled.

Impeccable manners can nuke unwelcome intruders. Who was I, this sleek repetition of my credentials seemed to beg, to invade the Irons ether?

But the problem was mine: I had nothing to say. Without an ice breaker, I froze, my body reacting as if his smile were saber-fanged.

If you don't recognize the symptoms of social death, stop reading. You are a mathematician of genius, ruler of a minor principality, or possibly a sociopath. It may amaze you to learn that for many, even mild socializing is pathogenic. Such as the financial company directors, sent a questionnaire for a leadership course, which asked: "What in your work is most difficult?" As a chorus they replied: "Small talk with clients."

THE ANATOMY OF SMALL TALK

Small talk has always had a bad name. The earliest reference in English, Lord Chesterfield's of 1751, is to

> a sort of chit-chat, or small-talk ... the general run of conversation in most mixed companies.

Stunted conversation, in other words. Like women, small talk has been derided as trivial, empty, even frigid (a 1905 tale refers to "her colder, small-talk manner, which committed her to nothing"). As ever, prejudice masks insecurity and misunderstanding.

A character in Bernhard Schlink's novel *The Homecoming* observes:

> I am no good at small talk: I can never quite find the right tone to make the weighty sound trivial and the trivial sound weighty.

But small talk is neither a synonym for trite, nor about scaling topics to a set size. It can be many things: preamble to a meeting, networking, gossip, an exchange in the queue at the post office. At parties where guests are like bees bumbling flowers, it is a frivolous end in itself; for geishas, it is work. And wherever it occurs, however artless it seems, it is essential. As the wife reproves her husband in *The Painted Veil*:

> *If people only spoke when they had something to say, the human race would soon lose the power of speech.*

→ Rule one: Small talk conjures intimacy

Anthropologists liken small talk to grooming among primates, largely because it stimulates the snug sense of belonging that makes socializing a joy. Likewise, some academics stick it in a narrow box marked "phatic" speech, those remarks meaningful less for what they say than for what they signal. For instance, idle comments about weather are phatic because their meaning isn't the information they contain—anyone can see it's a lovely day—so much as what they signal about the speakers' relationship: emphatically, you're on friendly terms.

This view minimizes small talk's multifangled role as conversation's warm-up act. Robert Louis Stevenson explained:

> *A good talk is not to be had for the asking. Humours must first be accorded in a kind of overture or prologue.*

Not only does small talk enable the big by scouting topics, but it sets conversation's tone, pace, and rhythm; scanning sensibilities, locking on to affinities, massaging minds and goodwill. All of which makes it a virtuoso instrument of social orchestration. What's not to like?

First, we do it most among strangers. Second, it can feel pointless. (The softer the topic, the harder the sell.) Third, it is bitty, quick-fire, demanding disproportionate amounts of energy, rather like badminton, and pressure to perform may be cramping. (Who enjoys sparkling to order?) Fourth, as we send out grappling hooks, we expose ourselves, and if our offers are rejected, we feel rejected. It's a striptease-cum-beauty contest.

This is why even Lady Florence Bell—a tireless Edwardian promoter of conversation, who launched Winter Gardens for the poor to congregate in on dark, lonely nights, away from the demon drink, and who was so far from shy that, by her daughter's account, she treated life as a play with "herself ... the leading personage in the drama"—even she so loathed small talk, so yearned for set phrases to stand in for it, like the preordained pieties that nuns "are obliged to say" if paths crossed at the convent, that she wrote a ridiculous book of them, *Conversational Openings and Endings.*

Wrong, wrong, wrong. The honor of small talk lies in paying others the compliment that they're worth talking to, the power in sparking the everyday magic of intimacy. Hell when it fails, it is eminently worth doing well, as the intimidated financial company directors understood.

THE RISE OF SMALL TALK

While most Anglo-Saxons joke about mothers-in-law, native Australians have "mother-in-law" tongues, with dedicated vocabularies for use on taboo females. But such impressive verbal voodoo is fading along with other formal and deferential modes.

People are different, and it's daft to treat everyone the same, as did Sir Walter Ralegh's brother Dr. Gilbert, "a Man of excellent naturall Parts" who "cared not what he said to man or woman of what quality soever," winning himself the accolade of sixteenth-century Britain's "Greatest Buffoon in the Nation." Yet growing numbers of us opt for the buffoon stance.

Psychologist Steven Pinker observed:

Younger Americans try to maintain lower levels of social distance.... I know many gifted prose stylists my age whose one-on-one speech is peppered with sort of and you know, their attempt to avoid affecting the stance of the expert.

It's not just to be cool; in multicultural settings, hooked up through global commerce, or at international conferences such as the esteemed Pinker attends, user-friendly, low-key lingo translates more readily. But artful small talk is defter at making friends than what Chesterfield belittled as "sort of chit-chat." Or any other, kind of, like, you know, verbal padding.

→ Rule two: Artful small talk is the social compass

Rather than assume intimacy through blunt language, small talk creates it by pumping out friendly vibes and establishing connections between speakers who meet as equals. (Something of a cultural novelty, born in the assembly rooms Chesterfield patronized, which may explain historic disdain for small talk, as an upstart tradition that forced men to listen to—*ugh*—women.)

Its added bonus is the firing neurons and fizzing hormones that come of light stimulation—all of which enhance adaptability, indispensable to social survival in fast-moving, pseudo-egalitarian society, where talent for whisking up intimacy creates leaders among supposed equals. For instance, in ordering staff to "Call me Tony," ex–Prime Minister Blair astutely claimed friendship's privilege without conceding authority, making it harder to challenge him. Well, do you fight a mate?

The social instinct that made Blair an alpha operator is hardwired in us primates. Science writer Matt Ridley noted, before resigning as chairman of troubled building society Northern Rock:

The top male chimpanzee in a troop is not necessarily the strongest; instead, it is usually the one best at manipulating social coalitions to his advantage.

We all must build coalitions, but as Ridley's fate testifies, this is an increasingly unwieldy task. Count the masks we wear, assigned by us, society, other people's perceptions.... Shifting between roles, projecting different faces, is stressful (tellingly, the financial company directors hated *combining* small talk and business).

Humans are territorial animals. Exposure threatens us. Understandably, we feel the lack of a social compass. For sure, I dread what Philip Larkin called, explaining his refusal to be Poet Laureate, "Pretending to Be Me." But to fear small talk is to miss its opportunity. It is the social compass, and with it, we escape self-consciousness.

DISABLING SHYNESS

Would you believe a professional performer finds small talk especially daunting? Ask Judy Finnigan, the chat-show host whose warmth makes her a friend to viewers:

The idea of conversation with strangers fills me with horror. When I'm with friends I'm totally relaxed, but with other people ... I just don't like the whole small-talk thing. I even hate going to premieres now. I know that sounds ridiculously spoiled, but there it is.

But her trepidation is reasonable. Famous people suffer the vast disadvantage that strangers imagine they know them intimately, which makes the task of building intimacy rather lopsided, and instant niceness the order of the day. Nonetheless, even for non-celebrities, who before entering a pub endure, like Kitty in *Anna Karenina*, "a young man's feelings before a battle," and who bow down in thanks before the DJs waging war on conversation everywhere—including my hairdresser's, where it's being drummed out by the unstoppable march of techno—what makes small talk a tall order is performance pressure.

➜ Rule three: The more engaged we are, the less nervous we feel

Research has found that with a serious topic or a good friend, we measure a conversation's success by how enthralled we were by what the other person said. Whereas, the less familiar the other person, the more trivial the topic, the likelier we are to rate the experience by our own performance. An exception is between long-term romantic partners, when neither a topic's gravity nor either party's performance appears to effect post-conversational satisfaction—the negative interpretation being that they've stopped listening, the rose-tinted that they're so at-one that the relationship is one unending symphony of sensitively cadenced talk. You decide.

Setting lovebirds aside, it seems that if we're not invested in a discussion, or whom it's with, we're self-conscious. Therefore the shortest path to bearable small talk must be to make it more involving—that is, to value it. Emotion inhibits this. However, harnessed by small talk, emotion is also the solution.

➜ Rule four: Convert fear to imagination

Philip Larkin's friend, novelist Kingsley Amis, suggested that human history is the tale of man, an animal, striving to forget he is an animal. Emotion exists to remind us of the truth. Embarrassment is the nephew of an ancient monster, fear. In bad cases we long for the earth to open and welcome us back, like the worms we were before life grew so complicated.

As anxiety prowls for evidence you'd be better off inside a large paper bag, nervousness ensures these fears come true, every time. Although such feelings are common with strangers, small talk is a correlate, not—as many small-talk haters assume—the cause. The true horror arises from self-consciousness: the feeling you're on show, which paradoxically sabotages self-awareness, muffling your sense of the topic in hand, and, worse, your sensitivity to interlocutors.

But fear is merely dyspeptic imagination. Set it to work on thinking about the other person, remembering that he, if a stranger, is at an equal disadvantage, and embrace the opening courtesies, equivalent to those nosy things dogs do sniffing each other out—as an opportunity to express your feelings. Unless, that is, they resemble those of the man who crushed an old friend of mine. They were on a train, heading to an academic conference, sharing pleasantries and peanuts. Then, having inhaled the nuts, the other man picked up his book (almost certainly by Schopenhauer) and handed my friend the empty packet, saying:

"This is all our conversation is. Exchanging rubbish."

THE PRINCIPLES

All relationships serve self-interest—after all, the laughs and tears we share with friends are fringe benefits. Cynical? Hardly. This is what makes them meaningful. Similarly, conversation thrives if it is purposeful, so let artful small talk do the reconnaissance, delineating common territory and seeking a mutually agreeable direction in which to amble. Very often its point is no fancier than to find the point in talking to someone.

Not always easy. But as anyone fond of pubs or beauty parlors knows, chat need say little to be pleasant. Whatever the context, old friends or new, it is best if speakers respect five principles:

Put others at ease
Put yourself at ease

Weave in all parties
Establish shared interests
Actively pursue your own

These combine into the following strategy:

→ **Rule five: Approach small talk like a treasure hunt**
Tools are:

Elicitors: open questions—e.g., "Have you come far?"
(a House of Windsor special)
Neutral topics
Observations on your environment
Ice breakers: humorous questions and remarks
Suggestions
Enthusiasm

The most productive spirit is pioneering: sincere, curious, light, humorous. Radiate pleasure and non–Schopenhauer fans usually take it personally, opening like flowers in the sun. The only trouble with enthusiasm, as the wrung-out wife of an ebullient acquaintance confided, is you can drown in it. So if in doubt, leave it out.

→ **Rule six: Start in neutral**
Ladies and gentlemen once kept commonplace books, magpie hoards containing scraps of literature, historical facts, bon mots— any bauble that snagged the owner's fancy—that were consulted and memorized before engagements, lest opportunity arose to flourish them and impress the company.

Dare you disturb the universe with a tag from Ovid? Alas, today it's dangerous to presume shared knowledge or values, let alone puff your plumage. Better to think, as you approach that door, what is in the news, fashion, cultural affairs—whatever piques you. Try to combine elements in surprising ways. ("I was thinking of entering this outfit for the Eurovision Song Contest"; "I see you're wearing Manchester United's colors.") Ideally frame them to cascade clues about the other person. I wouldn't dream of suggesting you copy actress Imogen Stubbs and invent something. . . .

> The Time I Died, *I think we called it—and tested it out at a pretentious party. The collective response? "Oh, God, yes, so moving. I loved that book."*

No, no, much nicer to mine uncontroversial territory. Keep it light: an observation, question, a thread to weave to something new. And revelations are out. I've never forgotten my first goring by an ex-boyfriend's horn-hided ex-belle: "Did he tell you about the abortion?" Or my own clunker to an ex-colleague—standard-issue, but still toe-crushing, and pointless: "Any more children?"

If the answer's no, he doesn't want to say why.

ACTS OF PROVOCATION

Some approaches ask for trouble—which might be just the thing to pep talk up. Compare "I'm not sure about the coffee here" with "This latte's like breast milk." Between prejudice and opinion lie discussion and disagreement. But easy does it. Beware:

Generalizations:
Can appear pompous, shutting off discussion.
Personal remarks:
There's no accounting for neurosis. For example, "I hate being told I look well," confided a radiant beauty. "It means I'm fat."

Unsolicited advice:

A charming fellow restaurant diner once told me, "Order the fruit: It'll do your skin good."

Health, wealth, creed:

If you must know, there are other ways to find out.

Boasting:

Let them see how marvelous you are.

Moaning:

Need I explain?

Bitching:

A hostage to fortune. Do you know them well enough to trust?

Teasing:

Do they share your sense of humor?

Too much information:

Enough said?

Unwarranted sympathy:

Who wants to feel pitied?

Telling a woman where she bought her dress:

Obscurely insulting, and a form of boast.

"What do you do?"

We've all asked, but who enjoys reheating their CV? If he loves his work, you'll hear soon enough. And you don't want to come over as a status sifter or salary sniffer, do you?

If on the receiving end of this question and feeling puckish, why not take this ex-escort's advice: "I say I'm a brain surgeon and see how they react." Or copy ad director Vick Beasley, and print bogus business cards (hers read "BDI" for "Beasley Detective Investigations": extra credit went to those who detected the pun).

Be prepared or toads shall hop forth from thy mouth. Like my unlucky friend who fell mute, to hide the effects of goldfish-bowl chargers of wine served by her boyfriend's intimidating older friends. But the soigné hostess wasn't having any of it and kept asking about her legal course. Somehow my friend spoke: "Don't worry your pretty head about it."

The shame outlived the hangover.

↪ Rule seven: Find an incentive for talking

What do you want to talk about?

To save time and tedium, seek what your fellow talkers would like. With antennae tuned, you can find common ground fast, then dig in. Trail topic bait, pouncing on subjects that light them up. Just one word—"sports"—is a personality biopsy; gouts of useful information usually spurt forth. Or, if in season, mention Oscars: Either they won't care, or they'll discuss films, gowns, or whoever's blubbing acceptance speech. Voilà your conversation's direction: another topic, culture, conspicuous consumption, or the grisly trade in emotica.

Watching faces also stems catastrophe. (I still picture my dumb-struck Anglo-Indian friend, Anil, at a barbecue, as evening darked to night, and I happened upon him cornered by a beery Blimp, who it transpired had been calling him "O'Neill" and descanting on how Albion was awash with foreigners.)

Floundering? Then fabricate an incentive. Generous small talk automatically has a point, not least for you: Jonathan Haidt, author of *The Happiness Hypothesis*, found "kindness and gratitude activities" the most enduring of mood improvers. I know a hotel publicist who finds the perpetual obligation to chat to strangers occasionally stifling. She wards off insincerity by finding ways to help: a restaurant tip, gallery to visit. This tactic works both ways, since being asked advice is flattering. Maybe the other person knows a good butcher, book? A gift for a glum aunt? Specific inquiries reap detailed answers—richer small-talk material.

↝ Rule eight: Tickle boundaries

Discussion should enlarge by exploratory increments. Pace matters. Too neutral, too long, and you'll both transmit beige personalities, but accelerate to war's evils right away and her son will be a brigadier. Instead, use discreet hints to flush the other person out.

If in doubt, the stair to intimacy has four steps:

Courtesies ("Hello, how are you?")
Trade information ("So what brought you here?")
Trade opinion ("Isn't this music unusual?")
Trade feeling ("Yup, I hate it.")

Pose questions that circle the personal, noting whether the other prefers a sharp or gentle approach, and adapting accordingly. And although small talk aims to please, don't make this too obvious. Unlike journalist Piers Morgan who, in an uncharacteristically beseeching mood, asked Diana, Princess of Wales, what it was like "being Diana":

"Oh God, let's face it, even I have had enough of Diana now— and I am Diana."

Helpful of her to point that out.

It could have been worse: She could've said, "So ..." This tends to rear up then gently die after the preliminary flurry when basic parameters are established (who you are, why you're here). For such moments, we have ice breakers. The best are funny. Such as the occasion Diana's alleged bête noire, Prince Philip, went to dine with the governor of Agadir, and the British delegation was alarmed to see no cutlery. Not that this was unusual in Morocco, but nor was the Prince known for his sensitivity to foreign ways. Yet into the couscous plunged his fingers. "Don't you find," he said, "eating with a knife and fork is like making love through an interpreter?"

→ Rule nine: Build talk up to scale

Turn observations into discussion points by tagging on a question. For example, "It's a beautiful evening, *isn't it*?" or "I can hardly keep up, there are so many great American novelists/new restaurants/ways to lose money these days, *aren't there*?" The implied compliment to listeners is that you value their opinion.

More provocative opinions can be smuggled in, potential offense cushioned by the note of query. But watch your tone: Agreement-seeking can be discreet bullying. Or worse, in the case of the acrid yoga instructor who strode up to my friend, in the process of executing a perfectly humble down dog, and said: "Have you ever been to a yoga class before, because this is an advanced class, isn't it?"

Just as hazarding a topic you've no passion for is unwise—without an opinion, it's a dead end—so you should aim to raise a subject with a follow-up comment or question in mind. Had I prepared one for Jeremy Irons, I could have averted full-body blush. Had I been less self-conscious, I might have seen what we already had in common: the place. If only I'd asked him about the exhibition. If, if, if ...

THE ALGEBRA OF A FOLLOW-UP: AN EXERCISE

This is a topic-creation scheme. Instead of dollops of heavy material, information should be drip-fed. Try combining these ingredients:

A   Situation—where you are; what people have been talking about

B   The other person/people

C   What you would like to know

Bald statements are hard to respond to (hence those fond of them seem pompous). Instead, fuse observations with questions that invite more than yes or no.

For example, at a welly-wanging contest held in Scotland by your pal Seamus:

A + B + C   =   "This is my first welly-wanging contest. You look pretty handy, Seamus. What is the best way to hurl a Wellington boot?"

A + (CB)   =   "These wellies are light but not very aerodynamic. How are yours?"

(AB) + (BC)   =   "Much as I love Seamus's welly-wanging contest, rowing across the loch gets harder every year. Have you come far, Jeremy?"

(ABC)   =   "What film other than *Welly-Wanging* should I bet on winning an Oscar?"

➜ Rule ten: Be optimistic

Worried something isn't worth saying? Heed the anonymous author of 1673's *Art of Complaisance*:

> *The readiest way to become agreeable in any Conversation, is to banish all distrust, and to be confident that we are already so.*

And what makes anything interesting? Well, how do you know a poem is a poem? Because it's marooned in white. Two things make its words art: the mind that selected them, and readers' faith that the choice was meaningful. And if you want to hold something up for consideration, it is already interesting: it interests you.

No idea why it attracts your attention? Mention it anyway; someone else might have a clue. With an open mind, you might learn something new about you. And try to extend the courtesy. If "So ..." is small talk's hardest word, nastiest is "No." As James Joyce found, meeting fellow *belletrist* Marcel Proust:

> *Our talk consisted solely of the word "No." ... Proust asked me if I knew the duc de so-and-so. I said, "No." Our hostess asked Proust if he had read such and such a piece of* Ulysses. *Proust said, "No."*

Conversation hinges on reciprocity. You may sing like a nightingale on the dullest of subjects, but eloquence is no use, no matter that you're Joan of Arc or Joan Rivers, if nobody can answer you. If you speak, and I don't, a contract is broken. However, it isn't necessary to match word for word, revelation for revelation; the trade is emotional, not informational. What matters is to hear the invitation in what someone says: to speak, or to listen.

TYPOLOGY OF BORES, CHORES, AND OTHER CONVERSATIONAL BEASTS

DEMOLITION BALL   *Pendulor blockheadibus*

Demolition Ball will let you get a word in edgeways. But don't mistake these interludes for him listening. In the lags between tirades, you can almost hear the groan of mental machinery as he swings back, preparing for the next attack.

Whatever you say, however you say it, DB will find something objectionable. Whether or not it is what you actually said. Why let facts stand in the way of a good argument?

His enthusiasms are little easier to take than his hates. Positive, negative—every opinion is delivered with such ferocity that people appear always to agree. It's easier.

The unfortunate by-product of rolling over to DB is that it appears to confirm he is right in all he says. This is particularly harmful since DB's operatic ego is in fact host to a tragic character, an aged toddler, still reeling at the discovery that he is not, as Ma and Pa suggested, the font of the world's hopes, dreams, or wisdom. So the older he gets, the higher disappointment mounts, and DB punches out with ever greater force.

Tactics: Facing a monster, it's tempting to play dead. Instead, do as Perseus did to the gorgon Medusa: Hold up a mirror to turn him to stone. It is because DB can't master his emotions that he messes with other people's. So step back, calmly identify contradictions in his arguments, and watch him writhe.

Can't be bothered? Then treat him like a tot: Laugh or hug the helpless critter.

Pluses: In a Whatever world, DB's conviction that some things need saying, sense and sensitivity be damned, is rare. Consider him a whetstone to sharpen your wits.

3

PAY HEED

On the Acrobatics of Attention

When Marilyn Monroe married Arthur Miller, obtuse observers were confounded: What could an intellectual possibly have to say to a helium-headed bombshell?

But if Laurence Olivier is to be trusted, Monroe, not Miller, got the fuzzy end of the lollipop. He wrote to Noël Coward from the set of *The Prince and the Showgirl*:

> *The blond bottom looks and appears to be very good indeed. . . .*
> *Arthur talks a great deal better than he listens, but I never*
> *found his talk very entertaining.*

Of all deterrents to conversation, most off-putting is the notion that great conversationalists are great talkers. Luckily, it's wrong. Conversation is two-way, three-way; as many ways as there are people. And however entertaining a night with Oscar Wilde might have been, compared to Arthur Miller, it would have been as spectacle, preferably at a distance, or you'd have risked supplying the warp for his wit.

Talk has hogged the limelight in part because listening lacks glamour. Politeness ordains it a duty, which has been mistaken for a measure of conversational power, with listeners the weaker vessel, to be filled by speakers' potent spirit. So thought society Rottweiler la duchesse du Maine, daughter-in-law to Louis XIV:

> *I adore life in society: everyone listens to me, and I listen to no one.*

Unsurprisingly, her fashionable reign was brief.

→ Rule one: Great conversationalists listen more than talk

Surely the main reason listening is overlooked is that its masters deflect attention and cast it flatteringly elsewhere. Nonetheless, unlike madame la duchesse, the great French *salonnières*—who did so much, as historian Benedetta Craveri remarked, to make conversation "a game for shared pleasure"—placed "talent for listening" above speech, rating the brilliance of in-house wits according to the polish of their politesse.

Well, of course: If nothing else, drawing out other people is canny social politics. Stefano Guazzo, author of *Civile Conversation*, advised:

> *Keepe the mouth more shut, and the ears more open. . . . In companie [ye] shall get the good will and favour of others, as well by giving eare courteously, as by speaking pleasantly. For wee think, they thinke wel of us, which are attentive to our talke.*

It can be the path to power. Witness the career of eighteenth-century courtesan Elizabeth Armitstead, who began in brothels yet bagged a top politician hubby, slinking into polite society by the grace less of her "arts of display and seduction," than being a "sympathetic listener," able to "make every man believe himself the centre of the universe."

And for any misguided person who imagines this is just for girls, another lady (opinion is divided as to whether she was Winston Churchill's mother or Queen Victoria's granddaughter) captured the difference between captivating talkers and heart-stealing listeners in two prime ministers:

> *When I left the dining room after sitting next to Mr. Gladstone, I thought he was the cleverest man in England. But after sitting next to Mr. Disraeli, I thought I was the cleverest woman in England.*

Whom would you prefer? In short, stuff duty. Far from talk's demure shadow, listening is its creative partner, able to shape conversation, forestall faux pas, forge connections, direct discussion, reap information and joy.

See how easily Dolly Parton bewitched this middle-aged magazine interviewer:

> *She totally focuses on me: how many female superstars could I say that about?*

Or was it Parton's opening gambit that won her over?

> *"I saw you in the corridor and I thought, 'Who is that attractive young woman?'"*

Actually, both.

Great listeners are irresistible because they sense what we want to hear. Soothing noises are part of their art. At its heart lie techniques to seduce purses, votes, and minds.

THE RISE AND FALL OF THE EAR

Ears aren't just acoustic channels or pincushions for fashion statements. Their use and abuse as symbols throughout history tell a tale of social change. Where once power lay with gods, kings, and armies, whom ordinary mortals had to placate, in our rackety world, with the assiduous propitiations of advertisers and other media, everyone seems to be grabbing at our attention, and we seem to listen less and less.

Ancient Egyptians exalted the aural organ to combat deities' and monarchs' indifference. Statues of pharaohs had jumbo flaps to display—and doubtless encourage—their willingness to heed the people. In hieroglyphics, the ear represented divine hearing, and worshippers left votive ear sculptures at temples to implore the gods to lend them theirs. Hear the longing in this three-thousand-year-old hymn (etched with forty-four ears) to the god Ptah: lord of Truth, great of strength, the Hearer.

Christ's final miracle before crucifixion was to replace the ear of the high priest's servant Malchus after the enraged disciple Peter struck it off: an act of forgiveness that serves as an emblem of Christ's openness to hear the prayers of all.

More sinister iconography adorns the Rainbow portrait of Elizabeth I, a branding exercise that depicts the childless monarch as divinely youthful (aged sixty-seven) and all-seeing, in a cloak spangled with ears and eyes; a baldly coded warning to any subject minded to foment dissent at a time when the succession remained uncertain. No wonder, condemned after a disastrous colonial exploit, Elizabeth's erstwhile pet Sir Walter Ralegh instructed his son:

Publicke affaires are rockes, private conversacions are whirle-pooles and quickesandes. It is a like perilous to doe well and to doe ill.

(Likewise, the Queen's motto was the repressive *Video et Taceo*—"I see all and say nothing." Never mind that she rejoiced in conversation, in several languages at once when ambassadors came calling.)

Rather gorier propaganda took place in Japan in 1597, with

the erection of the *Mimizuka* or "Mound of Ears" outside Kyoto. This grim shrine contains ears and noses of up to forty thousand Korean victims of overlord Toyotomi Hideyoshi's territory grabs into Korea and China (1592–98)—an obfuscation that couldn't mask his ventures' ultimate failure.

Martial madness turned silly in 1739, when Spain and Britain began what the latter dubbed the War of Jenkins's Ear, named for a British captive who lost his to a Spanish privateer's blade in 1731. It was handed back with the words, allegedly,

"Take this to your king and tell him if he were here I would do the same to him."

Instead, seven years later, Jenkins flourished the wizened item before Parliament, demanding retribution, and the conflict raged for nine wretched years. But this noble revenge story masked the war's somewhat ignoble origin in a squabble over Florida colonies.

In the last century, the ear became a source of horror, figuring disconnection and alienation—whether in the lobe that crazed Vincent van Gogh lopped off as a love token, the severed ear that besoils a white-picket-fence world in the film *Blue Velvet*, or the one sliced off a cop taken hostage in *Reservoir Dogs*.

THE DYNAMISM OF LISTENING

As art forms go, listening is a real Cinderella, little studied, scarcely taught. Yet there is no doubt it activates intelligence: Infants snatch up words, with a vocabulary of up to five thousand by their fourth year, largely spoken grammatically, whereas deaf children unschooled in sign language or lipreading are severely mentally impaired. Are these dynamic skills, found in no other species, acquired simply by hanging around?

Not a chance. The opposite of passive, listening is an activity and it wires the minds of those of us who are lucky enough to be wired for sound.

→ Rule two: Listening is the mother of relating

Feedback is neither silent nor invisible. It precedes talk and is first evoked by baby talk, what speech professionals call "motherese." Although baby talk may sound like nonsense, it is instinctive and universal. Studies have found even premature infants automatically play goo-goo games with parents, and by four months they chime in to nursery rhymes, and, giggling, will mess with the beat—in effect, cracking musical jokes. Parents are no less programmed than their sprogs; as a child develops, baby talk unfolds in remarkably similar patterns across the globe, whatever the glottal idiosyncrasies of the parents' mother tongue.

In essence, it's a foundation course in the wind instrument, the voice, which is far and away the most complex sound system we can hear in nature. When the adult voice lifts and dips, roaming around inside and elongating vowels (consonants, the percussion section, are taught later), the exaggerations of pitch and tone sculpt points for the infant's untrained auditory cortex to seize hold of, educating it in how to differentiate sounds, and later words, from the voicestream.

The importance of baby talk to malleable young minds is evident in the case of so-called wild children, who, having grown up without human contact for the first several years of their lives, never learn to speak. But more than language, when the infant gurgles back to the parent, the two are duetting. Such musical companionship informs and enriches intellectually and emotionally, grounding babies in taking turns and timing: the key to social harmony.

By contrast, if babies are understimulated, they suffer. Depressed mothers' infants, who tend to experience lower pitched, less frequent vocalizations, are relatively flat, and clumsier at joining in, taking turns—negative feedback that gives their mothers less to grab on to, weakening the parental bond further. It would be wrong to accuse the poor mums of passing depression on. Rather, insufficiently turned on to the world, their babies struggle to gauge feelings or express their own.

Attention-deficit disorder, formerly known as annoying brat syndrome, is a clumsy term for a pervasive social blight: bad listening. I don't just mean those trying, shouty kids who hear nothing at the word "No" but an instruction to turn up the volume. However, they're a poignant illustration of what becomes of people who don't acquire, for whatever reason, the raft of facilities that we compact under the term "listening," skills that children saw more of in less distracted times, but which are today increasingly scarce—whether in classrooms, pubs, clubs, or at dinner parties.

Can we improve?

You might think, why try? Are we not doomed, set from the crib to our happy or unhappy parent's wavelength? Indeed, because we learn to listen before we speak, analyzing it feels odd. But it isn't impossible, and it's worth it. Throughout life, listening makes us articulate, creating knowledge, attuning us to others' rhythm, helping us feel good. Like every aspect of conversation, it can be done better. Or worse.

In theory, it consists of two skills:

Projection: displaying listening
Detection: interpreting meaning and sentiment

In practice, detection breaks down to six tasks:

Hearing messages
Understanding
Remembering
Interpreting
Evaluating
Responding

But six is too modest a number. Words' melody maps the emotional curve of meaning, and as those who suffer from autism find, without sentimental equipment—what Jane Austen termed sensibility—following conversation is tough. So nimble listeners leaf through a mille-feuille of different messages: not only assessing context and sense, but gleaning speakers' motivation, personality, agenda, mood, indigestion, sobriety ...

That is, listening is harder than reading runes. Yet, by adulthood, most of our interpretative software is such that a study of people listening to football results found that

> as soon as the name of the second team is read out, you know straight away what the result is [win/lose/draw], even though you haven't heard the score yet.

In another, from recordings of "forty seconds of surgeon-patient consultations" in which words had been wiped, leaving only tone, listeners could deduce which surgeons had been sued for malpractice. Surprise, surprise, they were the ones who sounded overbearing, not sympathetic. The moral of the story is that listening binds people to us.

→ Rule three: Listening is the mother of invention: we make it up as we go along

Although we might imagine we hang off a person's every word, this is a trick of our con-artist minds.

Three factors make listening creative, setting aside the not inconsiderable matter of weighing up the myriad meanings in every utterance. First, memory forms, as Plato observed, on a warm wax slab. Most messages self-destruct within half a minute, conversation following a thirty-second short-term memory track, which is built and dismantled as fast as its engine moves. So we lose the thread, or as actress Ronni Ancona apologized for a tangent:

> My train of thought fell into my stream of consciousness.

Second, listening is selective: We zone in on a voice, even if others in the vicinity are louder, in what linguists dub the "cocktail-party effect." Third, however much we might wish to, we cannot hear everything. Expert Jean Aitchison explained:

> [If we] assume an average of four sounds per English word, and a speed of five words a second, we are expecting the ear and brain to cope with around twenty sounds a second. But humans cannot process this number of signals in that time.

Like inattentive yet imaginative secretaries taking dictation, our Houdini brains don't absorb every unit of each word but surf sound, improvising, glossing, and predicting. Such feats show how listening elasticates our minds, springing us to conclusions with a gymnast's grace. Is it any wonder that occasionally we slip, detecting words on the tip of another's tongue, and bite back before they have spoken?

→ **Rule four: We're boundless adepts at piecing sense from nonsense**

Listening, like housework, is observed more in the neglect than the performance.

While no great treaty could have taken effect without arduous hours of ear industry, history's annals yield largely negative examples. If Henry II and legend are to be believed, four daft knights misconstrued a rhetorical question, "Who will rid me of this troublesome priest?" for orders to dash off and dash off Thomas à Becket.

Critic Kenneth Tynan built a theory of Tom Stoppard's plays on one odd remark: "I am a human nothing." (In fact Stoppard had said: "I am assuming nothing.") John Mortimer found Kingsley Amis's revelation "I hit my son with a hammer" almost as suggestive. Alas, no Oedipal tale, it was not novelist Martin, but Amis Sr.'s thumb that was black-and-blue.

These accidents happen because when we listen we iron out confusion with extraordinary, sometimes alarming efficiency, as was demonstrated in a 1967 "alternative psychotherapy" experiment. Subjects—college students—asked questions, receiving yes or no answers from a therapist in another room. Except there was no therapist: The experimenters had decided what responses would be given in advance, pre-preparing random sequences of yes and no. As a consequence, one guinea pig was advised first "no" then "yes" to stick with his girlfriend. However, although

> *he expressed surprise at the "yes," responding that he had expected a "no" [he] then looked for the pattern that made this [contradiction] intelligible. Students commented that the answers had a lot of meaning.*

Our ability to find patterns of meaning in the most arbitrary data is supreme, as was proved by similar tests, which created "poems" from random lines in an anthology. Does such interpretive creativity destroy the notion of art? Not a bit. These experiments underscore that without interpreters, all meaning, all art, is air. In this sense every artwork is collaborative: a conversation between creator and viewer, writer and reader. (Suggesting that a monkey manacled to a typewriter for long enough could indeed type work attributable to Shakespeare—provided a human being in another room had even longer to explain why Shakespeare had written such tripe.)

And the improvised sense-jazz of conversation is surely the ultimate artistic collaboration. Excuse me if this sounds pseudy, but aren't you impressed how inventive we are?

↝ Rule five: Signal attention to show you are happy to listen

However, the rewards of listening aren't always obvious. Once I believed it a chore. Specifically, my first night at college, in the pub, sandwiched between two dry crystallographers for whom I served less as jam than bland conversational glue. I wondered whether, given limitless nods, smiles, and Really?s, I need ever speak again.

But I was being lazy, projecting satisfaction, instead of seeking an incentive to talk. And if attention is disengaged, what of communication? In a tart letter, Jane Austen mocked two women who "spent their whole time in what they called *conversation*" yet

> *there was no interchange of opinion and not often any resemblance of subject, for Mrs Thorpe spoke continually of her children, and Mrs Allen of her gowns.*

Who enjoys the sensation that someone has lent you his ears, retaining his mind for his own, private use? However, very often this impression is unwarranted, because many who appear distracted are anything but.

How to Listen Actively:
A Signaler's Guide

Strong listener reactions elicit livelier speech by projecting interest. Physical cues are: Face the speaker, make eye contact, nod, smile, let emotions animate your face.

By way of experiment, fix an expectant gaze on a silent person in a group, as if they are about to say something fascinating. How long until they speak?

Take audible affirmative action too. "Wow!" "Really?" and "You didn't!" inane if insincere, are powerful used appropriately. "Never interrupt," a cliché of conversational etiquette, should be ignored. Good interruptions aid the flow. Such as:

Supportive comments:	to encourage or evince sympathy, like ticks in the margin of your homework ("I so agree," "Exactly," "No!")
Overlaps:	when thoughts run gaily together
Summaries:	to clarify meaning, ensuring the right message is heard

LISTENING AS SELF-EXPRESSION
AND REPRESSION

Signals are one thing. A responsive listener also shows, and knows when to veil, his feelings. Or does he?

In the 1960s another experimenter, computer pioneer Joseph Weizenbaum, created Doctor, a software program that adapted a psychotherapy technique for bouncing back patients' statements as questions:

User: *I have been rather depressed lately.*
Computer: *Are you depressed often?*
User: *Yes, almost all the time.*
Computer: *Why do you say yes almost all the time?*
User: *Right now I feel like I could cry.*
Computer: *Is it because right now you feel like you could cry that you came to me?*

One morning he was appalled to discover his transfixed secretary at a computer, unspooling her sorrows into Doctor's clunky, copycat code.

I'm not shocked Weizenbaum was shocked (contrary as it seems, given that this confirmed his program's success). Each of us swims in an amniotic consciousness, and we love, need, to feel understood, in order to dilute the solitude of our condition. So the thought that an echo is sufficient to convince us we're being listened to, that the bogus Doctor could seduce the secretary, carries the degrading suggestion that much of human complexity—those worries and wonders we store up and long to share—may also be illusory, empty, and that we are mere bundles of reactions, mysterious, and meaningful only to us.

Such fears plague modern man, and to an extent explain the value vested in expert ear-givers—father confessors, therapists— who restore faith in empathy as an art akin to shriving the soul. And whose friendship we needn't risk, troubles we needn't take on in return: a relationship dead-end, compared to fruitful exchanges with friends. Consolingly private, but pretty barren, this seems a perfect manifestation of the depressing direction conversation is taking.

→ **Rule six: Good listeners share a virtue: imaginative hospitality**
On the upside, Doctor's success indicates how accessible are the basic tools of empathy. Nonetheless, for meaningful understanding, imaginative engagement helps.

Its qualities have been quantified in an "empathic communication coding system" designed to assess physicians' listening, which placed greater value on showing than telling. From best to worst:

LEVEL	TYPE OF LISTENING
6	Shared feeling/experience
5	Confirmation of an emotion's legitimacy
4	Pursuit of the topic
3	Acknowledgment
2	Implicit recognition (but changing the topic)
1	Perfunctory recognition (autopilot)
0	Denial/contradiction

(I doubt this system advises British GPs to listen for a paltry average of three minutes before interrupting patients and telling them what is wrong.)

An open mind puts the censorious self on hold while a speaker speaks. In theory. In practice, since listening is a process of selection and creation, with our inner voice providing a running commentary, mind clearance is difficult.

To improve, try to notice how you listen. Do you hear people out? Or are you, like me, so eager to show empathy that you're prone to talk over them?

And be aware of how you don't listen. Detecting the message in what someone says—the motive, goal—is guesswork of an eye-blink, which lends it the false, often deafening power of instinct or intuition. Ralph Waldo Emerson caught the difficulty:

> *What you are sounds so loudly in my ears that I can't hear what you say.*

In conversation, as music, it is easier to hear a false note than identify its source. Our minds are astonishingly able at judging, creating rules of thumb, prejudices. Holding back—not immediately attributing our irritation to the other person's character, but pausing to examine why we're annoyed—serves us better.

↦ Rule seven: Trace the emotional line of expression
Superagent Mark McCormack urged aspiring tycoons:

> *Hear what people are really saying as opposed to what they are telling you.*

Likewise, actress Harriet Walter advised would-be Cleopatras wrestling with Shakespeare's verse to "hear the need" in a character's speech—that is, find the emotional code to unlock its meaning.

Like arrows, words have impact through force and direction, but their point hits home only when listeners can account for where they are from and where they aim. And differences in conversational style add another "direction" that can, if misunderstood, lead to a personality clash. According to discourse analyst Deborah Tannen, a barrage of questions punctuated by finger jabs is a friendly fumble to most New Yorkers; to a Californian, it is assault.

So reserve judgment, bearing in mind:

A speaker's native and personal style (his "Omigod" may
　　not be blasphemy to him)
How his words relate to the conversation so far
How his words relate to the agendas circling beneath
How emotions inflect what he says and what you hear

And try to follow the emotional roller coaster implied by tone and
pitch, as well as posture, facial expression, and gestures.

SYMPATHY SHUTTERS: A GLOSSARY

Thou shalt not give advice: the undeclared commandment of
the Samaritans' helpline. Advice is a peerless strategy for not listening, and many words of seeming empathy are double agents,
closing down talk the speaker would rather not hear, or criticism
cloaked in sympathy.

Here follow some false friends, which appear to hold out
comfort but, like a cross wielded at a vampire, aim to drive others'
woes away. In addition, some handy water-treaders that sound
supportive without agreeing (ideal for tricky conversation).

LINE	SUBTEXT
"Poor you!"	"Victim *again*—do we detect a pattern here?"
"You are in the wars!"	"Why do you keep picking fights?"
"Yes, when I did X ..."	"Back to my favorite subject: me."
"The same thing happened to Y ..."	"You're not the only one with problems!"

LINE	SUBTEXT
"She didn't!"	"Stop exaggerating."
"I can see why you felt that way."	"Are you, perchance, being unreasonable?"
"If I were you, I would . . ."	"Thank heaven I'm not!"
"That's awful!"	"Enough already."
"I understand."	"And have for twenty minutes. Where's your fast-forward?"
"Why do you think he said that?"	"Look in the mirror, honey."
"That must have been hard."	"But note my use of the past tense: Move on."
"Next time . . ."	"New topic, please."
"Can't be easy."	"Hey, could be worse."
"That's hilarious!"	"I don't get it."

→ Rule eight: Hear the unstated

Comic Joan Rivers says no to shrinks ("There goes my act"). Poet Rainer Maria Rilke was little more enamored:

> *Something like a disinfected soul results from [psychoanalysis], a non-thing, a freakish form of life corrected in red ink like a page in a schoolboy's notebook.*

He was too suspicious. Responsible therapists tease out discontinuities and slip-ups in what patients tell them, not to smooth away quirks of personality, but to unearth tensions and conflicts, and break down hidden causes of pain—painful as this enzyme may be.

In any situation understanding is deepened if we listen out for insights lodged inside inconsistencies and non sequiturs; telling details that can identify the knotty kernel of a misunderstanding from which problems have grown, or reveal interesting kinks in a mind's architecture.

For example, Elizabeth I shot down rumors of a dalliance, vehemently denying "anything dishonourable"—then spoiled it by adding, so what if she led a "dishonourable life"? As queen she "did not know anybody who could forbid her." These statements coalesce the conflict she faced between being a woman, servant of chastity, and a monarch above men's laws—a conflict that, in a cooler temper, she strove to put on ice by assuming the sterile role of Virgin Queen.

On a practical level, when you hear a contradiction—say, the airline claims your flight's cancellation is not the same as bumping you off, therefore compensation isn't due—unpack it. Not only can this be therapeutic and forestall misconceptions, but you may cajole someone into revising his tune. (For extra intimidation, write the explanation down, calmly checking spellings and punctuation—see *How to Complain*, page 249).

Attend to speech patterns too, as these are living autobiographies. If the new boyfriend gabs in unalloyed jargon, clichés, or swear words, what does this say? If the prospective client talks down to you, how will he do business?

And heed omissions. What does the estate agent pass over in silence? If the car dealer keeps returning to the design, ask again how the machine moves.

LET HER EAT CAKE

Philosopher J. L. Austin suggested that statements have three dimensions: words' sense, the meaning implied by that sense, and the speaker's underlying aim. This idea suggests a recipe for X-ray listening.

Take a statement: "Marie Antoinette has eaten all the cakes."

Now picture it as the message iced on a three-tiered cake: the top layer consists of the message's meaning (what the speaker is saying); the middle, an implied opinion tucked inside; and at bottom, the speaker's sly conversational purpose.

Icing: "Marie Antoinette has eaten all the cakes."
Top: Greedy Marie Antoinette looks fat.
Middle: Fat is not a good look.
Bottom: She makes me sick; I wish she made you sick too.

This prompts a final question, the plate: Why is this speaker making this statement?

The answer depends on your view of the context. In this case, I imagine my bony speaker addressing a boyfriend, who, his eyes lost in Marie Antoinette's creamy cleavage, replies, "Let her eat cake," wishing she'd let him scoop up the crumbs.

↦ **Rule nine: Listen to construct the meaning you want to hear**
When the reluctant suitor Ziggy told fellow *Big Brother* contestant Chanelle that he wanted "to finish this," she shot back, "This conversation?"

It took him another week to dump her.

Her rat-trap response demonstrates how effectively replies can nail the meaning of a preceding sentence—whether or not this happens to be what a speaker intended. Similarly, paraphrases elucidate speakers' views, and may sneakily alter them, tossing them back, refashioned in so pleasing a style that others happily mistake them for their own—spinning conversation wherever you would go....

For this reason, La Fontaine compared a skilled conversationalist to "the bee who gathers honey alike from every different flower." He might have been describing Lord Rendel, politician-friend to egotist Gladstone, who could

> start a new trend of thought with the most innocent suggestion; some challenging remark, casually interposed.... With the gentlest pressure on the rudder, he could give a turn to a conversation, confirm or moderate a trend of policy.

Effective listeners reach inside minds to place a hand on conversation's controls, an ability that helps avert the danger to every bearer of bad tidings: getting shot. Like business consultant Rick Huttner, who inoculates clients to unpalatable truths by building rapport, using listening and questions to train them to his way of thinking.

> I respect all the input they give me. I listen for what they really want from their lives.... [The job] is really listening, listening, listening and at the appropriate time adding something to the conversation, and then change happens.

Thus advice emerges as the product of a joint-thinking venture. Which, of course, it is.

So before saying something challenging, see if skilled midwifery can't persuade it out of the other person's mouth:

Listen
Wait to be sure a speaker is finished
Question
Summarize
Empathize
If you must, offer a different view

But you may get further saying nothing at all. Pop artist Andy Warhol might have been a big noise. Still, he understood listening's craftiness, according to singer Deborah Harry:

"He was a terrific listener, that was his genius really. He just sucked it all in, and made a point of never saying too much. That's a skill," she says, and to prove the point, stops and smiles.

Not least of listening's virtues is that it reminds us to cherish silence.

TYPOLOGY OF BORES, CHORES, AND OTHER CONVERSATIONAL BEASTS

THE APOLOGIST   *Perfica nervosa*

She's so, so sorry. She's three minutes late. Her fault: The trains weren't working. She's always expecting them to be—silly her—that's probably why the drivers strike! Has she ruined the meal and everything? And dear me, she's only brought wine, chocs, flowers, no cheese. Sorry, they were clean out of Lafite '78, she had to settle for '75—isn't it awful how old bottles' labels peel off, all that nasty dust. And it's such a pity the roses look as if their petals will drop off next week. If only she'd brought a nice bush....

While having her over for coffee is trying, steel yourself before tea at the Apologist's glossy-mag-proof home. As she wheels out the feast (only truffled unicorn; the phoenix got burned), pointing out asymmetrical holes in her home-fribbled fig focaccia, if you don't hug her, you'll club her.

Although bent on increasing others' happiness, the Apologist has much in common with her introvert sister, the Paranoid. That is to say, she is a mite selfish. In her relentless quest for perfection, she neither hears the pain her sonorous angst inflicts, nor senses that self-flagellation is inverted boasting, compelling others to give reassurances that, as a result, are never entirely sincere.

Tactics: If you care about the Apologist, don't be drawn into her sadomasochistic reward system: Shut down the apology airspace to set her free. If she starts, laugh and change topic. Or say if you didn't know better you'd think she was fishing for compliments.

If you don't love her, the same tactics apply. Otherwise she'll drive you nuts.

Pluses: Maddening, yes, but the Apologist proves how hard it is to be nasty to someone who beats you to it (a useful ploy to remember when you're in trouble).

NOTE BENE
Sorry, But, the Celebrity Apologist: The public display of supplication has become an inevitable chapter in the narrative of any self-disrespecting twenty-first-century celebrity. A jolt of scandal, plus foaming bootlick to the people that a waning star has let down (all potential exercise-DVD/redemption-memoir purchasers), may offer a brief sequel in the public eye. But never confuse a good-hearted Apologist with this suppurating imposter, Sorry, But.

4

THE REST IS SILENCE
On Not Speaking

Silence's advocates tend to be discreet. But unusually self-effacing journalist James Hughes-Onslow spoke out after someone complained that, for all his juicy insider knowledge, having him to dinner was like "feeding a corpse." He argued that this was polite:

> *Any intervention of a merely factual nature would probably bring the conversation to a complete halt.*

Do you hold back? Despair of those who do? However lively your patter, however focused your charm, occasional air pockets in conversation are unavoidable. Whether they're golden, or deadly, is debatable. But then, the same is true of talk.

When Egypt's pharaoh sent Solon, founder of Athens' democracy, an animal to sacrifice, he took the chance to test the Greek's famed wits. Would Solon kindly select which part of the beast he judged best, which worst, and send both back? By return came a single item: the tongue.

If words may be misread, the trouble with silence is it's nothing if not ambivalent. Since it requires discipline, it has long reflected power, and been affiliated with both good and evil. While the Roman goddess Isis vanquished "the lamentable silences of hell," to

Quakers and Buddhists freedom from the word brought higher consciousness. However, these days the negative view is in the ascendant.

The noisier life becomes, the more technology and social isolation gnaw at face-to-face talk, the less conversational silence seems to be valued. Residents of febrile urban environments dread it far more than those reared in gentler, rural settings—as if the absence of speech were as threatening as a Pinter pause.

To me, rising hostility is slightly paradoxical: If we don't converse so much, you might think we'd feel easier with silence. But it also seems logical, as an extension of our declining prowess at reading conversational subtleties. Certainly, the bias is so entrenched that research finds hesitant speakers are routinely taken for doubtful characters: either mad, sad, shifty, or—a telling contradiction, this—powerful. Meanwhile powerless preschool tots are being diagnosed with "selective mutism" (fear of speaking in social situations), a condition formerly known as shyness, that is dosed with Prozac.

There's bleak humor in busy parents contracting out responsibility for their offspring's social graces, like this father, flourishing a check at an analyst:

> *"Ask any price you want. My son doesn't talk. So do whatever you want as long as you make him talk, and then let's not talk about it any more."*

But when did speech cease to be a freedom and become compulsary? Is silence an illness? And what parent licenses strangers to "do whatever you want"?

Whatever is going on, it is sick (if happy news to Pharm-Corps).

It is time to speak up for silence.

→ Rule one: Confidence not talking increases confidence talking
That those who fear silence also grasp its strength is clear from the popular belief that quiet people are arrogant, with some justice in the case of U.S. President "Silent" Cal Coolidge, whose disdain spayed many a conversation.

"How could they tell?" asked Dorothy Parker, on hearing he was dead, and it's thought that it was she who enlivened a dinner by saying she'd bet on getting more than two words out of him. His reply? "You lose."

But the prejudice is more often a projection of self-doubt, as when American *Vogue*'s Anna Wintour became a target to murderous ex-reporter Peter Braunstein:

> *There were many high-profile editors and God knows they had big egos.... But Wintour? She just never talked to peons like us. It was beneath her.*

Braunstein's inadequacies reflect a widespread (fortunately rarely homicidal) malaise. In individualist society, if self-promotion seems nigh on compulsory, those who don't play the game may seem above it all, and above us.

Hence a newspaper interviewer felt moved to note that Churchill's biographer, Martin Gilbert, was unafraid "to leave long pauses as he mulls over a thought or searches for a precise word"—correctly implying that self-restraint and pedantry, handy traits in a historian, are eccentric nonetheless, signs of social deviance and awesome self-assurance.

Are silent people a danger to polite society? The unconfident ones are, according to research that finds that lonely people fear silence most, with anxiety about how to fill it, or seeming needy, compounding the problem by cramping their conversational style: Too scared to ask questions, offer opinions, their introverted habits of speech pretty much guarantee more silence.

Perhaps the chief conversational threat of a quiet person, however, is that his sphinx-like bearing acts as a verbal laxative on those less able to keep their own counsel. Believe me, I know. A former boss was a clam. During one of his rare after-work outings, desperate to fill a void, I began riffing (I knew not why) on the unlikely, not to say barking, possibility that a business rival's bizarre taste in white, pointy loafers had contributed to his recent coronary.

Then I glanced down. What did I see on my boss's feet?

Yes, it's worth getting to grips with silence.

⇢ Rule two: Silence is meaningful

You may imagine that silence says nothing. In fact, in any spoken communication it plays a repertoire of roles. Just as, mathematically speaking, earth should be called sea, since most of the planet is covered in it, so conversation might be renamed silence, as it comprises 40 to 50 percent of an average utterance, excluding pauses for others to talk and the enveloping silence of those paying attention (or not, as the case may be).

Outside speech, silence serves as background, frame, or cue to talk (like the white page around the words of a script, plus added capacity to give emphasis or tug the playwright's sleeve and beg further and better particulars, if anything's unclear). And within speech, it can be a unit of communication or punctuation to pace, pattern, and shade meaning.

Conversation gourmet La Rochefoucauld distinguished between the "eloquent," the "mocking," and the "respectful" silence, as if there were clear-cut types. However, no silence is inherently good or bad. Yes, sometimes it expresses empathy and promotes good talk; others, confusion and distance. Then there are silences of power—as a shield, weapon, or to encourage others to speak. But silence never comes with a label attached, and ambiguity multiplies, since each instance is custom-made. We each have a personal dictionary for interpreting the unsaid, and while your pause may be devoid of intent—say, you're thinking or breathing—it always conveys a message if a listener interprets it as meaningful. All of which increases silence's potential to wound and confuse.

I remember the call from a friend.

"I'm pregnant," she said.

The moment stretched.

"Silence," she said, by way of prompt.

Rude as it seemed, my silence wasn't empty, but clamorous with questions and emotions. So I quickly said, "Wow. Are you happy?" Then immediately wished I hadn't.

Rather than let silence get the better of you, appreciate the virtue in its flexibility: a communication tool that's as versatile as the queen in chess. Heed Benjamin Franklin:

> As we must account for every idle word, so we must account for every idle silence.

Which sounds onerous, but on the contrary, you've everything to gain. Discreet conversational omissions can fuel thought, exercise tact, prompt laughter, drama, flush people out, and push prices up, or down, swifter than any fast-talk. Or as Aelfric Bata, tenth-century monk, teacher, and midget (proudly signing work *brevissimus monachus*) scolded novices:

> It is stupidity to be so talkative and full of words. Chattering garrulity and garrulous chattering are hateful to God.

→ Rule three: Be a connoisseur of pauses

Listen carefully and dumb silence tells you plenty—after all, the pause is for thought.

Two kinds occur in speech: for breath or hesitation. Only around one in twenty are the former, because respiration automatically slows when we talk. (Maybe the abbreviated monk Bata was right, chatterboxes really are dumber, their poor gray cells starved of oxygen.) Often these fall at grammatical breaks, where in writing would be punctuation.

Far more suggestive are hesitation pauses, which comprise between a third and half of ordinary speech, and can pop up anywhere in a sentence, grammar be damned. And, despite our popular mistrust of halting talkers, linguists judge hesitations as marks of "superior" spontaneous speech; like fins breaking the water's surface, they indicate thoughts snapping and circling, as speakers plan ahead.

Whereas, for at least one disgruntled academic, smooth talk betrays a phoney:

> *Either [speech] has been rehearsed beforehand, or the speaker is merely stringing together a number of standard phrases she habitually repeats, as when the mother of the 7-year-old who threw a stone through my window rattled off at top speed, "I do apologise, he's never done anything like that before, I can't think what came over him, he's such a good quiet little boy usually, I'm quite flabbergasted."*

So don't be down on gappy talkers. Rather than indicate hedging, their broken sentences may stake out high-grade truths.

Alternatively, they could be super-manipulators. Masters of silence may be taken for master talkers—not always a mistake. Infinitely foxy French statesman Talleyrand sat up at night, polishing his epigrams. Then he

> *would often sit through a party without saying a word, but then suddenly come out with a sentence which people said was the sort they never forgot.*

Well-honed shafts of wit strike harder, resonate further, than buck-shot bon mots because listeners must give greater weight to each word (as a cracking twig can convince the lone traveler that a host of dangers lurk in the shadows).

Notice how speakers use controlled pauses, like stage managers, to prompt others to talk, to clarify meaning, to increase drama or suspense. A pause may say, "Wasn't that something!" or "Listen up!" Or draw attention to what a speaker isn't saying, inviting listeners to fill in—as wicked Iago does throughout Shakespeare's play *Othello*, misleading the imaginative Moor. Or mark a channel hop, as a speaker brakes before—ahem—changing subject.

Frequently pauses are tacit invitations to others to speak. If unsure whether you're being asked to leap in, note turn-taking's three laws:

> If a speaker invites another to speak, he must stop and let the other start.
> If nobody has been invited, anyone can speak next.
> If nobody volunteers or has been selected, the speaker may go on (but is not obliged to).

→ Rule four: Use pauses creatively

Investigation into music's physiological effects has found that listeners' pleasure and relaxation peaked, if that isn't a contradiction, not during slow movements but at junctures of silence in a melody, when tension breaks. This shows how subliminally manipulative silence may be, suggesting why the great waves of a rousing harangue of a speech, such as Hitler went in for, are so effective. How easily may entranced listeners mistake the rapture they experience in the interludes for a mark of the righteousness of the words?

But pauses are just as easily a force for good. Listen to how newscasters' seesaw cadences help words slip down—even though in some respects their delivery is utterly unnatural. And while it's well known that listening to music impedes students' concentration, fewer of us are aware that silence enhances intelligence. A 1970s "wait-time" study in American schools found that if teachers gave students just a few extra seconds to answer questions, their responses and engagement greatly improved, as did their year-end examination results. Equally, evaluation of psychotherapy has found that sessions in which the least is said are most effective.

In part this is because the longer a pause lasts, the more meanings germinate in speculative minds; like the lull before a joke's punch line, a long pause deepens reflection. Indeed, silence's spirit of incantation may be very sexy, cloaking the reticent speaker in mystery. Scantly interviewed icons, such as Greta Garbo or Kate Moss, metabolize this into mystique, and women who gripe about male emotional inarticulacy persist in swooning over word-shy hunks, like *Pride and Prejudice*'s Mr. Darcy, who seem impregnable to pressure to talk. Why say she looks good enough to eat with a spoon if you can say it in an indolent glance and let her imagination roam? Practice the seductive art of tailing off ...

And see if you can't splice a few more breaks into your speech to underscore what you've just said, to build anticipation, swell significance, slow pace (useful in arguments), or grab attention—if only to free a moment to break off and meet listeners' eyes. Your words will weigh heavier, you'll seem more self-possessed, and others will listen closer.

→ Rule five: Silence pressures others to speak

Alexander Pope dubbed silence the "varnisher of fools, and cheat of all the wise!" Occasionally, it creates too positive an impression, as film executive Kate Philpot discovered when overstretch led to breakdown:

Too tired to speak in meetings, I would just smile and nod, hoping nobody would notice. Ironically, given the chance to talk uninterrupted, clients sang my praises and recommended me to others.

Her tragicomic predicament illustrates how effortlessly silence compels others to talk—a chance to gain information and insights, as well as speak volumes about your confidence. In power games, be aware of three tactical properties: as silencer, shield, and negotiator.

For Sigmund Freud, rebuffing a bumptious writer, it was a blunt but effective instrument:

[Freud] made no answer and was not troubled by the silence this caused. It was a hard silence, a sort of weapon in his hand.

Use silence to kill. Asked a nasty question, pretend you didn't hear. Don't want to say why you're late? Don't, then. Not reacting also guards against unhelpful revelations, whereas hasty complaints provide recipes for how to wound further. And it overrides embarrassment, as a Frenchman found, watching eighteenth-century Londoners relieve themselves into chamber pots in, *horreur!*, the dining room—"undisguisedly," and at "no interruption of the conversation." So if you screw up, shut up: Talk will perforce move on.

Silence can sidestep commitment, signaling acceptance without an irretrievable yes, since tacit consent is always deniable. Instead of disagreeing, saying nothing keeps channels open, defusing potential confrontation. It also turns tables, forcing others to plead their case. (How weak Richard II seems in Shakespeare's play, for all his eloquence, before the quiet avenger and future king, Henry Bolingbroke.)

Maintain silence as a smoke screen, forcing opponents to speculate what you're thinking, hiding, planning.... This may inflate their perception of your position. What is more, if they're ferreting around, wasting time, worrying, you've weakened them—so the illusion is eminently material. And always wait to respond to an offer: If he comes back again, you know he's desperate. Even on the phone or face to face, hold back. The pressure to fill silence is so alluring that he may just improve it.

Remember what CJ, the merrily tyrannical boss in the 1970s BBC series *The Fall and Rise of Reginald Perrin*, would say, as he kept underlings waiting outside his office?

> *One, two, three, four,*
> *Make 'em sweat outside the door,*
> *Five, six, seven, eight,*
> *Always pays to make 'em wait,*
> *Nine, ten, eleven, twelve,*
> *COME!*

➙ Rule six: Silence is a window of opportunity

Of all silence's powers, perhaps greatest is the chance it gives you to mend a hole in conversation, winning everyone's gratitude. Or, if you prefer, to kick talk into touch and skedaddle. Either way, politeness requires that you revive talk first.

First diagnose the silence: Is conversation dead, or has it skipped a beat? If so, why? Miscommunication? Too much information? An agenda better saved for another day? A faux pas?

Think hard. In my experience, offense can bud out of anything from scorning lemon yellow cars, calling a child "little devil" (admittedly, it was a christening), to querying the name Kenton (her husband's).

Once you have identified the cause, smile, invoke a new topic, or prepare to say good-bye.

And if ever in future silence troubles you, try to count the ways in which it is full. Welsh poet Dannie Abse recalled life with his late wife:

> *There are so many different qualities of silence: the breathless silence that follows a war explosion; the stony silence of a religious sanctuary. There is also the agreeable, comfortable silence of two people who love each other and who have lived together for years. I knew that silence.*

Maybe for a moment, words are unnecessary. Maybe something better has passed: something understood.

TYPOLOGY OF BORES, CHORES, AND OTHER CONVERSATIONAL BEASTS

LIMPET   *Nugo pendens*

Limpet tries to blend in. He shows no sign of life. It isn't clear who invited him, or why. But as he clings to conversation, rocklike in silence, he stands out ever more.

Alternatively, garrulous Limpet sizzles with news you've already heard, stories that end well before their telling is told; impervious, indestructible, like a fossilized creature mysteriously reanimated. Oh yes, she says (and this explains everything) she's known the host an age. But thank heaven for Facebook. Otherwise, they'd have, like, totally lost touch!

To either species, grim or garrulous, time is an abstract notion. Limpet adheres like a useless limb, unbudgeable by hint or yawn, and drags at conversation until all others' spirits are limping.

Tactics: Show Limpet the kind of interest he must experience rarely—how else has he developed such a concrete coat of a personality? Perhaps a story lies behind the creation of the carapace. Ask questions, explore passions: You might prize off the shell to find a remarkable person.

Pluses: Limpet reminds us that anyone is boring if he outstays his welcome, and that diverting others is a duty—its neglect punishable by withdrawal of social security.

5

FIT SUBJECTS

On Topics in Search of Good Homes

W hat do you want to talk about?

This can be a question of social life or death. One Hollywood producer feared for Victoria Beckham and her husband, the ageing soccer player David, on moving to LA:

> *They're good-looking and rich, but I don't know where they're going to fit in. . . . They don't really have anything anyone wants here. I mean, they're not going to be in movies. You're certainly not going to see them at Warren and Annette's for dinner, talking about politics. They're going to have to find an "issue" if they want to be taken seriously: maybe something like breast cancer or the environment.*

A pet subject is the only passport to some circles. In less elevated settings, to be without a cause may not make you a rebel, but you had better have something to say.

You need a topic.

TIMELESS MEASURES FOR
TAILORING TOPICS?

We think of topics as abstract nouns with capital letters—Love, War, God—but the terrain shifts with time and tide. A minefield once yawned between men and women, so much so that evil Queen Victoria strove to deter suitors for her youngest daughter (whom she wished to retain as a companion in old age) by expedient dullness. One man recalled:

Sitting next to a beautiful princess is a reward for bravery in fairy stories, but if the gallant man were popped down every night next to Princess Beatrice, he would soon cease to be brave. Not that she has nothing to say, for when the subject moves her, she has a torrent, but what with subjects tabooed, the subjects she knows nothing about, and the subjects she turns to the Queen upon, there is nothing left but the weather and silence.

Still, rationing spurred ingenuity. A debutante snaffled Britain's richest duke with graceful disquisitions on "ghosts and the royal family," honoring the double-edged ethos that gals should lead conversation, but never, ever come over as clever. My granny held that wherever she was, however grim the circs—and as a nurse in the Second World War, grim they often were—babies and the price of fish perked things up. But her modest topic store would not stretch far today.

Now information is wireless and free-range, no princess may be sequestered from it, however high her tower. And if Granny's generation could confidently assert do not discuss War, Politics, Money, Sex, God, or Death, such iron certainties toppled before the Iron Curtain, attitudes drifting from nothing to anything goes.

It might even be argued that conversation skills have slackened because we're spoiled for topical choice. Imagine the stamina necessary to eke out ghosts and the royal family over the duration of a dinner date, before tabloids made them such toothsome subjects.

Yes, we have it easy. But as anyone who has put her foot in it will testify, there remains such a thing as the wrong topic of conversation. How do you tell?

By the silence.

⇢ Rule one: Good topics create talk

Far from fixed Abstract Nouns with Capital Letters, the elusive What we are talking about keeps moving, slipping down side alleys, emerging as something else entirely, due to conversation's spirit-charging ability to summon up ideas.

It's the law of the conversation jungle: Either fresh talking points sprout from the old, new ones are grafted on, or the whole fragile ecosystem conks out.

⇢ Rule two: Topics are unstable mixtures of attitude and subject

Aristotle had a neat concept for explaining what enables topics' polymorphous perversity: the active intellect. In brief, inside Homo sapiens' lively mind lie imaginary versions of the world, and in the collective craft of conversation, we trade perceptions and ideas: a wondrous capacity that has enabled us to transform each other's views and, with them, the world.

On the small scale, simply exchanging words is alchemy, altering topics each time they pass from person to person. Just as syntax, the arrangement of words, shapes meaning and clarity, so conversation has its own dynamic syntax, as thoughts conjoin and separate with the ripping speed of Velcro. The better they do, the better we get along.

→ Rule three: A topic's fitness endures with the thrill of the chase
In an ideal world, as the libertine author of 1673's *Means to Oblige in Conversation* wrote, a subject, "the quarry of two heated minds, springs up like a deer out of the wood." However,

> *There is nothing in a subject, so called, that we should regard it as an idol, or follow it beyond the promptings of desire.*

As for where to hunt, his advice was simple: "Speak ... to the purpose." Which seems sensible: The original Greek word, *topos,* means "place," so a topic can hardly be out of it. (The word is Aristotle's, from his *Ta Topika*—"On Commonplaces.")

→ Rule four: Topics must be relevant and accessible
That is to say, a good topic is whatever you want to discuss, and most fertile are those on which anyone can comment—the richest, like evergreen pop icon Madonna, morphing before they date.

But hang on, aren't some topics bad?

Yes: generally the ones we gossip about, then regret at our leisure. Like this seventeenth-century English lady, Lucy Hutchinson, repining her racy youth, before Civil War divided cavalier from puritan, and Charles I from his head:

> *I was not at that time convinced of the vanity of conversation which was not scandalously wicked. . . . I became the confidante in all the loves that were managed among my mother's young women; and there was none of them but had many lovers, and some particular friends beloved above the rest.*

Can't you sense her yearning to say more about these "particular friends"? And doesn't the fact that virtue starches her lips increase your desire to hear, three-plus centuries on?

→ Rule five: Questionable subjects whet appetites

Scandal and conflict have ever been the spice to conversation. In the Bible's first chat, Eve and Eden's serpent discuss pilfering the tree of knowledge, and the earliest recorded literary dialogue, in the Mesopotamian epic *Gilgamesh*, is between a father and his hunter son, fretting about the hairy ecowarrior sabotaging their traps. The association remains fitting because although, as Aristotle suggested, accessible topics hail from the common ground, hot topics map fault lines and points of difference.

Paradoxical? Hardly. Without such border skirmishes, where would we be?

In a dull, silent world, free of opinion and all the troubles and triumphs it brings.

What we really want to talk about are pleasures, frivolous matters of taste (market researchers confirm this: Launching a pop group or a chocolate bar, they court neighborhood cool-makers, but not for conversationally unfriendly products like life insurance). And perils, as well as those piquant phenomena that don't quite square with our notions of how life should be. In other words, when it comes to good and bad topics, puritan and cavalier attitudes continue their squabble, speaking in us with forked tongue, as we shiver at a murder, deplore a film star's cellulite, and get our juices flowing.

Hot topics' appeal isn't entirely prurient. We huddle around them like a fire, trading titbits of information, taking intoxicating nips of Schadenfreude, to render the monsters out there a little less scary and reassure ourselves that we aren't alone in our fears, or that worse could happen, indeed has: to somebody else.

The best topics—even the bad—make us feel better, one way or another.

THE CHOICE

So which subjects should be hoarded for sustaining conversation, and which froth up a light chat? In his *Art of Pleasing in Conversation* Cardinal Richelieu (the real one, not the *Three Musketeers* villain, although they've plenty in common) counseled:

> *Obscure Sciences and great Affairs must have a less share in their discourses than agreeableness and diversion.*

But jolly humanist Erasmus ridiculed sententious attitudes in the tale of a banquet:

A guest sat by the fire. Another said, "I want to tell you something."

"Is it serious?"

The man frowned. "Not merry."

"Then save it," said the guest. "Serious things after the feast."

He was not happy when he saw his burned cloak.

There is no formula. Instead, read the mood, and bear in mind that edgy subjects, though risky, tend to trail conga lines of meaty potential topics. And whatever you pick, it will say something about you. . . .

THE MENU

BIRTHS, MARRIAGES, AFFAIRS, DIVORCES, DEATHS?

A category better known as local news. Learning what has befallen family, friend, or foe is great. Provided it is your family, friend, or foe. Like many wines, local news may bring transports of delight in its native land, but it doesn't necessarily travel.

Still, gossip is conversation's bread and butter (two-thirds concerns our local world). The word originates from Old English *godsybb*—"spiritual kin" such as godparents—and it still serves as social glue, reinforcing ties of kith and kinship. Just as apes groom to bond as much as to clean, even salacious talk is a form of solace and back-scratching. Its devilish reputation is deserved insofar as it features material we may not mention to the parties concerned. But talking behind backs forestalls exchanges like this:

> Friend (who shall be nameless): *Hello, Mrs. X. Where's your husband?*
> (Pause. Mrs. X turns green, gulps.)
> Mrs. X: *"He died two weeks ago."*

To me gossip is a growth industry, ever more essential in atomized urban society, as family ties weaken and networks grow wider, looser, and diffuser, and most bonds are inked in friendship. While monitoring a virtual crowd of Internet pals can accentuate loneliness if you're not truly in touch, gossip remains friendship's primary medium, as well as being good for business. If I could, I'd buy shares in it.

Risk: Misjudging your audience; too much information, too little
Opportunity: Information; titillation; unearned sense of
    superiority
Scenario: Reunions; christenings; bar mitzvahs; and (at low
    volume) funerals

Sex?
Once upon a time my friends and I shared further and better particulars—for research, you understand—but detailed accounts have been off-limits since the last door slammed on my teens.

Does sex talk turn you on? Does your listener want or need to know? Certainly, the Mitford sister, Diana Mosley, found it dry fare at a lunch with the aging widow Wallis Simpson, Duchess of Windsor, who was evidently keen to remind guests that a king had once preferred her charms to ruling his country:

> *Pathos personified, about nine people including a nurse (in a green silk dress) & she (Duchess) tried to get the ball rolling by saying how nowadays people are only interested in SEX, well as we were all well on the way to the grave the ball refused to roll.*

Risk: What you think flattering may not be if your listener's mind's eye isn't soft-focus

Opportunity: If it turns you on

Scenario: Locker room, doctor's surgery, bedroom, bathroom, kitchen …

CURRENT AFFAIRS?

A fair bet once. But as a surfeit of topics rush in via radio, TV, or Internet, like Cleopatra, 24/7 news "makes hungry where most [it] satisfies." Hourly are we buffeted by vistas of calamity, but our relation to it is image-deep—dulling shockability, jading interest. So where our grandparents avoided talk of war out of consideration for those who wished to forget, we are likelier to shun it out of boredom or that guilt-salving euphemism, compassion fatigue. Not that we think of it like that. In fact, we'd rather not think about it, since it makes us feel futile.

Nonetheless, discussing big stuff with baby boomers remains more mind-expanding than numbing, thanks to their halcyon memories of 1960s protests. And many—their mortgages paid off, their offspring schooled and resolutely deferring the production of time-consuming grandchildren—are also doing something concrete to set the world to rights. Let them fire you up and you might find yourself getting out there too.

Risk: Depression; tedium; argument; revelation of dubious beliefs
Opportunity: Catch the latest; quell a bore; have a row; raise consciousness
Scenario: Student union; pub (for sports haters); dinner party; AARP holiday; sixtieth birthday

HEAVY WEATHER?

The British classic. Where others have climates, UK skies are ruled by the capricious goddess Weather. Except, with climate change, weather has gone global—no longer a demure neutral topic of discussion, but a titan, hauling an unruly retinue of visions of imminent, overheated apocalypse, as we dodge hail in July, sunbathe in October. Want to talk about it? Do canapés go with melting polar ice caps? Up to you.

I say, reclaim weather; acquaint yourself with its fluffier side and go cloud spotting.

Risk: Cliché; inconvenient truths; environmental depression
Opportunity: Remember umbrella/sunblock; better than old ladies' bunions
Scenario: Start of conversation; passing time of day with strangers on street; anywhere. Go on. If only for one day a year, imagine how nice it would be.

IN GOD/STATE/KING WE TRUST?

The forces that shape us are sometimes fascinating, sometimes dull, and always divisive. Formerly, such topics were forbidden from mixed company, but this stricture is at an end. However, if you want to curdle a conversation, toss in a remark about your Undear Leader. You'll soon learn who is a political animal, and who doesn't give a monkey's.

As with current affairs, discussing creeds, whether social, political, or theological, can coagulate conversation, since it reminds unbelievers how little dust our little lives, for all their busyness, actually raise. Worse, many of those who rise on hind legs to such topics are ranters and ravers, who talk as if atop invisible podiums.

Take this scene in Katherine Mansfield's story "Germans at Meat." The other hotel guests are agog that the narrator might not want a baby (in fact she is ill):

> "Germany," *boomed the Traveller, biting round a potato which he had speared with his knife,* "is the home of the Family."
> *Followed an appreciative silence.*

Minds worn shiny by prejudice offer few conversational footholds for those who don't mirror their opinions. So before you ask, ask yourself: Do you care about the answer? Equally, do you mind too little? If, like pioneering psychologist William James, you regard religious belief as a vehicle to convey us through choppy existence, to prick another person's convictions is to tinker with the engine of meaning in his life. Equally, to press your own on him is in effect to demand that he show you his, since conversation is a trading game. Who would do either?

Someone itching for an argument is who. Thin-skinned nineteenth-century painter Benjamin Robert Haydon, a committed Christian, griped about a dinner party:

> *Shelley* [the Romantic poet] *opened the conversation by saying in a most feminine and gentle voice,* "As to that detestable religion, the Christian ..." *I looked astounded, but casting a*

glance round the table easily saw by [Leigh] Hunt's expression of
ecstasy and the women's simper, I was to be set ... vi et armis.

Admit it: Baiting is fun.

Risk: Depression; tedium; argument; revelation of dubious beliefs
Opportunity: Tranquilize bores; wind someone up; get down with
a teenager
Scenario: Drinking holes; rallies; temples; academic gatherings;
golf course; after Christmas lunch

MONEY?

If two-thirds of the average conversation consists of window-
shopping one another's lives, naturally the price tag arises. Nonetheless, traditionally money talk is taboo.

Food writer and successful businesswoman Prue Leith recalled:

In my family, you never discussed food, money and sex. Only
complete vulgarians discussed them. I think that's absolute non-
sense. Food, money and sex are all great pleasures in life.

Of course money is fun. If you have it. If not, it may be a talking
point—but a pleasure? And advertising wealth exposes insecurity.
Take note, self-declared tycoon Peter Jones:

If there has been resentment about my success it's gone unno-
ticed, because I simply wouldn't care. I am positive there are
people out there who are jealous.

Er. He is positive. Therefore, he cares.

If money talks to you, make no mistake: Others' envy funds the
pleasure. Be subtle, as a 1587 conduct book advised nouveaux riches
brides:

Guide your guests around the house and in particular show
them some of your possessions, either new or beautiful, but in
such a way that it will be received as a sign of your politeness
and domesticity ... as if showing them your heart.

But after your latest acquisition's price has been tagged, really, what more to say? Despite strong recent growth, this conversational weed shouldn't be mistaken for a fecund topic.

Risk: Unpopularity; crassness; mistaking price for worth; silence; "So what?"

Opportunity: Funny, perhaps, as ABBA suggested, in a rich man's world ...

Scenario: Office; accountant; estate agent; bank; marital bed; divorce lawyer

HERE COMES TROUBLE?

"How are you?" To which the reply is: "Fine. You?"

Any alternative should be broached with caution. Unless, that is, you wish to bring conversation to an end; in which case, trouble talk is a swift means to do so.

In general, inquiries after health and happiness are not diagnostic. Their aim is the friendly gesture, doing the metaphorical job of a wave as we pass someone's home: If not on intimate terms, rarely do we expect to be invited in and told how unhappy he is. (Similarly, Anglo-Saxons routinely close conversations with symbolic invitations to "see you soon," as a foxed Russian acquaintance found, turning up on London doorsteps as she thought had been arranged.)

While you may consider painful topics, like scabs, best picked in private, in Turkey, however, complaining is art, with seven different verbs to capture its nuances. Of Istanbul students surveyed,

30.4 percent identified "personal problems" as their top topic, 37 percent of women selecting the slightly grander "problems for students/the young." Some argue this predilection expresses a national romantic, melancholy streak; others blame fear of the evil eye (unguarded talk of fortune is asking for trouble). But I see the pleasure of whining, with the right person, as philosopher Francis Bacon wrote:

> *Communicating of a man's self to his friend works two contrary effects, for it redoubleth joys and cutteth griefs in half.*

Complaining can be modest, extremely funny, and gory details are bliss. A cynic might add that tales of misfortune—told sparingly, with wit—stoke popularity. A Machiavellian might go further and tell you the novel *Vanity Fair*, Thackeray's masterly mockery of social aspiration, features a gentleman who did "little wrongs" to neighbors "on purpose, and in order to apologise for them in an open and manly way afterwards"—and for his troubles was "liked everywhere," earning a lucrative name for honesty.

Risk: Lost prestige; attract/be trapped by losers; self-pity; yawns
Opportunity: Feel better; make others feel better; analyze
    problems; laughs
Scenario: Best friends; mothers (in limited doses); lovers (ditto);
    frenemies (when moaning is coded showing off—as in "I'm so
    busy, with my projects/babies/holidays/work-life-holiness
    balances to juggle")

TRUE CONFESSIONS, SECRETS, AND LIES?
Blame Freud, blame TV, blame the Pill: the twentieth century saw a mass deregulation of taboos. But while our hot-lipped media imply that anything is up for discussion, unsolicited revelation

from non-friends remains a burden. Spare a thought for hairdressers and bartenders.

Although morsels of mischief pep up talk, overdone they leave a sour taste. For conversation to feel truly intimate, traction between minds and an easy flow are what counts.

Risk: Bad name; bad aftertaste; offense; do you know who you're
    talking to?
Opportunity: Thrills; spills; risk; they might show you theirs
Scenario: Father confessor; doctor; therapist; best friend; officer of
    the law

DEARLY BELOVED?
Romance, pets, and children fall under what I term the Baby Problem.

Why are babies boring? They're not. As P. G. Wodehouse observed, many resemble homicidal fried eggs, and of course, in little blossom's greedy gaze we see the wonder of the world reborn. The problem is their makers.

Hormone-foamy, exhausted, or plain self-centered, parents, like lovers, fondly imagine that what makes them happy is equal cause for celebration to the rest of us.

Well, I'm happy you're happy. And as it happens, I like hearing about affairs of the heart and children; I love talking to said miniatures, and I enjoy patting dogs. Do I want details? A recital of little Timmy's latest trumpet-tooting triumph? Oh, a *story*? A real live anecdote? You're on.

But my, how fast stories about children grow; must be pesky time that goes slow.

However loved-up you are, it's no excuse to ditch conversational technique. Litanies and lists do not a tale make. Keep a long story short to make the pleasure mutual.

Risk: Tedium; envy; the opposite of envy
Opportunity: Laughs (now or later)
Scenario: With other interested parties; at school gates; featured in
    deprecating jokes, etc.

HOBBIES, SPORTS, ARTS, BOOKS, FILMS, MUSIC, GADGETS, WIDGETS, AND OTHER ESOTERICA?

With fellow enthusiasts, go for it. Even with the uninitiated, a light
top note of tidbits and trivia make conversation sing. Aside from
radar for identifying common ground, discussing extracurricular
interests has the advantage that enthusiasm spawns enthusiasm.

Poet Leigh Hunt, who cheered on Shelley's teasing of Benjamin
Robert Haydon, seemed to have forgotten his meaner streak when
he advised:

> Topics fittest for table are cheerful, to help digestion; and cor-
> dial, to keep people in heart ... reminiscences, literary chat,
> questions as easy to crack as the nuts, quotations flowing as the
> wine, thoughts of eyes and cheeks blooming as the fruit.

The Romantic era may be over, but even acid-tongued comic Ricky
Gervais admits: "Nothing makes a connection with me like a piece
of art, a song or a painting.... I'd rather gush about something that
changed the world than be embarrassed."

Try to imbibe a bit of culture; if only to distract yourself from
routine matters. Should you be too busy for firsthand research into
the latest must-read/-see/-listen, take heart from Pierre Bayard's
How to Talk About Books You Haven't Read:

> Among specialists [literary critics] mendacity is the rule, and we
> tend to lie in proportion to the significance of the book under
> consideration.... The books we talk about are only glancingly
> related to real books.

The oddest interest can ignite a conversation. Whatever grabs you. In moderation.

Risk: Riding hobby horse into ground
Opportunity: Information; warmth; passion
Scenario: Anywhere. Up to a point.

IMMEDIATE SURROUNDINGS?

What is going on? What prompted the smile that just scudded across your companion's face? Why did that woman wear that dress? All such minor mysteries may be enlisted for your battle against silence.

The joy of topics triggered by your environment is that because they occupy common ground, they limbo dance under the usual etiquettes and you may raise them, interrupting a given line of discussion, without offense. So if bored, keep eyes and ears skinned and you can bounce talk elsewhere. Be imaginative ("Nice flowers" is not juicy). And cautious. Jibe at the man in the mauve catsuit and he will be her dad.

Risk: Is it worth talking about? Can you make it worth it? Is it safe?
Opportunity: Distraction; filling gaps
Scenario: Anytime; anyplace; anywhere

THE OTHER PERSON?

Smooth-talking Disraeli remarked,

Talk to a man about himself and he will listen for hours.

But don't enter your interlocutor's private space without invitation. Wait to ask what he does, if he's married, has kids, until he's flagged these topics as safe. Take the side route, and stalk subjects that excite him.

Risk: Is it interesting? Is it safe?
Opportunity: Big returns for small investments of enthusiasm
Scenario: Need you ask?

WHAT NEXT?

And finally, the topic so overused that we're hardly aware it is one: arrangements.

Many conversations round off in an exchange about the next occasion to meet/talk/do business. So if you want to say good-bye, but not forever, ask, "When can we do this again?" This sends a polite but unambiguous message that this conversation is already in the past.

Risk: Making false commitments
Opportunity: Getting on with your day
Scenario: When the end is nigh

Here ends my menu. Perhaps yours is longer. Whatever subject you choose, let it matter. G. K. Chesterton was right:

> There is no such thing as an uninteresting subject; there are only uninterested people.

Neither an encyclopedic imagination nor a spontaneously combustible topic makes conversation whoopee if speakers don't engage. It became clear to me that a job interview masquerading as lunch had turned belly-up when, without warning, my would-be employer began rabbiting about her cat (she hoped, by obscure methods, to "raise Sheba's consciousness").

What went wrong? Hard as we'd tried, I didn't care about her interests, and the indifference was mutual. We had failed to tie our topics together.

TYPOLOGY OF BORES, CHORES, AND OTHER CONVERSATIONAL BEASTS

SHOWGIRL   *Ostentatrix ludi*

You smile. She laughs. You say she looks well. She says you look incredible. You have a new job. She just bought her company. Going on holiday? Guess who is heading into tax exile. . . .

Showgirl understands that life is competition. Anything you can do, she does it better, with knobs on, and glitter, and if you're lucky, lucky, lucky, she will tell you how.

Men, call them Preens, employ similar methods. But Showgirl respects a distinctly feminine tradition. If she had an emblem it would be a tiny silver spade, disguised as an accessory. Although insecure to the bottom of her high-kicking heels, she never undermines directly. Rather, she takes every opportunity to smuggle information into conversation to big herself up, most perfidious, as a worry preying on her mind. Will her cloth-of-gold gown shed dodo feathers at the Academy Awards? Will she be shuttlesick on her voyage to Venus? Will that rock star stop trying to convince her he isn't gay?

Invariably thrilled to hear your plans, Showgirl does all she can to advance your cause. But isn't it odd how often she converts your news into ways she can be of help?

You'll never leave her company walking taller. That little spade builds her foundations by nicking earth from yours.

Tactics: Isn't it gratifying she wants to impress you? Her machinations are also painfully informative, given she targets your weaknesses: Listen for what riles you and you'll hear your insecurities talking. With this guide, set about shoring up your perimeter walls.
Pluses: There is something breathtakingly brazen in how Showgirl boosts her interests. Such focus, drive, chutzpah: useful armor, and worth assuming from time to time.

6

INTO THE GROOVE

On Steering Controls

I f having nothing to say is bad, too much is possibly worse. Millionaire American politico and doer-of-good Arianna Huffington "bubbles over with questions":

> *"Do you like to dance?" "Can we talk about perfumes?" "Do you think the breast stroke is more feminine than the crawl?" "Do you like Leonard Cohen?" "What do you think of my lipstick?"*
>
> *She says this is all part of her innate "capacity for intimacy."*

But gush and it may wash over them.

"Only connect," wrote E. M. Forster in *Howards End*: a motto for life, but it does as well for conversation. At its best, in animating our views, conversation reveals who we are, and when sympathies chime, we relate to one another. Slipping between topics makes connecting possible.

Even military men should cut a tippy-toed dash. Captain Orlando Sabertash's 1842 gent's conduct book advocates

> *a graceful and pleasing manner . . . from "grave to gay, from serious to serene."*

Sound silly? Think of a person you met recently. Do you remember what was said or how you felt talking to him? Emotion dwells in the memory longer than the neatest verbal twist, and whatever topic you discuss, conversation's visceral pleasure emanates less from the beauty of words than the harmony of its pace, rhythm, and flow.

→ Rule one: Flowing topics smooth social dynamics

Jumpy talkers unsettle us by darting from topic to topic, like squirrels in a forest fire. Wordsworth's friend, the opium eater Thomas de Quincey, suggested all would run smoother if we appointed a "symposiarch." A similar approach is used to broker talk in fashionable "dialogue" workshops, at which mediators instruct speakers to pass batons, even bananas, to divvy up airtime (only the banana-clutcher may speak). But isn't that bananas? Think what is lost if you can't share the insight a remark has sparked, or overlap sentences—in terms of spontaneity, ideas, momentum, connection . . .

Like the industrious fairy-tale gnome Rumpelstiltskin, who spun straw into gold, dexterous talkers transmute dross subjects to dazzle by spinning threads that draw people together and lead to new treasures. But magical as it may sometimes seem, conversation's flow proceeds by cues and signals little more complex than traffic lights. However, because we follow them, like rules of grammar, largely unconsciously, and often converse with our minds elsewhere, or running ahead to what we want to say next, signals can be missed or skipped. Indeed, many encounters go wrong purely because topic signaling is on the blink. We just don't notice. Instead we blame the situation or the other person: so gauche, rude, dull! Or become defensive, inhibited, and stop doing our bit to tease out common ground—shortsightedness that cheats us of fun and friendship.

E. M. Forster was on the money. "Only connect." Topical connections are the joinery of relating.

→ Rule two: Bid for a topic tactically
Throughout conversation we broker topics. Negotiations can be comically protracted.

> *"Does this red top go okay with my coloring?"*
> *"Yes, dear."*
> *"You don't think it's too loud?"*
> *"No, dear."*
> *"It doesn't clash?"*
> *"No."*
> *"It's just the way my hair's been acting lately . . ."*
> *"You look fine."* (*Sound of TV channel being switched.*)
> *"I DYED IT GINGER LAST NIGHT. HAVEN'T YOU NOTICED?"*
> *"No, dear."*

But bidding is simple. I offer a subject—"Hear about Fred and the banana split?" And you either agree—"No, what?"—or bid for another—"Yeah. But did you hear about Mary and the Hells Angel?"—or, if a you're real schmo, offer nothing more—"Yeah."

Nonetheless, how we bid alters conversation dynamics. The options are:

DIRECT BIDS
Statements: *"I have to tell you about Fred, the biker, and the vanishing banana."*
Questions: *"Heard about Fred's Hells Angel?"*
Previews: *"Guess what Fred's done now?"*

INDIRECT BIDS
Oblique comments, statements, or observations: "Fred is in
the custard."

Your style of bid indicates whether you wish to lead discussion.
Open bids—*"They say Fred is brilliant"* or *"Heard about Fred?"*—let
the other person either react passively or take charge of developing
the topic. Closed bids—*"Tell me about Fred"* or *"Guess what Fred
did"*—leave no room for maneuver. So be wary of bidding as an
expert—*"Let me tell you about my ormolu clocks."*
In sensitive situations, indirect bids tactfully point out the door
without forcing the other in. Say someone else mentioned John's
striptease at the harvest supper, you might ask the guilty man: "You
partied out?" And if you can't ask where Jean's been, fish: "I would've
invited you but there was no answer when I called."

→ **Rule three: Exercise editorial rights in your reactions**
Just the tone of an answer is illuminating, able to signal desire to
spin in a given direction (green), support without furthering a topic
(amber), or enough, already (red):

Green: Add new material to be developed (*"Fred, eh? Fearless
for his height."*)
Amber: Neutral, no extra topical reference, adding nothing
(*"Poor Fred."*)
Red: Yawn. (*"Uh-huh."*)

Be aware of how your responses actively select topics by shining
a light on what interests you. Think how to train it. For instance, I
met a man, call him Jake, who boasted: "I have a weakness for fast
Italian cars." I said nothing. He elaborated:

"Laid my hands on a beaut of a Testarossa. Bright green. Can do up to 220 mph on a fast road. Dealer couldn't sell them for horse meat at first, Ferrari discontinued the run, but now there's hardly any, they're worth a mint."

Each extra tot of information was the seed of a new topic. Had I smiled and said, "Ferrari?" at "Testarossa," this would have focused his mind on that marque as a subject to expand on. If I'd said, "Gosh, where can you drive that fast?" after "fast road," that might have steered us away. Stupidly, I smiled, wasting a month's ration of "Really?"s.

How you structure statements may engender or neuter talking points. Consider these reactions to "Silent movies are so evocative":

"I don't remember any. Maybe because I'm obsessed with words."

"You're right, they're hypnotic. Maybe that's why I find it easier to remember scenes from talkies. Or that could be because I'm obsessed with words."

Same information, different message. The first says: "I have completely different opinions. Want to hear about me?" The second shows respect and supplies at least three fresh topics (hypnotism, favorite scenes, words).

Conversely, play a defensive game with amber signals; use clichés to suggest a topic is not for debate, or flattery and polite comments to baffle difficult topics, e.g., "That is an interesting question." (See Chapter 13.) The subtlest curb of all is not matching enthusiasm: "Oh yeah?" softly spoken announces that this news is already stale.

"THE REASON I CALLED"

You feel it circling. A shadow passes overhead. For some reason it doesn't swoop. Instead, the person at the other end of the phone chatters on. But you aren't fooled. You know this conversation is heading toward something—something you probably won't want to hear.

Who likes being ambushed? But, charming as wittering may be, it may be kinder—not least to your schedule—to open conversational airspace and guide the agenda in to land.

First, step back, highlight the oddity of the call: "It's been a while since we spoke."

No response? Hint you know something's up: "Everything all right?"

Does she say, "Fine"? From a friend, this answer should make you nervous. Take courage: ask "So what can I do for you?"

"Oh. I— No, nothing."

Now you have a choice: press on—"You sure?"—or take this at face value and let yourself off the hook—"Right. Only, I was in the middle of something ..."

If she doesn't spit it out now, don't worry. She'll be back.

STAGING TOPICAL TAKEOVERS

Fed up with Ferraris? Time to change the subject. But take your listeners with you. There are six methods to shift between topics without audibly scraping gears. Pick yours according to whether the subject you wish to introduce is a

Shift: New
Contrast: Variant on a line of discussion
Familiar: Extension of the given topic

The fresher a topic, the greater the work required to weave it in. This is marked in how we speak, whatever our language. Evaluations of French and German speakers have found that pitch and volume rise according to how new a topic is. So use your voice to grab attention. (Monotone speech is uninvolving because so much of words' meaning—their emotional force—is lost.)

Now choose your topical knitware. Consider these links marketing tools, pitching a topic by connecting it to the other person's needs, wants, hopes, and fears. Better still, be gossipy, introducing a tinct of secrets hidden, details forbidden. "Well—No, I'd better not say" makes anything twice as interesting. Want to wind somebody up? Root the topic in her insecurities. ("Talking of Christmas, Aphra, how's the diet going?")

1. Topic-tying: Good old grammar. To keep clear, ensure listeners grasp which "he" or "it" is in play, even as you introduce new "hes" and "its" as you go along.

2. Step-wise progression: Good for complicated subjects. So, to explain that your job at the café is hell, you might say, "First the bananas arrive, then the Hells Angels, and then Fred throws a wobbly with the custard"—progressing to the conclusion: "It's hell!"

Bridging components—"first," "then," "after that"—create coherence by presenting elements as part of a story. Not only do they help reach topical destinations, but they are invaluable for escaping one you don't fancy. For example, ending a relationship you might begin: "It's not you ..." At first, this is clichéd. But go step by step, itemizing issues you wouldn't wish to foist on the other person, and the topic ceases to be "You're dumped" to become "Tomorrow begins my quest for Shangri-la."

3. Touching off: Trade off previous talk, introducing a topic by latching on to something mentioned earlier. Say, "As you rightly said, bunions and wellies don't mix...."

This is endearing, in a subliminal way, as it demonstrates how engaged you are. We're all suckers for apt quotations. Think of the cheap laughs TV quiz-show panelists bag by referencing previous jokes. It isn't so much that what they say is funny, as it shows off their quick wits, and we feel included—somehow, recognizing the allusion makes us feel wittier by association. Similarly, in the frame of a conversation, a touch-off, witty or otherwise, enjoys the privileged status of an in-joke.

4. Thematic touch-offs: Topics may springboard to others by touching on shared themes. Such leaps of thought ask us to attend to buried meanings—the implied, the unspeakable—giving a certain frisson. Indeed, half the pleasure of conversation with old friends is how much of it may be woven from thematic touch-offs. It feels like glorious mind reading, because it is.

Hence thematic touch-offs are among the fastest ways to feel more connected to strangers, as well as escape a dull topic. Be warned: They can seem random. If in doubt, make the link explicit: "Kangaroo keeper? Wouldn't a pouch be cool! I hate handbags."

5. Triggered topics: Triggered topics also play off previous talk but are even more unruly, conversation's equivalent to tickles. A keyword—say, mention of a friend's labor—might cue a fresh topic ("Speaking of monstrous births, seen Hilda's kids?"). Or the trigger might be a pun. If you're walking in the park and you say, "Ice cream?" and he says "I can make you," this Platonic friendship may be up for review. An added bonus is that, as with topics triggered from observations of your surroundings, these bypass the etiquette of bidding for a topic.

6. Listed topics: Or agendas, as at business meetings. These require no topical interweaving, and make lousy social conversation, e.g., catalogs of activities in reply to "What did you do on holiday?" However, invoking the *idea* of listed topics can be handy.

For example, to cut off her inventory of buffet dishes served at the Hotel Paradiso, say, "Now, the other thing I wanted to mention is that …" At a stroke, you've introduced the impression of an agenda, implicitly declared the previous subject closed, and conveyed that your time is limited, even if hers is not.

TOPIC PLASTERS AND SIGNALS: A GLOSSARY FOR GLUEING TALK

Out of inspiration? These nifty words and phrases cobble together the unlikeliest topics.

If you're truly in the doldrums, try the ones with stars: All by themselves, they should provoke fellow talkers to return to the floor with a fresh topic.

CASUAL	RETROSPECTIVE
"Hey"	*"Well"
"Listen"	*"Anyway"
"Guess what"	*"Still"
"You have got to hear this"	*"Did I interrupt you?"
*"Erm"	*"As I was/you were saying"
*"Right"	"I meant to say"

CASUAL	FORMAL
"Let's see"	"The reason I called"
"Now then"	"This might interest you"
"Now, here's the thing"	
*"So"	

OMINOUS
"Incidentally"
"By the way"
"I was wondering"

→ Rule four: Dare to be conventional

You needn't be a smoothie to win points for keeping talk going. As a teenager I was prissily averse to platitudes, clichés, and never knowingly remarked on the weather. More fool me. Stating the obvious is perfectly acceptable. And a little local knowledge can pay dividends.

An agonizingly gauche banquet very nearly wrecked President Nixon's historic visit to China, by showing how little each side had to talk about, despite their nations' supposed new understanding and the efforts American delegates had made beforehand to learn the use of chopsticks (famed TV reporter Walter Cronkite sent olives flying), not to mention a White House memo containing useful conversation tips such as "The Chinese take great pride in their food and to compliment the various courses and dishes is also recommended." While Nixon traded insipid remarks with the Chinese prime minister, his secretary of state, William Rogers,

told long stories about his hero, the great golfer Sam Snead, to the Chinese Foreign Minister, a tough old revolutionary who had no idea what golf was.

If only Madame Mao had been there. Then Mrs. Nixon could have salvaged the moment with this age-old Chinese conversation opener:

"How is Your Excellency's favored wife?"

To which Madame Mao would have replied, equally conventionally,

"Thank you, the foolish one of the family is well."

TYPOLOGY OF BORES, CHORES, AND OTHER CONVERSATIONAL BEASTS

THE GRAND INQUISITOR   *Sciscitator nasutus*

You may imagine you have embarked on a light chat. To the Grand Inquisitor, this is contact sport. Neither has she a private thought, nor encountered a private grief. No topic is too sensitive to be aired, shared, and shredded. In her favor, her candor matches her nosiness.

A fine specimen at a dinner was a radio deejay who eagerly asked each guest's age, leaned in for a closer look, cocked her head, and said: "Are you sure?" Later in the meal she cried out: "Ladies, who do we fancy, handsome Henry or sexy Simon?" Then she smiled at the man beside her, neither Henry nor Simon, saying in a voice of unutterable pity, "No, not you."

Her husband, also neither Henry nor Simon, grimaced. "Her family call her the social hand grenade."

Tactics: Don't be offended, be awed she's made it so far, missing so many filters. People like her build business empires. Watch carefully. If only to replenish the stock of your *Shut-up Shop* (see Chapter 14).

Pluses: A great how-not-to, valiantly she proves why social protocols exist. Watch her at work, carefully noting the boundaries as she crashes through.

7

DO GO ON

On Wrangling Boredom

"As I was saying ..."

Yes, he has been at the smoked salmon blinis. You turn your head. He mistakes your ear for an invitation and leans a little closer, his canapé breath hot on your cheek.

"What I was saying was ..."

He stops. Out shoots his glass. A passing waitress tops it up: his fourth refill. How long have you been trapped?

The bore totters, regains his balance, and looks you up and down, confused.

"What's your name again?"

Your eyes coast over to your friend, chatting merrily. She sees you, smiles, carries on. Damn her.

He notices.

"I'm sorry, am I boring you?"

"No," you lie. "Not at all. Please, do go on."

He beams, then frowns. "Now, what was I saying?"

Boredom provokes desperation. It was either that or disco rage that propelled my father from a Christmas party to walk seven icy miles home. A friend of mine consoles herself in similar circumstances by writing—on her ankle, with the toe of her shoe, under the table where no one else can see: "BORED," "I'M DYING," "HELP," "THE END IS NIGH."

History does not relate if anyone has in fact been bored to death, although the entertainment provision in many care homes for the elderly suggests this is not for want of trying. When you're cornered by a bore, the sensation of life ebbing away—and going on elsewhere, where the people laugh and the sun still shines—is palpable, and painful.

To be boring is beyond bad manners. It is theft. Take that lady who wouldn't dream of picking your pocket, yet thinks nothing of squandering your time, detailing the plot of a book you already said you've read. What is she thinking?

The short answer is: She isn't. While boredom is easy to recognize when you're inside it, it's more difficult to tell if you are its cause. But it is your duty, and in your interests, to try.

Are you an unwitting time thief? How to judge? How to stop? And can anything be done about those dullards guaranteed to bore all of the people, all of the time?

Absolutely. Although our social lives might improve if we could sort bores from non-bores, the word's a label, a perception, not an essence of soul. That dolt may think the same of you, or pep up given encouragement. Bores are made, not born.

Good news! Redemption is possible. Instead of hunting tame bores, then, the task is to truffle out instances of the verb, "to bore," explore its causes, then trample it.

WHAT IS BOREDOM?

Historians argue that boredom isn't a timeless human dilemma, but rather an evolving concept—wafted across the English Channel, ghost of the dandified *ennui* that held court among moping

French aristocrats before the guillotine intervened. They have a point.

Though a sin, medieval "sloth" shares little of modern boredom's character. If you spent your peasant days hacking a living from unyielding fields, rustling up tithes for fat abbots, you would not be bored, but fervently desire, as old graves do, "Rest In Peace." Peace and quiet were valued commodities then, not boredom's yawning ladies-in-waiting.

The antisocial sense of the verb "to bore" sauntered into the language around 1750, on the arm of the expression "French bore," "boredom" making its belated literary debut the following century, with languid Lady Dedlock in Dickens's *Bleak House*. Lexicographers can't decide how it came to mean what it does, or displaced its ancestors—apathetic "accidie" (affliction of famished monks, tormented by pre-lunch sugar lows in the form of "noonday devils"); peevish "spleen" or mundane "dullness" (as defined by Samuel Johnson: "to make dictionaries is *dull* work"). My theory is bores got their name because they bore a hole in conversation out of which enthusiasm rapidly drains.

If the notion was born of the age of industrialization, on a practical level tedium today is mass-produced by leisure, be there nothing to do or so much choice none seems worthwhile. The latter is commonly diagnosed as an illness, "options paralysis," and privileged Westerners seem to be suffering an ennui epidemic (in 2007, 36 percent of Britons, beneficiaries of the world's fourth largest economy, rated themselves "very happy," compared to 52 percent in poor, gray 1957). Feel-good businesses are booming and we have a brand-new science, "positive psychology."

The idea of a Well-being Institute at Cambridge University (est. 2006) may strike you as certifiable, but boredom is no laughing matter. It drives change; indeed, anthropologist Ralph Linton argued:

Capacity for being bored, rather than man's social or natural needs, lies at the root of cultural advance.

And it raises conversation to art. France's first salon began in tedium, after a twelve-year-old Italian newlywed, the Marquise de Rambouillet, arrived in Paris in 1600, found nobody to talk to, and imported *conversazione*. Salons became sanctuaries from the dull court, *salonnières* became unbeatable talkers (excluding unmentionable courtesans, see Chapter 10), and grave topics flourished, inadvertently helping to finish off their stifling world. Shortly before the Revolution, the Prince de Ligne observed:

In salons these days one speaks of politics and finance where once one spoke of nothing but love.

WHAT MAKES A BORE?

Boredom has two causes: too much of something (overload renders all information equally meaningless) or too little. Similarly, there are two extremes of bore. At one end stand those besotted with their own voice; at the other cringe feeble, silent types.

Most conspicuous are the former, who draw all life and light to themselves and, like black holes, give none back. Disgraced media baron Conrad Black was a world-class attention thief. Blessed with an excellent memory, his social climbing consisted of courting famous people with lectures on history and current affairs (at dinner).

The latter sort, stealth borer, is subtler but no less selfish, so conversationally risk-averse that when persuaded to speak, he says effectively nothing: either clichés and platitudes (silence thinly disguised) or remarks that lead nowhere.

For instance, the stealth borer says, "Yes, I went to Japan once." You say (excited: first hard fact), "Did you! Where/When/Why?"

"Um. I forget/Ages ago/ Holiday."

On a good day he'll add, "It was nice."

The antihero of Herman Melville's story "Bartleby" is typical. "Pallidly neat, pitiably respectable, uncurably forlorn," he replies to all requests

in a singularly mild, firm voice, "I would prefer not to."

Don't pity Bartleby. His bogus shyness is contempt, buried in a coy shrug. Stealth borers may find the rest of us boring. Talking to one of them is like putting coins in a slot machine that doesn't even cough up the flashing lights.

It's tempting to ignore bores, but switch off and the conversational circuitry soon breaks down. Hence creative solutions are preferable. I don't say it's easy. Bores aren't good company, because it doesn't occur to them that they're anything less. Maligns sense no obligation to engage others' interests; benigns fail to perceive that their interests aren't universal. All inhabit a pre-Copernican universe, in which they are the axis about which the world spins.

In essence, they lack nerve endings, like Christopher Monkton, third viscount of Brenchley, a conundrum of a man, who lost a million pounds on his (he thought) "insoluble" Eternity puzzle, yet seems immune to embarrassment:

[He] talks with irrepressible good humour and impervious authority on this and any other subject I raise, from the Forestry Commission (spectacularly incompetent) to the Guardian (ditto). He laughs without restraint at his own anecdotes. He is not a man, you might say, who seems plagued by self-doubt.

Funny as bores may be in retrospect, talking to them presents conversation's highest challenge: to make the bore interesting.

First, diagnose the boredom, including your role in it.

At root, the bore is someone you don't want to listen to. Although there are therefore as many varieties as people to be bored by, the structure of every boring conversation is basically the same: a conflict of interest played out as hostage situation.

Boredom fills the deficit between the attention a speaker demands and the interest he commands. The more intrusive the bore, the less entranced you are, the more confinement chafes—pain magnified a thousandfold if you're stuck.

Contextual variables—loud music, hunger, tiredness, bad temper, urgent desire for a pee—play their part. And of course, although someone may look bored, eyelids droop for many reasons. Telepathy has a way to go, but when conversation stagnates, we may interpret the signs and make a judicious guess as to whether we're with an unresponsive Bartleby, or ourselves acting the part of an impervious Black.

→ Rule one: Read the listener
Be reasonably confident your listeners' interest is lost if:

> They reply with monosyllables, random comments, new
>   subjects, silence.
> Their eyes wander or assume a fish-on-slab glaze.
> They glower, never nod, keep twitching their watch cuffs.
> You find yourself repeating yourself.

Chains of "reallys" are not dialogue. And don't be encouraged if their tone lends "Hmm" a sleepy question mark (translation: "Like I care?").

Barring sleep, physical clues to listener fatigue are ambiguous. Some people pitch forward when they're interested, but settling back also equals settling in for a meaty chat. Whatever body language experts claim, crossed arms signal concentration or fed-up-ness as much as defensiveness, and one girl's eager grin is another's clenched, mute "God, you're weird." There is no universal grammar.

Reading ennui is not an exact science, more a descriptive art. As logically it can only be, given that boredom—an instinct for social survival, evolved over countless generations—makes itself known first in feeling. Nonetheless it is amenable to analysis, which offers clues to how to fight it. By way of experiment, if you're really bored, divide the minutes a person takes up (T) by your level of interest in what they have to say (I) (from a low of 1 to a high of 10). This is their Tedium Index (T/I). The higher the number, the greater the bore.

There is a further nuance, in that most people's interest rate, however high it soars initially, will deflate with time.

→ Rule two: Keep it brief

Sadly, listening talent is on the wane, with patience in dwindling supply. So if your listener looks tired, or your Guinness is still brimming, its foam flat, and everyone else's glass is half-empty, shut up. Every subject has its use-by date.

SHUT-UP TEST:
Imagine you're soft-boiling a modest egg.
Have you talked more than three minutes?
This better be a great dinosaur egg of a fascinating topic.
Stick to the point. If they want more, they'll ask.

This advice may puzzle raconteurs who believe themselves marvelous conversationalists—writers and actors in particular. The likes of Gore Vidal and Peter Ustinov are lionized for their ability to sustain lengthy anecdotes. Personally, I'd rather eat glass than sit next to them. Virginia Woolf, too, was a conversational dominatrix. Her biographer writes, apparently approvingly, of her amazing

> *flights of fancy, her wonderful performances in conversation, spinning off into fantastic fabrications while everyone sat around and, as it were, applauded.*

Leave it out. They want theater? Let them buy a ticket.

Good conversation is a team sport; pace and energy keep it alive. The poet Shelley captured the giddy joy of high-tempo rallies with Byron:

> *the swift thought*
> *Winging itself with laughter, lingered not,*
> *But flew from brain to brain.*

And if you want each word to sink in, take a leaf from poetry. Researchers Marc Wittman and Ernst Pöppel have found that our brains prefer data sorted into three-second bundles—be it in music, speech, or poetry. This bias transcends cultural differences:

> *Experiments were conducted using poems in different languages that were spoken aloud. Independently of the language, it took the speakers circa three seconds to recite the individual lines.*

We're all suckers for this rhythm. How else to explain the mysterious power of three? "Education, education, education," cried the politician. "Love, love, love," chorused the Beatles . . .

Better, then, to ditch three-minute declamation for three-second sound bites.

Long Time, No See

The old friend is an old friend for a reason. You know, she knows, but it's impossible to ignore her without offense. For a nippy, packaged small-talk getaway, turn to Aristotle, who argued that stories have a beginning, middle, and end. Equally, a catch-up conversation will gallop by if structured to deal first with the past, the present, then future plans, a strategy that also creates a natural exit.

For example:

PAST	—"Hello. How long has it been?"
	—". . . !"
	—"Wow. Wasn't that at X's? How is she?"
	—". . . ?"
TRANSITION	—"No, I haven't seen her for a while."
	—". . ."
	—(Awkward pause.)
PRESENT	—"You living around here?"
	—(. . . !)
TRANSITION	—"That sounds great. We're hoping to do that one day. Any tips?"
	—(. . .)
FUTURE	—"Excellent. I'll remember that. Oh, look, I'd better catch up with Y before he leaves. It was great to see you. Let's do it again sometime."

→ Rule three: Take turns

Your listener remains unresponsive? Dispirited as you may feel, don't give up.

Note the Latin *conversare* means "to turn around often." Sharing is the core social principle, and most people like talking about themselves, so unpack your conversational tool kit to help him join in. Frame questions to offer scope to roam on to other subjects (not "Do you like chocolate?" but "Can you believe cocoa is a health food?"). Equally, when—if—you're asked a question, supply an answer they can mine, don't bat it straight back. That's not playing the game.

I know a diplomat's son whose childhood was awash with insipid drinks parties. He and his siblings survived the small talk by setting challenges (odd words to weave into conversation, e.g., lecithin, penguins, telescope, fanny). Today he's ace at converting questions into questions, flicking on the conversational ball. Finding out what he thinks, on the other hand, is like catching eels with chopsticks. Sometimes it's tiring. But still, at least he acts interested in me. There are superbores, invariably male, capable of consuming five courses without asking any questions of their companions, usually long-suffering females. (Traveling alone, especially by air, pack earplugs.)

→ Rule four: Act interested to be interested

How we behave contains numerous instructions as to how others should treat us, so one of the most effective tactics against boredom is refusing to acknowledge it.

This applies both when bored and when you suspect you're at fault. At a friend's birthday I met a man who, when I excused myself (nature called) said mournfully, "I'm very boring." At once I believed him, even as I loudly disagreed, then had to wait five minutes before dashing to the loo. Worse, till that self-pitying moment, I'd liked him.

If ever tempted to say "I'm boring you" take this as a warning from your subconscious and say good-bye instead. And remember, to be bored or boring isn't affable. Often it is the bored person's fault: a failure to engage with the other person's point of view. In that frowning toad may crouch a prince, so give him the benefit of the doubt and smile encouragingly.

Perhaps the most important revelation of the Tedium Index (above) is that the intensity of a listener's engagement materially alters the value of what is said. The more interest you bring to conversation, the more interesting it will be. Even if you fake it.

Why bother? Enthusiasm—originally, Greek for "possessed by god"—kindles energy and warmth through the friction of thoughts darting back and forth. Just like magic.

So detonate your bore with this tactic, from a journalism course's seminar on pepping up dull interviewees: Whip the droning along with monosyllables—"Yup … yup … yeah … right … wow!"—all the while smiling, nodding, doing lively things with your eyebrows.

When speaking, act animated and you'll not only carve up the sense of your words more clearly, but seem more engaging too, as politicians appreciate. They karate-chop the air, to lend gravity to the hot stuff steaming from their mouths, a venerable tactic. In Attic Greece, Cratylus disguised his flummery by

> *hissing aggressively and shaking his hands; for these things are persuasive* [to people], *because the things they know become tokens for what they do not know.*

He played angry, they believed he was justified. Alas, it worked for Hitler too.

→ Rule five: Scavenge for material

Nothing to inspire you? Excuses, excuses. Imagine doing zip all, beautifully, full-time—and having to entertain bored masters, potentially on pain of death? Courtiers, muzzled by etiquettes and sheer monotony, somehow unraveled viable material from their cocooned existence. Their techniques repay study.

Sei Shōnagan, a tenth-century Japanese lady and the empress's chief wit, was more constrained than most. Sitting behind a screen (one could not be seen) dueling poetic ripostes with a man, was life at its most thrilling, and writing verse, off the cuff, in public, a frequent, terrifying ordeal. Relief came in light conversation. What, in such a shuttered existence, did she talk about? Her technique was to watch everything closely, sucking joy from minutiae: the hush of blossom falling, ice shavings sweetened with syrup, snow on a sunny day.

Look around and you'll find endless material. Like bitching, only nicer (if you avoid needless risk: remember the mauve catsuit), observations bond people by ranging them metaphorically side by side—facing outward instead of at each other, wondering what to say.

Admire the whiskeys behind the bar, wonder how so many Scottish islands can support distilleries. Does that arch frame a bucolic bosky view? Did you love climbing those kinds of trees when you were a child? Is that man over there wooing that woman? You like that necklace? Then admire it. Observe the effort the boring host has made, aloud. He may light up. You might jump-start something new.

→ Rule six: Watch the waffle

Equally sharp was Shōnagan's eye for bores. High on her list of "disagreeable things" comes the "insignificant person who talks a lot and laughs loudly" and "uses too many words"—unaware that he is ridiculous, too self-involved to recognize that his listeners are better informed. Overlook Shōnagan's snobbery and here is the bore's fatal flaw: significance.

It's generous to offer listeners more than one topic; blather on and you'll seem self-obsessed, and rightly so because, if only out of naïveté, this shows no awareness of the imperative to focus discussion and invite others to sign on to a topic.

If listeners can't relate, every word is a waste of energy, like throwing a ball without taking aim, which is why all tangents and remarks that loop nowhere are freighted with boredom—whatever their inherent interest. And verbiage is certain to wax listeners' ears. I heard a woman put down a slavish man (he was in love; she feigned not to notice): "Gee, you're spewing inanities this morning." But he wasn't. He was trying to impress her, in self-consciously florid terms. So if on the receiving end, listen harder: Within the pomposity may be a pearl worth knowing.

Or not. For a time I worked at an arts institution. To stay awake during epic meetings, I translated, silently, into English, the jargon-laden prattle (most of which turned out to be about money). But the director had a useful catchphrase for silencing quarrels: "I take a Brechtian stance on that." Nobody could answer back because they couldn't understand.

I left.

→ Rule seven: Divert, don't dictate

Ideally, conversation takes us out of ourselves. This is totally at odds with the bore's social strategy. Some bludgeon with fixed opinions, others rule with silence, and all dictate to conversation, by being its dead center. What to do? Soldier-philosopher Sun Tzu observed, "The highest warfare attacks strategy itself." To beat bores, challenge their monopoly, and their tactics: Divert them.

Sociologist Max Weber compared ideas to railroad switchmen,

able to redirect a culture's evolution. I'd add that they fuel the engine. Why not attack a monologist's monoculture with a virus: a fresh idea? Just don't thump invisible lecterns or neglect to observe your listener: Ask yourself, is this news to him?

Teasing may also throw bores off their well-worn tracks. I watched a self-important politician melt when a flirt tweaked his ruddy nose. Still, gently does it. If cheeky courtiers quickened the pulse of their jaded patrons, some went too far. The earl of Rochester, Charles II's on-off favorite, got the boot for this squib:

> *God bless our good and gracious King*
> *Whose promise none relyes on*
> *Who never said A foolish thing*
> *Nor ever did A wise one.*

But the king soon fetched him back. Life grew too dull. (How could he do without the man who began a poem *"Her father gave her Dildoes six?"*)

➜ Rule eight: Use the difficulty
Don't forget, a little learning can be a fun thing, sprinkled on the right company.

As the anthropologist said, boredom spurs invention. Follow the example of novelist Sir Walter Scott and milk for information:

> There are few persons from whom you cannot learn something, and ... everything is worth knowing.

The exception, in my experience, being an aficionado of Swiss fridge magnets. (The cow, when you wagged its tail—guess what? It went moo.)

Still, as your bore talks you through his client list for the umpteenth time, try to capitalize on this opportunity to polish conversation skills. If he's exceptionally nasty, you could play Outbore the Bore, doing unto him what he has done to you. But I doubt he'd notice, and you'd soon bore yourself.

Is boredom ever a virtue? Psychotherapist Adam Phillips reckons it's a "developmental achievement" and that adults are "oppressive" to demand that children

> *should be interested. . . . Boredom is integral to the process of taking one's time.*

Perhaps he's right, we're too quick to cry "bore." We entertainment-rich consumerists are all a bit like Charles II: We demand to be amused.

Recently I took a train from London to Bath, in the designated family carriage. Most passengers read or snoozed. But one boy whined and moaned, all the way to Bath. The same boy whose top-drawer laptop computer delighted everyone else with top-volume war-game noise, all the way to Bath.

Every so often his parents told him to shut up and play his game, then went back to their books.

The elderly lady opposite me muttered, "He needs a good talking to."

We exchanged a grimace, went back to our books.

In retrospect, I feel sorry for that boy: unable to amuse himself, and his parents acting as if this was solely his problem. Couldn't they have talked and played together?

Adam Phillips might argue that he needed to be ignored.

Believe me, I tried. I should have talked to the old lady instead.

→ Rule nine: Closed minds are bored minds

The rough manners today bewilder older generations. Grannies lament the toys kids are given—when we were young, they say, we made our own fun. Old bores?

They know far better than TV-drenched we how to tell stories, take turns, listen.

Then again, in her old age, Rebecca West had unforgiving memories of meeting Nobel laureate W. B. Yeats, who "boomed at you like a foghorn." The younger writer had far preferred frisking with other young writers present, and decades later remained astonished that

> *Yeats wouldn't join in, until we fussed round and were nice to him.... What he liked was solemnity.*

Yes, even in her dotage, it didn't occur to West that the grand old man of letters might justifiably expect these literary whippersnappers to be interested in what he had to say.

That whiskery chap with the slow way of speaking has a trove of experience. So be patient, let him share it. You'll be the richer.

→ Rule ten: Be kind to the bore
One day, he could be you.

TYPOLOGY OF BORES, CHORES, AND OTHER CONVERSATIONAL BEASTS

DEAF IN BOTH EARS   *Ambiaures inauditae egotissimus*

Least forgivable are those ostensibly interesting bores, bereft of curiosity, complacently accustomed to consider being in their presence a privilege. Anyone who has been pursued by famous, rich, or older men will recognize the problem. You say gold digger; I say danger money.

With a shrug DIBE kills the question he dislikes. With a swivel of the eye he heckles any other who durst hold the floor.

"The point is," he says, a prehensile fist smashing the table, if you venture a comment that strays from his preferred narrative line.

But while his self-importance often reaps fat rat-race rewards, DIBE usually has a dead-eyed spouse in tow, as well as an entourage of failed relationships—consoling testimony to the social limits of tunnel vision.

Tactics: Remind DIBE you exist. Make comparisons, seek advice, offer counterexamples to curtail the monologue: "Reminds me of when I did X." If DIBE is toxic, attack the core: smugness. Sympathize at each boast: "How awful-looking after so many houses!", "Don't businesses like that go under?"

Pluses: Since the demise of *Dynasty,* how many opportunities exist to pity the spoiled rich? Those sad, lonely billionaires . . .

8

WIT TO WOO

On Humor as Social Engineering

Is your catchphrase "Just joking"? Perhaps it's time to revise your repartee. How about this:

> *Two cannibals, eating a clown. One says to the other, "Does this taste funny to you?"*

It worked for Tommy Cooper, the madcap magician-comic, who knew well that humor, like clown meat, is a matter of taste. But now, if I told it, quietly, in a quick, breathless burst, I guarantee the gag would pass you by.

I never crack jokes. Not that I don't try to be funny; I just prefer a side approach, smuggling humor into comments so that, if nobody notices, the custard pie is not on me—or so I like to think. Why bother at all? Robert Louis Stevenson nailed it:

> *Talk has none of the freezing immunities of the pulpit. . . . A jest intervenes, the solemn humbug is dissolved in laughter.*

If nothing else, Harvard University investigators have found that those who stride on life's sunny side outlive misery guts, which may well be because they are not lonely, since humor is the electricity of intimacy. It helps us forget ourselves, braces emotional suspension, exercises minds, garnering friends and power, from bedroom to boardroom.

Cicero recalled Julius Caesar as a young lawyer:

so superior to one and all in wit and repartee that, even in fo-
rensic speeches, he prevailed over the arguments of other advo-
cates with his conversational style.

Anyone can profit from humor. Yet I'm not alone in my fear of skidding on the banana skin of a slack wisecrack, nor my tendency to chuckle at the merest sniff of wit from someone else. Such cowardly tendencies are prudent social politics. And for all the mystique misting ideas about what makes something funny, laughter turns out to be an ultrapractical conversational fix-it. Eight times out of ten, wit has nothing to do with it.

What can this mean? For a start, anyone can be funnier—without being funny—if he appreciates how laughter works.

THE SOCIAL CONJUROR

Imagine there was a magic word that could, like a snap of the fingers, wind someone up, calm him down, make him listen, draw him near, send him packing, change the subject, or let you say what you want and get away with it?

There is. It's "Ha-ha-ha." And that's not all it can do.

Neuroscientist Robert Provine had a hunch that laughter was more significant to communication than some fellow academics credited. With difficulty, he raised funds to investigate twelve hundred "laugh episodes" (moments of dialogue followed by laughter, in typical social situations). To his amazement,

only about 10 percent to 20 percent of prelaugh comments were
estimated by my assistants to be even remotely humorous.

Typical laugh-getters included "I know!", "Look, it's Andre!", "Nice meeting you too," "What can I say?", and "How are you?"

If rarely a response to humor, what is laughter for? Provine speculated it expresses "grunts and cackles from our animal unconscious," hand-me-downs from ancestor apes. Perhaps. We can't ask them. More useful is the notion that, like so much else in talk, laughter is a grooming device for smoothing and restyling interaction.

→ Rule one: Laughter is a social organizer
When we "get it," "it" is not only the joke, but the effervescent intimacy with everyone else laughing. And in those eight out of ten cases where no joke is in sight, laughter serves as social punctuation: Like an exclamation mark, it says "*Really* good to meet you!" or "*Andre*? So it is!" On an emotional level, this shows approval: "I'm talking to *you* and I *like* it!" On the practical, it denotes a change of topic.

So to laugh after "What can I say?" is a way of saying "Not a lot on that topic! Any other offers?" And at Andre's arrival, its punctuation opens a gap in conversation, to let Andre in, or let out the person who spies him (noticing being a classic conversation getaway).

Laughter also opens trapdoors in serious moods, and we use it tactically, as a matter of Machiavellian instinct. For instance, most of us laugh after raising troubling topics, a reflex that gives listeners two options: to laugh too, or to react seriously and talk. Hence we're wise to quip at our blunders. If others laugh, the moment is burst, conversation levitated out of awkwardness, and speakers are returned to an equal footing. No matter if their first impulse was to laugh at you, now it is with you: Your quip gives permission.

This illustrates how laughter not only gives conversation rhythm, but also regulates intimacy, releasing tension, communicating emotion, performing a similar job to those dials you twiddle on stereos, equalizers. Without its pulse, talk feels dead and social syntax buckles, because in very precise ways, laughter synchronizes conversation's dance. Muff the joke, miss the beat, giggle too late, and you'll soon feel out of the loop—making humor a status game.

→ Rule two: Laughter is a status moderator that can lift you up or down

Casanova trod the knife edge in 1750 Paris. New in town, seeking friends, he was chatting to a plump man at the opera when he spied a lady, "covered in jewels but enormous in size":

> *"And who," I asked my fat neighbor, "is that fat pig?"*
> *"The wife of this fat pig."*
> *"Oh! I beg a thousand pardons."*

Luckily the man, "choking with laughter," promptly asked him to dinner, a coup later crowned when an aristocrat sneered that an actress admired by the Italian lothario had "terrible legs." Casanova replied:

> *I cannot see them, monsieur; and anyway, in judging female beauty, the first thing I set apart are the legs.*

The fortuitous pun won him "immediate standing."

But the easiest way to make people laugh is be their boss. I remember, a lowly assistant and new to a company, making a barbed remark in a meeting. Silence. Then the man next to me repeated it, and everybody needed straitjackets. Maybe they didn't hear me, maybe they disliked me, maybe my timing was way off. I prefer to think the problem was social position. Until this point I'd communicated in shades of blush, whereas he was resident funnyman—far better qualified than me to be funny.

→ Rule three: Humor melts barriers

If I'd been more laid back, however, banter might have brought me real influence. On-target laughter is a powerful weapon. Fourteenth-century artist Giotto vaporized social boundaries with backchat, winning the friendship of the King of Naples.

One scalding summer's day the king said, "I'd stop painting if I were you."

"I would too," said Giotto, "if I were you."

This seems ample proof of George Bernard Shaw's claim:

To tell people the truth, you'd better make them laugh or they'll kill you.

You can get away with murder if you make people laugh, because a minor mental explosion disables thought and body. Sportsmen exploit ridicule to scuttle opponents' concentration. In particular, Australian cricketers are maestros of "sledging," aka ball-breaking. My favorite was yelled as England's Phil Tufnell moseyed over to the wicket:

Oy, Phil, lend us your brain? We're trying to build us an idiot.

Similarly, bons mots are slicker than pig grease for squeezing out of tight spots. Ninon de Lenclos, *salonnière* and calumniated pioneer of rights for women, such as changing lover every three months, sharpened her wit repulsing amorous suitors. Just as well. One day the queen, pressed by scandalmongers who accused Ninon of poisoning the flower of French youth, sent an order to quit town for "a convent [*couvent*] of her choice."

"I pray you," Ninon told the messenger, "say I choose the Grands Cordeliers."

Punning on *couvent* (also "monastery" in French), she had selected one whose monks' debauches were legendary. The stunned messenger returned to the palace and repeated her word for word.

"Fie, the villain," said the queen, laughing. "Let her go where she wants."

Comic Steve Allen explained the paralysis caused by laughter as a "short-circuit" because humor plays games with our mental processing. The brain begins

> *filing away the material according to what appears to be its face-value meaning, when suddenly ... our consciousness perceives that there is more than one interpretation of the material. The brain is therefore momentarily startled, and its normal function interrupted. We suddenly face the fact we have been tricked.*

The tingly adrenaline rush that follows makes it harder still to be angry at the laughter's cause. Happily, this mind-body trade flows both ways, and physical ruses can tickle an unsuspecting mind into feeling funny.

LAUGHTER WITHOUT WIT: SOME TIPS

Philosopher Henri Bergson observed that "all laughter is inherently social," and psychologists confirm that nothing eats away a sense of humor like isolation and its concomitant, self-consciousness. Conversely, there's nothing like other people to make us laugh.

Experimenters asked some seven-year-olds to listen to comedy tapes on headphones. Alone they laughed little, but with another child their giggle rate shot up. What is more, the closer they sat, the more both laughed. Even if only one could hear the tape.

Not only is laughter a reflex, but it is contagious. Hence broadcasters go in for "laughspeak," a giggly style of talk, to tame interviewees; hence laugh tracks are dubbed over sitcoms; hence, while traditionally it is wrong to laugh at your own jokes, laughter analyst Robert Provine found that speakers laughed on average 46 percent more than listeners. And just as it has been observed that we laugh harder at people we find sexy, so the reverse is true: the more you make others laugh, the more they'll be attracted to you.

All of which suggests some wit-free techniques for magnifying mirth:

Relax: be informal, focus on them (inhibition squashes laughter)

Stand close: the nearer, the more they'll laugh

Touch them lightly, occasionally

Use eye contact

Show your amusement

Don't fake smiles or laughs: always obvious (real smiles reach the eyes)

Be near laughing people, the more, the merrier

Bring others in (*note:* laughter's SOS will attract others, helping dilute bores)

Expect to be amused: optimism optimizes humor

Laugh at your own jokes, except in larger groups (with an audience, joking becomes performance, and the same criteria apply as for stand-up)

Drink alcohol

WHAT IS FUNNY?

If humor is organic to certain situations, can it be cultivated? What is funny anyway?

Defining humor seems almost the definition of foolish, like trying to sculpt sunbeams or bottle rainbows. Indeed, fitting farce ensued after Clarence Richardson, fifty-five, of Wessington, South Dakota, died in 1946, bequeathing a princely $30,000 to whoever sent his postmaster the best definition of "joke." Seven thousand entries in, the postmaster went to court, and the will was quashed on the grounds the deceased had been of unsound mind.

I suspect Richardson had an entirely healthy sense of humor. However, stern philosopher-wit Voltaire, a friend of Ninon de Lenclos, cautioned:

> A joke explained ceases to be a joke. Any commentator of bons mots is a fool.

Then again, Voltaire might have been protecting trade secrets. Although comedians harp on about how analysis destroys comedy, this is a bit like surgeons saying the leg is a marvel of nature and shouldn't be chopped up: So it is, but they still understand the mechanics, can dissect and repair it. What comedians really mean is that talking about what makes something funny isn't a barrel of laughs. But none can deny they work at it, and as Ninon demonstrated, a spot of apprentice work comes in handy.

→ **Rule four: We laugh hardest at the stuff that is hardest to talk about**

Comedy jigs on the borders of our discomfort zones. Ricky Gervais, star-creator of *The Office*, claimed humor has no taboos. But tampering with taboos, snapping at sensibilities, is comedy's raison d'être. Each joke has a victim: There must be an "it" to "get." Even if "it" is a belief, it is attached to someone, and a reductive view would be that the butt's invariably the listener, laughing at himself for being fooled.

However, lines of attack tend to be indirect. Anthropologists found that jokes in North American tribes skirt seven topics:

Sex and gender
Shortcomings or social deviance
Sickness, suffering, death
Religion
Wealth
Power and authority
Social stereotypes and relationships

These targets, sources of desire and weakness, strike nerves everywhere because comedy is a fairground mirror, monstering what disturbs us, making "it"—our fear, our folly—ridiculous. It defangs threats, deflates authority, transmuting the funny-peculiar into the funny-ha-ha, reminding us that nothing matters but plenty's worth knocking.

And we shouldn't overlook the enduringly popular, ever economical joke resource: its machinery. Wordplay, such as the pilloried pun, is humor's junk food, embezzling laughs from bamboozled listeners' brains. Unburdened of anything so portentous as a comical idea, the average pun has little to say for itself beyond "Duh, gotcha, filing error!" Which may explain why people are so down on them. Still, seven- to twelve-year-olds of all ages remain in thrall, including me.

→ **Rule five: The right target is what others are prepared to laugh at**

Jokes, like taboos, shift with society, and Russell Brand disproved Ricky Gervais on September 12, 2001, getting fired from MTV for hosting a show dressed as Osama Bin Laden. Brand had forgotten humorist James Thurber's dictum:

$$TRAGEDY + TIME = COMEDY$$

Although jokes thumb a nose at fears, they work best as "an epitaph on an emotion," not when feelings are live and kicking, and cracks at others' expense may cheapen you. So aim at listeners' assumptions. Even better, joke against yourself.

In unfamiliar terrain, only a bold, brilliant, or socially suicidal wit should tackle:

What others in the room look, smell, sound, feel, or taste like
Wives, husbands, kids, siblings, parents
Pets (wake me when it's over)
The poor and needy
Genitalia, odoriferous effluvia, biological hazards
Obscure hobbies, chess, philately, math, physics, esoterica
How wonderful life is, how brilliant you are
Plague, famine, war, pestilence
The horrid food/drink/guests (to the host)
The horrid host (unless it's you)

➡ Rule six: For wit to woo, better to amuse and be amused than ape a stand-up

Despite Britain's pride in our nation's sense of humor, a 2007 survey found the average citizen remembered only two jokes. Surprised? Don't be.

Social humor is generally triggered by situation, not ready-canned, and the monopoly conditions in which professional comics operate have none of conversation's companionable to and fro. Indeed, so antisocial is the audience-performer dynamic that jokes can de-emulsify conversations into gag contests—not always desirable. Be that as it may, professionals' comic wisdom can be culled to boost everyday wit.

Attitude: "Never, never try to be funny!" commanded *Producers* genius Mel Brooks. Following this advice doesn't mean never laughing; rather, relaxing to lower the stakes. Try quips, not shaggy dog stories, and smile. The more confident you seem, the less exposed you feel, the clearer your voice will be, and the funnier you'll appear.

Pitch Woo: If misjudging the audience is the commonest cause of humor failure, second is knowing the audience too well, and letting on, by jabbing at their insecurities. Don't tout your sharps, oversell, or announce, "Here's a funny one" before testing the water. Instead, do as comics do: Build rapport, lob the odd compliment.

Recognition: Read a group, ensuring it can read you. Humor has a regional accent, dramatized by actor Simon Pegg in this exchange between friends (B is British, A, American):

B: *I had to go to my grandad's funeral last week.*
A: *Sorry to hear that.*
B: *Don't be. It was the first time he ever paid for the drinks.*
A: *I see.*

Observe what makes listeners tick, ideally taking the truth and twisting it. Or as another comic advised, don't give a funny opinion; give an opinion in a funny way. Forget rococo riffs on harpsichords: People will more readily endorse the comic value you assign to, say, the horror of opening beer since the ring-pull's demise, or cadging a favor out of a miserly neighbor, or plowing through Ikea on a holiday weekend.

Style: Humor speaks with forked tongue—in double meanings, incongruity, image, metaphor, and so on—but overcomplicate it and no one will get it. A cleverly bowled joke deceives just enough to be caught; listeners' pleasure being in their mind turning somersaults, then making a clean landing. For instance, a phrase like "bungalow mind" places an extra processing load on the brain, which effort makes it stick.

So be economical, gulling listeners' imaginations into being your collaborators. Use as few words as possible; employ vivid, visual language, and act out stories with body and face. (Like actress Lucille Ball, who was so adept her scripts featured "light bulb" and "puddle up" as facial stage directions.) Dazzle your listener's mind's eye and he won't see a punch line hurtling at him.

Pace: Stand-ups say: "Never step on your punch line." Meaning: Savor the pause before a gag, defined by Franklin Ajaye as "the lighting of the fuse." When telling a funny tale, build suspense, let misunderstanding and expectation coalesce in listeners' minds, and adhere to the principle "Don't say it until you have to."

Surprise: No doubt Julius Caesar's witty conquests in court taught him:

The most powerful weapon of war is the unexpected.

Mix maladapted elements to wreak comedy havoc: Praise the bad, exaggerate, understate, fake anger, feign delight. Use inversion:

Rather than "What a big pancake roll!" say, as a lawyer did to me, "This pancake roll wants to devour me."

Humor works by guile, not advertisement, but play with comic expectations and punch lines may be discarded. A Bill Cosby routine began: "One time I had a sore throat, bad sore throat." He paused, preparing his audience for a joke, then resumed in a cross child's voice, "I have a sore throat." They cracked up, as much because the pause primed them for a gag.

Follow the Way of Woe: In funny-land nothing gets better: The trajectory is always bad gets worse gets more and more absurd. Such as the time I was whining about my expanding bottom. My husband—sighing, eyes shut, in bed—said, "Not at all." So in I hopped, to a loud crack. My side of the bed had gone through the floor. My husband groaned, got up, and we lifted it out. Another crack. The leg on his side had snapped. Finally, so did he.

THE ANATOMY OF A JOKE

Jokes embody in miniature the short, dapper definition of comedy given by the short, great Charlie Chaplin:

Two opposite ideas that collide.

The simplest come in two parts: the setup (building comic expectation) and the punch line (exploding expectation to reveal the skulduggery). Like mathematical equations organized on absurdist principles, a good joke's incongruous ideas are so deviously intertwined that the deception dissolves only at the end.

Think of it as a tale of two stories. If the setup implies one story line (the one listeners believe in), the punch reveals that a second has been tucked inside all along. But the equation never quite adds up. It defies logic, like a magic trick. The mind boggles, and so we laugh.

SETUP + PUNCH LINE = LAUGHTER

Or alternatively: INCONGRUITY x CREDULITY = *SURPRISE!*

To be effective, the first story, the setup, targets a specific audience assumption. Only if the aim is accurate will the trap spring, two ideas crash-bang-wallop, and then bumble about, rubbing their heads, quaking with mirth. This chicanery relies on intellectual prestidigitation; somewhere buried in the setup is a slippery item about which the joke turns, which stand-up Greg Dean calls the "connector."

Here's a Dean special:

For Father's Day, I took my father out—it only took seven shots. I could always drink him under the table.

This double-yolker has two connectors: "shots" and "took out" (both our flexible friends, puns). But the method only works if your aim is true, landing bang on listeners' target assumptions. Which is why the best jokes are

Concise (only telling details, no superfluous or repeated words)
Easy to follow (expressive delivery and weighted pauses, focusing attention on the connector and the reveal)
Timed to maximize misunderstanding and surprise
Save the punch till the last word.

Play it how you want it. Roseanne Barr's feisty Lady Caliban comic persona grabbed audiences by the throat, but liked to leave them hanging. She began with a premise, took a little journey ("the hook") drawing out the first story line, sinking it in listeners' imaginations, and then ...

Premise:	He comes in and he says, "Roseanne, why don't you try to be more aggressive in bed?
Hook:	So, I thought about it and the other night, we're lying there and he reaches for me ... and I said,
Pause:	
Punch line:	(screaming) NOOOOOOO!

And the target assumption? Barr's character: that she would want to please her man.

  Please.

→ Rule seven: Let humor shift the temperature

But the best humor is organic not premeditated—and medicinal, according to Norman Cousins, who beat 500–1 odds of recovery from an agonizing condition with an inspired hypothesis: If illness is psychosomatic, why not wellness? Treatment began with episodes of *Candid Camera*.

  Cousins's smart inversion has suggested a sneaky humor tactic. Why sweat up a quip if you can snatch laughter from the jaws of the social need it serves, by taking the mood and shaking it?

  To neutralize a problem, isolate, then ironize it. Use repetition. Say, she says, "Don't get me started ..." You say (warmly, not snootily): "Don't get her started." He spills wine? Say, *"My* shirt. *My shirt!"*

  Dropped a clanger? Make light: "Is it time to talk about the weather yet?" or "This reminds me of a joke. Shame I can't remember it."

Nervous? "Don't worry about my wobbly voice, I'm just terrified."

He said something funny but the feeling isn't mutual? Don't let silence gouge an embarrassing hole. A light eyebrow-raiser—"You!" "Honestly!"—is enough to let conversation continue smoothly.

We tease those we care about, because this flattering liberty assumes the other person will get the joke. Use the power. And if pressed by a pachyderm pest, try this boaster blunderbuss, overheard by cocktail-talk collector Andrew Barrow:

"Congratulations. Are you frightfully pompous now?"

TYPOLOGY OF BORES, CHORES, AND
OTHER CONVERSATIONAL BEASTS

CAN YOU BELIEVE IT?   *Mendax mirabundus*

Thank heaven for eyebrows. How else to sustain that look of amazement as Can You Believe It launches into another vertically challenged tale?

Few companions are as wearing. Coercive little phrases—"Wasn't that incredible?"—reach out from her flat-as-yesterday's-lemonade recitals, pulling her audience by the ear, demanding that they (a) show amazement and (b) wake up.

To an extent, such cues are welcome clues—how else to know which parts are meant to be fascinating? However, emotional stage directions preempt spontaneous wonder, and subject to such bullying, the rebel in us recoils while the nice conformist affixes a smile, wondering why we're annoyed as well as bored. (A fastidious friend took agin an old roommate at a reunion, not so much due to the exhaustive sermon on her visit to a cathedral, but because it ended in the command "Just think!")

What is worse, CYBI is so busy imposing reactions, she never learns what truly rocks our world.

Tactics: CYBI means well, and we've all been in situations where our excitement gets lost in translation. If it so happens that not only would you believe it, but you've a better story, take the floor (and give everybody some respite): say, "Yes, reminds me of when …"
Pluses: If you start issuing Wow!-prompts, this is your subconscious hinting that an encounter is on the slide. Seek more creative means of support, or get out of there.

9

HOW TO TELL A LIE

On the Detection of Untruths

It suits us to believe that liars are punished and their schemes backfire, but this is self-deception. There is a reason witnesses in courts of law tell the truth, the whole truth, and nothing but, so help them God. If we went about our business voicing our every suspicion, lust, and grievance, we too would need a divine bodyguard. Imagine:

"You as daft as you look?"

"My elbow has more personality."

"Your brat stinks."

→ **Rule one: Trimming the truth is a social skill**

Our species' success comes of sociability, serving four social goals—collaborative, convivial, competitive, and conflictive—none of which correlate with truth unmodified. While getting along means being trustworthy, could we gain one another's trust if we were totally honest?

Take the dilemma of vet Yoav Alony-Gilboa, eating rabbit at a "posh restaurant":

Halfway through I hit a bone and thought to myself, "This is not right." I checked another bone that, for a rabbit, shouldn't

be there, and it was. I realized we were eating a cat, beautifully
seasoned, tender and moist.... I didn't complain, however, as it
would have been too embarrassing for my hosts.

Sociability requires self-sacrifice, and kindness, self-censorship. Skipping awkward bits, sparing feelings, saving face: These are the lies that bind, invisible stitches of untruth, as we tailor conversation to our audience, but so intrinsic to the process that we scarcely notice doing it. Ideally.

But although lying is innate, found in gorillas and human toddlers, and deception well documented in grouchy infants who find instant succor in their parents' arms, tact is something only socializing can teach.

Worryingly, saving lies are falling from fashion. Confession is a flimsy alternative to a fully paid-up conscience, yet the often invasive mantra of "sharing" is little challenged. The soap operatics of self-revelation are free to all in the access-all-areas info swamp that is the Internet, with scanty particulars on full display. And the "home truth," seldom less than self-serving—a warrant to bully or pass problems on, breaches of social trust in the name of honesty—passes for virtue.

An unsuspecting friend received a call from a recovering addict, an acquaintance long out of her life, who outlined the vintage sexual fantasies in which she had starred back at school—a violation prescribed by his therapist! Is this the road to responsibility?

➔ Rule two: Directness is a privilege of intimacy

A representative defense of directness comes from singer Mutya Buena:

"People say, 'You're so pretty but you're so rude; you shouldn't be
talking the way you're talking.' Excuse me? [Imagine extrava-
gant hand gestures here.] I can't help the way I am. I've grown

up with four older brothers so I've learnt not to take any non-
sense.... People seem to be intimidated by me, even small chil-
dren." She laughs. "I think that people took my bitchiness for
being horrible, rather than just being me."

Being herself means being bitchy but not being horrible? Such con-
torted thinking from such a bright woman shows how easily we
think well of ourselves, and how much is lost if we forget directness
is a right we earn. Only a friend can say you look vile as a favor.

HONEST DELUSIONS

Is directness honest? Depends what you call truth. Watching a philosopher grapple with it can feel like watching a fly fling itself at a
window, unaware that the glass it bashes (its perceptions) is both
what inspires its attempt to get outside, and the barrier to success.

We're all stuck inside ourselves; what we see is partial, and only
fickle language is available to comprehend it. Worse, our truths re-
side in memories, which aren't static entities but unreliable, imaginative acts, each recollection a minor physiological miracle, as
electricity and chemicals surge, switching on allied brain cells—
physical alliances that themselves ebb and shift with fresh experience and time's sifting sands. In a sense, we are but figments of our
imagination.

So why don't we go mad?

→ **Rule three: We're biased to believe and tell convenient truths**
In *Consciousness Explained* Daniel Dennett reflected:

Our fundamental tactic of self-protection, self-control, and self-
definition is not spinning webs, but telling stories, and more
particularly concocting and controlling the story we tell others—
and ourselves—about who we are.

Stories save us, thanks to our amazing capacity to fit evidence to expectations and believe the best of ourselves. Paradoxically, the self-serving editing by which we confect our identities shows how important integrity is to us, how much we long to be right—whether screwing a good deal, saying an affair hurts no one, or claiming bitchiness isn't rude.

By contrast, politic social awareness asks us to sense that truth is a contest between facts, their relevance and their meaning, which, like memories, alter with time and new information; to acknowledge that others see things otherwise, and our truth isn't The Truth. Thus conversational caution keeps us honest, by reminding us to take turns, hear other points of view, and frame our words accordingly. Thank goodness.

Imagine if truth were all that mattered, and a one-size-fits fundamental law identified it? We could forget ethics, humility. We certainly needn't worry about getting on, having a conversation. No, we could disappear up our fundamentals, stamp on all who disagreed, assured of our own supreme righteousness. Even former U.S. Defense Secretary Donald Rumsfeld, unbending in war, appreciated relativism:

> *Needless to say, the President is correct. Whatever it was he said.*

THE GOOD LIE: A USER'S GUIDE

So what is a lie? Concealment? Fabrication? Deception? Omission? A useful recipe for an active lie comes from William Hirstein:

> *I lie to you when (and only when)*
> *1. I claim* p *to you.*
> *2.* p *is false.*

3. I believe that p *is false.*

4. I intend to cause you to believe p *is true by claiming that* p *is true.*

→ Rule four: A bad lie is antisocial

If we accept the premise of doctors' Hippocratic oath (do no harm), we can define a bad lie by the test set in 1999 by the British judge who backed the Reynolds defense (named after the former Irish prime minister, who felt he had been libeled, but lost the case):

Is the untruth stated knowingly, maliciously, recklessly?

Which implies that:

→ Rule five: A good lie may mean sincerely well

This fits with thinker Bernard Williams's evocation of truth's dual personality, as consisting of sincerity and accuracy. The laws of good manners—don't impose, don't embarrass—resolve the problem of when sincerity and accuracy don't get along (you sincerely want to thank your hosts; mentioning the cat is superfluous).

And after all, competing truths redefine facts. Is the attentive, deferential doctor a docile wife or a walkover mother? Should she be? Different rules govern each role we play, and not framing our words to a particular situation or relationship courts hazard. (So if your sister had taken you to the restaurant, the cat might not be off-limits after all.)

Do as Emily Dickinson ordained:

Tell all the Truth but tell it slant.

TELL A LIE?

If we depend on convenient untruths, surely we need also to detect them. But while evolutionary psychologists view lying as an adaptation to aid social survival, one that hastened the growth of man's twisty-turny brain, evolution is rather lagging on our capacity to ferret out lies.

Investigations have found that the average person has a 40 to 60 percent chance of rumbling one, and professional lie hunters fare no better. And for each cliché about how liars act—they scratch their nose, fidget, their eyes roam, they look up and to the right—there is zero evidence.

Might as well flip a coin? Not quite.

Although each liar lies in his own way, all suffer three pressures:

emotional (nerves, excitement)
cerebral (they have to keep track)
behavioral (they try not to fidget, stutter, etc.)

These pressures produce clues that, if many appear together, may well tell a lie.

Non-verbal Clues
Eyes don't complete the smile
Decreased movement, gestures, blinking (the extra load on
    a liar's mind stills his body)
Seems uncooperative or uninvolved

Vocal Clues
Voice sounds tense, negative, its pitch is slightly higher than
    normal

VERBAL CLUES

Stories sound implausible, rehearsed

Statements are short on details, especially visual, sensual,
   spatial, or temporal (the liar is unlikely to observe a
   place was cold, smelly, dark, etc.)

Language is less immediate, more uncertain and negative,
   with passive clauses and indirect statements (e.g., "the
   man told me he felt ill" rather than "the man said, 'I'm
   going to vomit'")

Most reliable are verbal and vocal clues. Of course, abnormal behavior will be apparent only if you know what normal is (another
reason to prioritize face-to-face talk).

And be warned: Adroit, practiced liars doctor the facts to feel
like truths they can believe in. All tests agree that the best liars are
sales professionals. But for them, selling the hell out of a product
they don't rate isn't insincere but a sign of devotion—so by Bernard
Williams's measure, aren't they good, honest workers?

Whereas second-rate liars overcomplicate things, going out of
their way to avoid fabrication, preferring ambiguity to committing
to a yes or no. They omit information, claim a faulty memory, don't
answer questions, meet allegations with generalizations or subjec-
tive truths, heap up irrelevant details, as if to hide untruth in a
thicket of unrelated truth, and garnish statements with groves of
excess verbiage. They answer, as did one-time U.S. Secretary of
State Alexander Haig:

That's not a lie, it's a terminological inexactitude.

GUIDELINES FOR SNARING LIARS
(OR, ALTERNATIVELY,
NOT GETTING CAUGHT)

We're prejudiced in favor of words that confirm our expectations.
(Say what they want to hear; they will deceive themselves.)

We're biased to believe those we find attractive, friendly, and confident.
(We believe what we like to see: smile, meet their eye, dress well.)

The higher the stakes, the likelier they will seem stressed or rehearsed.
(Psych yourself down by shrinking the significance of the lie, and keep it simple, precise, and no quibbling.)

Falsification is harder than omission, so make them account for themselves.
(The best liars believe what they say. Stick to the truth, edited.)

Look for liars and you'll be misled by expectations. Instead, sieve behavior for indications someone may be lying. Does he look tense? Is he thinking hard? Playing for time?
(Don't overcontrol behavior: Fidgeting and gestures are normal.)

Don't rush to conclusions about whether odd behavior means someone's lying: Instead, seek explanations for any mismatch between what he says and how he acts.
(Imply alternative reasons why you might seem under pressure.)

Act suspicious and you put the liar on guard.
(Assume everyone is suspicious; act as if they've every faith in you.)

Increase the cognitive load: Ask him to repeat things, darting back and forth in sequence.
(Get the other person talking. Can you tell your story in any order?)

As he tells his story again, does his tone or style alter, the level of detail drop off?
(Lie as if reliving it, keeping immediacy and details consistent.)

Is he going out of his way to tell you something you didn't ask?
(Never lie unless you have to.)

And remember the clichés. To be believed, carry a hanky, and never scratch your nose.

How to Spot—or Mask—a Bad Idea

Verbal sharp practice may hone the appearance of reason. Equally, many a bad case has stifled a good idea. Don't be misled by rhetorical feints or, alternatively, miss an opportunity to beef up your argument. Here is a catalog of alluring nonsense, baseless assertions, and fallacious conclusions that arise in conversation at work, rest, and play.

The assertion-request
A blackmail technique for leveraging demands with an emotional but evidentially challenged premise. As in "Everyone has one, Mum. Why can't I?"

Character assassination

Ad hominem/feminam arguments discredit ideas by attacking
the advocate. Or conversely, they collapse distinctions between
actor and act. They call the child naughty because it has done a
naughty deed. Or call the man evil because they call the word
evil because, once upon a time, an evil use was made of it—
e.g., the plot-spur to Philip Roth's novel *The Human Stain*, a
misunderstanding over the word "spook."

If X, then Y

"If they hiked up your salary, then they should mine." Says who?
Note that "then" is not the same as "therefore."

"We have no reason to doubt"

But no reason to believe either. (Popular with politicians.)

Wrong case, right answer?

So they use a rubbish argument for why the sky is blue (Jupiter
spilled his ink). Does that invalidate the proposition?

Begging question

These clever smears can smuggle assertions into questions.
Such as "When did you stop beating your wife?" or "Ideal for
curing cottage cheese." Since when is cellulite a disease?

We are the great and the good; our agency is great and good.

Logicians call this the "composition fallacy"—assuming that a
group has the qualities of its members.

Britain is rich; every Briton is rich.

Oh sure. The reverse of the composition fallacy, this is the
divisive fallacy, which assumes all members share the qualities of the group. As in, "Each Beatle is a towering musical
genius."

If X, then Y. Not X, therefore not Y?

Not true! Just because the business made lots of money last year and we got bonuses, now the profits are down our bonuses shouldn't automatically flop.

Either X or Y. X, therefore not Y.

Again, says who? Why not both? Who says they're contingent anyway? For instance: "This pie tastes awful. Either the blueberries were off, or I forgot to add sugar. The blueberries taste funny. So I must have added sugar."

Bogus analogy

Misleading comparisons, comforting though they may be, lead to loony conclusions: "Shakespeare was a genius and he never learned how to use the Internet. Therefore I can still be a genius but foxed by Google." or "Saddam is like Al Qaeda. Therefore, blast Saddo, bye-bye Al Q."

What a dilemma!

Another either/or fallacy, whereby false equivalences are linked to form the basis of a decision. As in "Either I lose weight or I'll never be happy."

Unhappy averages

The golden mean fallacy is what democracy rests on: the notion that the best solution is a blend of all the different views out there. But think about it: If applied in the realm of interior decoration, the average wouldn't be golden, but a world in sludge gray.

Nice argument, shame about the premise

You can build logic on a wild idea, but it won't make the argument right. As in "In a world made of strawberries, sugar and cream would be fatal, due to maceration . . ."

Upgrading evidence

You may have data; this cannot determine ultimate values: "No skin cream smoothes more soothingly, say our tests on twenty-three women basted in it for a year. Ergo, this is the elixir of youth."

After X, therefore because of X

So she left after you burned the toast; that doesn't make Breville the reason why.

Do I smell fish?

Don't let a niffy red herring throw you off the scent: presented with data, question whether it's relevant enough to be called information.

Price = Value

Our management consultant cost a lot; therefore his advice is good? Well, if it makes you feel better ...

Value by association

The language of hope gums together spurious marketing claims. Regard with caution: "help," "like," "virtually," "acts," "works to," "can," "up to," "as much as," "looks like," "fortified," "en-riched," "strengthened," "fights," "combats." (All code for: "But not quite what you'd like it to do.")

You too!

Projecting the weakness of your case onto someone else. For example, the man accused of racism accuses his accuser of discrimination.

Minimization

So it was your first time. So you only broke one teacup. So? You broke it. (My catchphrase as a toddler: "Didn't mean to, doesn't matter.")

Straw doll

Redescribing someone's position to make it seem weaker: "You want to spend all day getting dusty and thirsty and burned?" "No, I want to go to the beach." "Oh."

TYPOLOGY OF BORES, CHORES, AND OTHER CONVERSATIONAL BEASTS

THE INSINUATOR   *Iago scabpickus*

Are you haunted by the third person? During arguments, does the same third party's name keep popping up? "*She* said you like mountaineering." "*He* told me vintage jewelry is for cheapskates." "*She* said you said that I said I didn't like her...."

This person is the Insinuator, often a nimble youngest child, schooled in sowing discord, using elder siblings as Trojan horses for advancing his own agendas.

Fishing techniques differ: Some Insinuators favor hooks, some flies; some scratch their catch's belly. But all want something, if only a reaction. To that end, annoyingly—this being the point—they'll assume private knowledge of your desires and dreams, then poke holes in them. Common baits are under-the-rib comments: "Bet you didn't like that," "Supposed to look that way?" or "You scrub up well."

The Insinuator believes himself a politician. In fact, he missed his vocation on the stage. This is never more evident than when he's delivering what he considers bad news. It isn't his voice, good though this usually is, soft as a velvety paw, the merest gleam of a claw in its anticipation of your reaction to what, sadly, he must impart.... No, it's how he engineers the blanks between words. The Insinuator is a Pinteresque purveyor of pauses—extended to span canyons, which panicked listeners populate with Bosch-like visions of horror.

The good news is the script usually falls short of its ... dramatic ... punctuation. No news can be that bad.... Can it?

Tactics: The lever of his power is irritation, so meet taunt with tease; he'll rise like a neurotic trout.

Pluses: If the Insinuator is hard to spot initially, once a victim, you won't forget.

10

PILLOW TALK

On the Languages of Love

Once, conversation was a dirty word, embracing every form of congress of the flesh. The association remains fitting. The way to a heart may lie through the stomach, but more potent are those aphrodisiacs fed via the eyes and ears.

Among the craftiest seducers were courtesans, prized since the hetaerae of Ancient Greece for their limber minds as much as their pliant morals. Many were poets, but their finest art was sales. Elizabethan traveler Thomas Coryat warned of the Venetian hired siren's

> *hart-tempting harmony of voice. . . . A good Rhetorician, and a most elegant discourser . . . shee will assay thy constancy with her Rhetoricall tongue.*

Nineteenth-century *grande horizontale* Esther Guimond remarked that it was strange "that we courtesans alone be worthy and able to converse with philosophers." But nothing pricks desire sharper than our erotic dream machine, the imagination, and ingenuity at caressing it upped a lady's price. And if agile tongues open purses, they engorged minds in the salon of her rival, La Païva, according to poet Théophile Gautier: "Conversation was always sparkling, original, rich in unheard-of ideas and expressions."

In our noisy world, words still arouse: Sex phone lines prove it. Yet when we like someone, we're often tongue-tied by nerves and adrenaline, elemental to sexual chemistry, and worry about finding the right words. This can be enough to silence us.

Is that such a bad thing? Across the world and time, people have lured lovers in a glance, à la Romeo and Juliet, in throbbing night-clubs, or like traditional Apache teenagers, whose courtship may entail sitting together for up to an hour in silence.

"It's better," said one seventeen-year-old. "You don't know how to talk yet."

Many techno-literati favor indirect approaches, like dater Andrew MacGowan:

> I knew what I wanted and the internet cut out the middleman. You can meet people in bars and clubs, but then the first element is attraction. I wanted to use a medium where you talked to someone on the phone before meeting and saw whether you formed a bond.

Yes. Then again, you lose the precious early bonding moments and the memories that form close up, as well as risk inspiring fantasies that bring needless disappointment when you meet. And can you know what you want before seeing it? Sex rewards serendipity.

Communication doesn't just create or conserve relationships; it is their essence, and face-to-face matters since so much lies beyond speech. I could tell I liked someone by the butterflies that jived in my belly when we met, and the daydreams after—second-guessing the meaning of a hesitation, a lowered voice, the shade of a smile; promises that neither email nor telephone deliver.

In eighteenth-century Madrid under the Inquisition, prohibition heightened desire and eloquence at expressing it:

> *On their walks, in the churches, at the theatre, [ladies] speak*
> *with their eyes to whomever they wish, and have a perfect com-*
> *mand of this seductive language.*

But the most spellbinding gaze speaks louder with words. Pick-up lines abound, and some work; however, subtler methods exist to ramp up tension, signal bad intentions, and ensure your pillow talk doesn't send lovers to sleep—not even in a relationship's mellow autumn.

SWEET TALK, HARD SELL: THE RISING PRICE OF NEGOTIATING FOR LOVE

Romance makes chess of the most humdrum conversation because in love and lust, all are strategists. We can't help it; millions of years' evolution and millennia of cultural change have conditioned us to massage our words to attract value-added partners. But recent decades have shaken up the curriculum of our sentimental educations, and romantic values have metastasized, with the length and style of courtship as unpredictable as ladies' hemlines. Conversation—seeing others' point of view, speaking to their desires—has never been as necessary.

For centuries men traded women in deals weighed by dowries, like so many gold balls and chains, and for all the mist swaddling romance, the marketplace persists and is increasingly volatile. In 1993 economists Theodore Bergstrom and Mark Bagnoli dubbed courtship the "waiting game" because in traditional societies, the richer the groom, the older he tended to be, and the younger his pretty bride. They predicted that as female autonomy grew, women would marry later, to men closer in age. Almost right; however, divorce and singledom are soaring.

They had overlooked the strains of negotiating for love in a free-market sexual economy. In *The Challenge of Affluence* Avner Offer demonstrated that as wealth rises, marital satisfaction falls. Why? Just as money doesn't end problems but precipitates new ones, so it is with choices. (Call it the quantity theory of insecurity.) Desires alter when we needn't wed to be kept, fed, or watered.

Ask model-actress-poet Jerry Hall, who in 1985, still embroiled with Mick Jagger, memorably drawled:

> *My mother said it was simple to keep a man, you must be a maid in the living room, a cook in the kitchen and a whore in the bedroom. I said I'd hire the other two and take care of the bedroom bit.*

By 2007, the focus was less on what she could provide than get:

> *You know the kind of guy I'm looking for? A guy on my own wavelength. A guy I can have a conversation with. I've tried toyboys, I've done lots of sexy guys, and some have been very smart and nice, but you can't talk to them about anything. Maybe I'm not going to enough cocktail parties.*

Hall could always take care of herself, of course. Nonetheless, this trend affects everyone in upwardly mobile economies. If we can meet our needs, we base decisions on wants and we want it all: to be caressed, supported, entertained, preferably by a partner of similar status, personality, IQ, and background (the well educated, far from less superficial, fret most about partners' "collective desirability").

But social change has outpaced biology and cultural ideals. Pregnancy remains a bigger deal than ejaculation, and cookie-cutter ideals of macho and girly, formed when sex roles embodied the division in male and female spheres, remain deeply embedded and still shape desires and tactics for meeting them; breast implants, for instance. Women still wish to be treated like ladies, men still wish to be "real" men; all want independence, but none, if they can help it, to pay the escalating bill.

→ Rule one: Romance is a dance and an audit
So romantic conversation today has to play some very old games, hurdle towering contradictions, scale skyscraping aspirations, as well as glean mate-rating data.

Luckily it is brilliant at the latter. Even a speed-date, the same duration as the three-minute pop songs and fox-trots our parents and grandparents had to tickle each other's fancy, is enough to assess if you two might have more to discuss. A survey has found that even though snap judgments rest on surface details, our instinct draws us to physical traits—age, weight, height—that, unlike eye or hair color, give ultrareliable clues to the socioeconomic factors we care about. And not forgetting our voice, which, from vocab to grammar to accent, is a treacherous informant on everything from geographical and social origins, to aspirations to temperament to health.

At the start of a relationship, then, the chief difficulty for would-be pillow talkers isn't so much working out if you share common ground as shimmying alluringly over it. Flirting is at a premium in contemporary metropolitan society, sexy because those who can get along have more options. And while nineteenth-century Japanese marriage codes allowed "she talks too much" as one of seven grounds for divorce, and while chaps once joked that they proposed marriage to fill an awkward silence (once the frantic blab of courtship dried up), nowadays settling down doesn't mean an end of conversation.

We should be so lucky. Today, quality communication is an almost oppressive ideal, expected day in, day out, in the talkathon of a long-haul relationship. Über-eligible über talent scout Simon Cowell rationalized his reluctance to get hitched:

The superstitious side of me goes, "I couldn't follow that." [My
parents] were as happy as I've ever seen two people, mainly be-
cause they never stopped talking. From the second they woke up
to the second they went to bed, yak yak yak, all day long—I used
to call them the chipmunks.

Except, when is there time for meetings of minds? Infatuation
must be hothoused (like all dopamine-releasers, it is an addiction).
But we have so much else to do, plus endless sexual window-shop-
portunities—from porn, to online dating services, to the ethereal,
not to say fictional, companionship available in virtual worlds.
Anyone may have a harem on his/her hard drive, and some may
think that if it steams their wetware, hardens their software, it's
good enough.

Other snipers are at work. Now sex roles are unmoored, modern
couples' lives must be custom-built and it's all up for debate: who
cooks, works, holds baby. As if the basic challenge—recalibrating
two people's wants and needs over the vagaries of time—weren't
enough. Never have men and women had so much to discuss. And
still we dream of The One. Then again, with artful conversation,
we might find him or her.

COURTSHIP, LOVE BOMBS, AND
OTHER VERBAL ATTACKS

Courtship does more than kindle intimacy, make loved ones
feel loved. Castiglione observed in his 1528 conduct book, *The*
Courtier:

If the means by which the courtier is to win her favour are to be
nobility, distinction in arms, letters and music, and gentleness
and grace in speech and conversation, then the object of his love

*is bound to be of the same quality as the means through which
it is attained.*

→ Rule two: The style of approach advertises, or masks, the game being played

Different means signal different ends, and ignorance is no defense
if hints are misinterpreted. Flirty G. B. Shaw reported how E. Nes-
bit, the nice lady who wrote *The Railway Children*, chastised him
(after "I refused to let her commit adultery with me"):

> *"You had no right to write the Preface if you were not going to
> write the book."*

So pick tactics, including pace, advisedly. Play slow, for risk as-
sessment and research, if intentions are serious, but if intentions are
light, so should talk be. Discreet messages are deeply influential
since they establish terms of engagement. For instance, scotching
the competition is an important element of the game and, argued
psychologist David M. Buss, a heterosexual woman looking for a
quickie should tell the object of her desires that a rival is a "tease"
(by implication, *she* isn't). However, for a slow-burn amour, better
call her a slut.

First, get his or her attention. There are two options: overt and
covert. One sends up flares, the other issues ambiguous smoke signals. Different means, very different ends....

Love Bombs

We've a rich tradition to draw on: Half of literature's pearls co-
alesced around the gritty challenge of breaking a chaste resolve.
"Had we but World enough, and Time," Andrew Marvell's narrator
chides his "coy mistress,"

An hundred years should go to praise
Thine Eyes . . . But at my back I always hear
Time's wingèd Charriot hurrying near

"Get a move on" never sounded so gorgeous. But how many more masterpieces will be written, in the West anyway, to beg a woman to strip? The obstacle race from lust to bed seems so short, with both sexes free to play for whomsoever they like. Still, transmitting the spark of interest, in spark-sparking style, hard enough when a boy had to traverse a ballroom to ask a girl the pleasure—and trek back to his laughing mates if she turned him down—seems little easier in the mosh pit. The Arctic Monkeys devote a song to the anguish of uttering a first word to a "future bride" on the dance floor (as if she could hear it).

For such dilemmas are pick-up lines, fishing hooks to snag attention and, in theory, lead to where up-chatters wish to go. Although the strategy—disarm by surprise—is sound, gambits tend to the crude, and always have.

In 1661, John Gough celebrated the end of the Puritans and licentiousness's return with Charles II's ball and scepter by publishing *The Academy of Complements*, a treasury of thesaurus-varnished lust for youths who'd witnessed little public flirting. In it, breasts are "twins where Lillies grow," "Ivory balls of listing pleasure," or "soft Pillows of love." (Do you like that positive visualization, steering her mind to bed?)

→ Rule three: Use outrageous pick-ups for fast-food love
The logic of a ready-baked pick-up is it takes pressure off the picker-upper, putting it on the picker-uppee to joke back. Alas, this is slightly flawed. Asked to perform, the logical response must be "Why should I?" How many strangers are game for instant verbal Ping-Pong?

Writer Toby Young went to mortifying lengths to find out, donning a surf-dude wig and brandishing ten lines from *How to Pick Up Girls* in ten Manhattan hot spots. Finally, in desperation, he whipped out the humdinger:

> *"Are those space pants you're wearing?" I enquired. "Because your arse is out of this world."*
>
> *She gave me a look of total amazement:* Did you really just say what I think you said? *Then, miraculously, she started smiling.*
>
> *"That's the worst line I've ever heard," she laughed. "I can't believe you've ever picked up a girl using that line."*
>
> *"You're right," I responded. "I haven't." Then, just as I was about to walk away, my new, be-wigged personality took over. I fixed her with an unflinching stare: "Until now, baby."*

A triumph, thanks to his quick quip. So much for the easy option.

A knock-back is odds-on unless the line's purveyor is Adonis or Aphrodite. Yet this is the cheap merit of cheesy pick-ups. They won't brain someone into fancying you; rather, they're tests to find out if they do. Admittedly, clowns can appeal. Comic lothario Russell Brand profited from childhood pester power:

> *Having to lobby so relentlessly to secure a pet [gerbil] set me in good stead in later life when seducing pious women. "Please take your bra off! Please?" "Can I see your bottom? Oh go on?"*

All the same, his Byron-nicked-my-eyeliner good looks must have helped.

A love-bomber who doesn't want to rule out long-term romance should keep it simple, using an ice-breaker, ridiculous flattery, or an off-center remark, avoiding the quick-fire banter conundrum by coming armed with a follow-up. Ask for a dance or buy a drink, and immediately you can ease into a gentler pace of talk.

Try to surprise. A creep I knew enjoyed fiendish success congratulating women's dainty teeth and ears, and publisher George Weidenfeld, whose conquests some considered disproportionate to his appeal (and allegedly furry derrière), used tactical psychology, praising intelligent ladies' beauty, and vice versa. Psychologists concur that gorgeous women seem to lack faith in their other strengths. Apparently this is not a problem for beauteous males; make of that what you will.

SMOKE SIGNALS

I offer no pick-up lines from women because I found so few.

Possibly because until recent decades women were under parental lock and key, possibly they were too shrewd to be overheard, but more likely because pick-up lines are the bastard progeny of courtly romance, of lovelorn swains hurling gravel at flint-hearted Madonnas atop unassailable pedestals, whereas women have their own tradition of strategizing with friends that starts in school.

Although clucks of hen-nighters aren't averse to heckling a hotty, and mores are changing, when looking for long-term action, females remain pickier mate-hunters than men, and by adulthood they've invested many hours in decoding and programming would-be loved ones. After this relationship homework, a bias against pick-up lines is understandable.

→ **Rule four: You're never sure an artful flirt is flirting, but you should want to be**

A pick-up line is as rude as a pinch on the butt, pushing for intimacy, yet leaving choice to the other person. So the picker-upper isn't only vulnerable, but he ditches seduction's mightiest weapon:

doubt. Whereas, flirting evokes a fugitive sense that intimacy *might* be possible.

It is an illusion any can nurture. The top-flight courtesan's true genius was surely in her reverse-sell, persuading clients she must be persuaded to tumble—and it was true; the best had their pick of suitors. And super-cocky male Jack Nicholson favors anti-pick-up lines, decanting the confidence of Hollywood sylphs with corkers like "When did you get pregnant?"

→ Rule five: Activate their interest by looking ready to be interested

To begin a flirtation, attract attention without showing your hand. The best signal of availability to talk was "Do you have a light?" Then, as eyes locked over the flame …

Smoking, rest in peace. Fitness lovers should buy a dog. Strangers happily coddle and compliment by proxy, so make yours a patable pet avatar.

Lesser substitutes include handing around refreshments at a party. Elsewhere, ask the time or where you can leave a coat. Or place yourself in the room's liminal zones, near food and booze. Don't look lonely: Talk to someone who makes you laugh.

Try an "accidental" eye-clinch. Move into the target's sightline, then do what anthropologists lyrically term allogrooming—i.e., twiddle your hair, lengthening the torso and narrowing the waist. (Men not blessed with Samsonesque lovelocks may fiddle with their collar.) Now catch the target's gaze, hold it a moment. Later, do it again and smile.

Just agitating your body can be enough. I watched actress Kristin Scott Thomas unman the Wolseley Restaurant with a feline stretch, and a minx do something horribly effective involving flashing marble-smooth, indubitably fragrant armpits. At. My. Man.

INVISIBLE FLIRTING

Can words convert attention to attraction?

As Yves Montand and Mae West proved, in the ravishment of hearts, you can talk, croon, or coo your way past an imperfect face. There is nothing like friendliness to hatch a romantic mood. Even in a laboratory, men given the mildest attention were found by behaviorists to believe that they shared interests with a woman despite reading unambiguous written evidence to the contrary.

Practice makes the flirt, so develop a habit of turning incidental transactions into satisfying interactions. This isn't about being cheesy, turning it on solely for those you find attractive, or faking it: Become a compulsive bestower of artificial sunshine and you'll drain your reserves. (A friend in PR attributed her divorce to being girdled in niceness all day—for which she compensated with a grand unloosening of barbs at the end of it.) Simply trade pleasantries in a queue, greet the waiter, the bus driver, chat while your purchases are scanned at the checkout. Immediately your days, and you, will seem brighter—a low-watt equivalent of the glow that people in love emit.

→ Rule six: Synchronize your speech

If you like what you're hearing, intensify engagement with a little romantic legerdemain, a tactic that should continue to work, however long you have been a couple.

Talk's rhythm, bounce, and flow conjure the delicious sense of having clicked, a process you can help along by becoming conscious of the other's pace, volume, and tone. Don't slavishly copy. An experiment on students concluded that only perceived similarity in speech rate increased social influence; extra slow or fast speakers were irked by overaccurate imitations, unaware of their own oddity, just as most of us fondly believe our voice to be deeper and richer than it sounds to any other (our skulls are hospitable to bass notes that scram when our voices project through air).

Also attend to your target's vocabulary. Words imply sensual preferences, according to neuro-linguistic theory, so adjust your vocabulary to appeal to the other's dominant sense. Listen. Is he visual? Or does he talk of feelings, textures, smells, sounds? Now echo this language in your speech.

You could try grafting yourself directly onto their romantic mainframe. Hypnotist Paul McKenna claims a friend (*friend*? pah!) uses speed seduction: "He asks [women] if they've ever been in love, and what they felt like, and then attaches himself to that feeling."

→ **Rule seven: Exploit rules of engagement**
Charm's good luck turns on a simple equation:

$$\text{Be interested} = \text{Interest them in you}$$

This can be a low-input endeavor. Women fought duels over the "polite and quietly humorous" eighteenth-century duc de Richelieu (model for Valmont, the rake in *Dangerous Liaisons*) because he listened. Smitten intellectual Emilie du Châtelet raved: "I can't believe someone as sought-after as you, wants to look beneath my flaws, to find out what I really feel."

Listening has the further advantage of unself-consciousness, and, relaxed, your confidence will unburden confidences. Director Ang Lee hypnotized actress Tang Wei into sharing

secrets I've never told anyone. Right away I can feel that he really wants to know me. Other directors look at you as a piece of flesh and refuse to meet your eyes. But Ang looked into my eyes. It was like he wanted to know my heart.

As with humor, those who are direct and clear (but not over-bearing) slip under our radars because their bearing implies that we're already intimate. Physical cues are:

Close distances
Eye contact
Touch

Move the other person to feel closer to you: Lower your voice, and your interlocutor will lean in and feel like an ally. What is more, primates are profoundly susceptible to mimicry, unconsciously mirroring each other. Watching somebody hold his breath, it's peculiarly difficult not to hold your own, and in police interviews, interrogator and suspect's body languages converge after three minutes (hence body language and its experts are always suspect).

So step nearer. Don't invade the other's comfort zone: The gentlest touch is effective. In a test, waitresses who grazed a customer's arm or shoulder when leaving the bill received 25 percent higher tips, yet customers were unaware of having been touched, let alone extra generous.

And verbalize the positive. Linguists term some impassioned talkers "high-involvement speakers." They favor:

Direct, strong language, full of positives and intensifiers ("must" not "could")
Few weedy diminutives (no "slightly," "possibly," "might have been")
Personal and relational pronouns ("I," "me," "we," "ours")

Just the word "we" can be enough to create a feedback effect.

Such is the power of social influence that high-involvers inspire hesitant speakers to talk more passionately, which may explain why opposites attract. By contrast, the gappiest conversation occurs when low-involvers meet. Instead of joking, expanding on themes, or offering fresh material, their comments peg limply off the surface text of what others say—unwilling to raise new topics, scared to pass comment—sapping vital forward momentum; a drag for everyone.

Trepidatious conversationalists with distancing verbal ticks are as difficult to converse with as pompous boors who cling to "I" instead of venture "you"; both make feeble talk-makers, entrenching their isolation by not building topical, or by extension emotional, connections. The diabolical cost of ingrown communication habits, in the worst cases, such as the angry young Internet addicts of South Korea, is that they incarcerate people within ingrown personalities. But for anyone, desire increases the social risks necessary to transmute an encounter into a relationship that might satisfy it. (Did your knees not knock in the vicinity of your first crush?)

So minimize the risk, look after what musicians call their "embouchure," and keep your spirits up with friendly chirps at people behind counters, on phone lines. Equally, if a shy mouse catches your eye, you can—must!—coax it out of the hole.

Wage war on shyness.

RAISING THE GAME

To ascend to romance proper requires that elusive devil, emotion, which scientists find consolidates and activates memory (as author Siri Hustvedt observes, "What we don't feel, we forget"). It makes sense to communicate memorably, stoking those stomach-plummeting sensations that ruthless salesmen exploit: doubt, fear of loss.

→ **Rule eight: Imagination feeds romance feeds attraction feeds
love**

There's nothing like uncertainty to make you think, giving romance
its tragicomic tinge, as is most perfectly realized in the novels of
Jane Austen. She knew whereof she wrote: Her own, ultimately un-
fulfilled, *tendresse* with Irishman Tom Lefroy had been nourished
by ambiguity

> *in a series of meetings, some of them accidental and some con-
> trived, at which feelings were only partially revealed, desires
> only half expressed.*

Be unpredictable, deploy silence; add layers of mystery, walk
away. And don't look too eager. Regency strumpet Harriette Wilson
inflated her market value with spirited perversity. Her memoir records first meeting the Duke of Wellington (it was she whom he
told, upon threat of blackmail, to "Publish and be damned!"). Having paid a procuress 100 guineas for his introduction, the old war-
horse took Harriette's hand. At once she withdrew it.

"Really," said the modest maiden, "for such a renowned hero
you have very little to say for yourself."

ON AND ON AND SO ON?

The language of love changes as relationships shift from lust to attraction to attachment. These are specialized activities: different
hormones, different behaviors, even different parts of the brain
light up with each phase. What we want of a mate—kindness,
warmth, openness—doesn't entirely square with the aggravating
erotic incertitude of infatuation. Yet most of us yearn for one person who can press all three buttons, and don't expect love to leave
lust behind.

Some doomy scientists argue that sexual destiny is inscribed before birth, with men likelier to be gadabout short-term maters the more testosterone swam inside the womb. (An indicator of *in utero* hormones is the length of index and ring fingers: if the latter is longer, apparently he may not be the marrying kind.) Yet myriad benefits come with pair bonds, and according to behaviorists, people disinclined to intimacy face "heightened stress and lower life satisfaction."

Luckily mind can rule matter. Artful communication lets lovers fulfill the three-in-one ideal, hopping between channels to meld the practicalities of cohabitation and cupboard love with affection, enthrallment, and animal desire. If communication falters, however, the firmest partnership may fall into the fourth, dead zone that psychologists dislike talking about: indifference.

So what is lovers' conversation like?

At first, urgent, hoovering up details in an attachment process similar to that by which babies imprint on parents, as we do what John Donne describes in his poem "The Sun Rising" and contract the world to our little room, frequently confecting our own baby talk too. To others nauseating, this private language can be enduringly powerful; even in the dog days of marriage, my husband can access it to shut me up. ("Choglet" remains particularly effective, when he wants the last in the box.)

As a relationship is established, conversation becomes less intense, but no less important. The joy of rubbing along, side-by-side, facing a shared future instead of drowning in the beloved's lash-wide stare, is a bond with exceptional practical benefits. However, as the thrill of performance, being witty, droops—with a sigh of relief, if the relationship is to be a refuge from the importunate world—the worth of keeping communication fresh remains correspondingly high. Get too cozy, stop entertaining each other, and undifferentiated coupledom can tip into complacency, boredom sneaking in with his pipe and slippers.

A fifty-six-year-old, otherwise happily married mother, still capable of orgasm, bemoaned the lack of ladies' Viagra:

> *I'm rarely in the mood.... I want something that will affect my state of mind before sex. I can still remember the level of interest I used to have. That's what I want to recapture.*

How depressing. There is an unimprovable mood enhancer. Not in the medicine cabinet: between her and her spouse's ears.

→ Rule nine: Communicate to stimulate imagination

Proximity doesn't equate with intimacy if you lose awareness and the relationship becomes wallpaper whose pattern you don't notice.

Some couples go to extremes to perpetuate exciting distance, like Gallic thinker Bernard-Henri Lévy, who addresses his glamour-puss wife by the formal *"Vous."* Others take a pragmatic line. Levy's countrywoman, Colette, earwigged on the conversations between "snobs of vice" in neighboring villas on the Côte d'Azur:

"Lend me your wife," asked a husband.

The other nodded. "If you lend me your eldest son."

Partners who care not to share re-charge all three levels of intimacy: they listen, say nice things, but also tantalize, tease—balancing the comforts of routine with surprise, never so stuck in their tracks that they forget to admire the passing scene.

To cultivate conversation, don't make it (and make it a chore). Enable it. Introduce spaces in the day where talk might flow, not cut off by other noise. Just being in the same room doing chores ensures companionship remains a relationship's hub and heart, unlike the hedge-fund couple outed as communicating by email—at home.

Turn the radio down, the TV off, face each other when you're eating, give the dishwasher a sabbatical, wash and dry up together. Then go for a walk. Give a dog a home. And hold a glance, remembering how it was when you couldn't be sure what that mind was thinking. Sure you can now? How presumptuous. Find out.

How to Fight

Ever felt trapped in a soap opera: same story line, faintly different script? You are. Most couples tussle about the same set of issues, and how tends to matter more than why. Psychologist John Gottman, at the helm of the U.S.'s "largest love and marriage lab," found that

some argue a lot but find that the thrill of making up more than compensates for the cost of the conflict; some argue very little, preferring to skim over disagreements and concentrate on the positive side of their relationship; and some spend so much time compromising that disagreements rarely occur.

These approaches work because resolution is not essential for conflict to be good, since airing problems releases tension. But two poison heart and health: carping, the steady drip-drip of contempt; or ignoring, denying a partner's point of view by withdrawal into silence. Although superficially different, both attitudes deny intimacy by attacking the central idea of a relationship: the shared bond. And by extension, immune systems, according to Gottman, with the attrition of stress leaving the henpecked and the cold-shouldered more vulnerable to disease.

Watch your argument tactics. There are six:

Pass: the complained-at ignores the complaint
Refocus: the complainer or complained-at shifts the subject of complaint
Mitigate: the complainer downgrades the complaint

Respond: the complained-at acknowledges the complaint's merit
Not respond: the complained-at denies the complaint's merit
Escalate: the topic of complaint expands, hostility rises

Hell-bent on breakup? Adopt either of the last two.

Otherwise, dilute gripes with positives—ideally, reckoned Gottman, a cocktail of five nice comments per negative. To me, this sounds as random as governmental exhortations to eat five fruit and veg a day, but can't be any more harmful. And stand back and pick a technique for difficult conversation (see Chapter 13).

→ Rule ten: Know when not to speak

Happy couples may duet, like Simon Cowell's mum and dad, from dawn to dead of night, but the least happy I know also keep babbling, like two-headed monsters; deaf, dumb, sadly not mute.

The difference is in imaginative sympathy, as defined by counseling service Relate: "Good communication, empathy, caring and emotional intelligence."

Which is why the faith that fostered a million therapy sessions— that if we have a problem, we must discuss it—should, in my opinion, come with a health warning.

Take the biggest interactive challenge a couple can face: when two become three. A study found that new parents routinely kept quiet on issues causing them grief, discussing only those on which they agreed. Initially researchers were shocked, but why deplete yourself quarreling over minutiae when huge change is already upon you? Partnership is a three-legged race that should make clearing obstacles easier—but will not if you keep stopping to debate whose leg goes where and why.

Relationships stumble if we forget that how we relate, converse, keep in touch, are their very substance. If there's a secret, it's the same as for any conversation: You get what you give. Negative, positive, at least 50 percent is up to you.

Spies set honey traps because love loosens lips. So relax, and if your pillow talk keeps you awake, I hope it's for reasons other than nightmares.

TYPOLOGY OF BORES, CHORES, AND OTHER CONVERSATIONAL BEASTS

BITCH *Canicula*

Bitch is a spin doctor by another name. Her smiles are sabers, her words knives, and her sallies detonate, like good jokes, moments after delivery.

Consider this, from hardy music perennial Keisha Buchanan of Sugarbabes, a charm fiesta in person, but who has the publicity savvy to rib her popstrel rivals in print:

Being famous, there's pressure to stay thin, but thankfully I'm in a group where we sell records based on our music, not what we look like. It's much harder for Girls Aloud.

How brilliant to suggest their asset, pulchitrude, is mere camouflage for other failings.

Bitching isn't exclusively female. Rap music proves men love doing it, if only beefin bout their bitches, and entrepreneurs and Ozzie cricketers excel. These gabsmiths prove the panoply of skills bitchcraft involves.

There are two branches: direct (vituperation, laceration) and indirect (rearview stilettos). The latter is great for bonding, bringing us together by focusing on a usually absent third party—what in drama is called an opposition figure—such as the snotty vixen, generally brunette, who makes you root for your Bridget Jones/Cinderella.

Indirect bitchery is therefore socially acceptable, provided you mask it; preferably, as bitching about an alleged Bitch. Direct bitchery is riskier (notice nifty Keisha Buchanan kept hers oblique: you laugh at her cheek, so are less inclined to condemn her). But always a guilty pleasure to watch.

Tactics: Don't mess with her: Bitch about her and win new friends.

Pluses: It's no fun being her scratching post, but eminently informative. She has a surgeon's eye for victim's vanities. Might she have a point?

II

THE FINE ART OF FLATTERY

On Love in Measured Doses

Confucius said:

Soft words and ingratiating expressions are rarely paired together with humanity.

But what did he know? Demi-deities have little call for compliments, being in the business of persuading us that their wisdom is superior. In mortal endeavors, to neglect them is less than human, and not a little daft.

Flattery fine-tunes conversational overtures and is an unparalleled instrument for making us feel good. Yet few aspects of interaction are so maligned. Why? There are suspicions of insincerity and manipulation, yes, but the underlying problem is difficulty.

Compliments require diplomacy as delicate as for buying presents. Every gift, by word or deed, reveals its giver's opinion, or misunderstanding, of the receiver. Indeed, compliments stake a claim for a relationship, by boldly assuming reciprocity. Better to give than receive; all the same, who doesn't expect something back?

➼ Rule one: Artful compliments are never too great to be returned

Flattery shouldn't be confused with bootlicking. Minimal effort and imagination can throw out delicious back-scratching hooks to bind people closer to us. To show you're listening approvingly, emulate octogenarian charmer Deborah, Dowager Duchess of Devonshire, who talked with

> *great economy and clarity, albeit punctuated with sudden bursts of flattery—"You are so right!" "Absolutely spot-on!"*

Incompetents think that more is more and overdo it, causing embarrassment, killing talk (if the flatteree doesn't know you, or is speechless, she will struggle to say anything back). It is worth remembering that flattery, far from self-abasing, is, as novelist Benjamin Markovits remarked, "sometimes the sincerest form of arrogance" and highly assertive. After all, to offer a compliment is to presume you are qualified to give it. Novelist James Salter mischievously downplayed his inclusion in critic Harold Bloom's hit list, *The Western Canon:*

> *The question is: does [Bloom] know anything? ... In the end, flattery is wonderful so long as you don't inhale.*

By contrast, Chaucer, father of English letters, well understood that writing his own *Troilus and Cressida*, a tale told and retold by the great classical authors, was a status-grabbing act, claiming a literary title for himself as much as his vulgar native tongue. But lest readers miss the point, toward the close he commanded his "litel bok" to go "kis the steps" where Virgil, Ovid, Homer, Lucan, and Statius had walked—an act of obeisance that, by implication, anointed himself their worthy successor.

→ Rule two: If flattery is self-serving, it should hide it

The underlying concept of flattery as indirect power play is best expressed in the musty phrase to "curry favor." To grasp fully its metaphorical sense, picture not a vat of simmering "favor" stew; instead imagine Favor, a handsome steed, being groomed with a currycomb. Never a straight bow of humility, paying homage is courtship, designed to massage the homagee's feelings and steer his responses in your favor. Ride him too hard, you'll both be saddle sore.

Heed the example of those repositories of royal caprice, court favorites, who only survived if they trained a discriminating eye on their job's two-way political function: as lightning conductor (on hand to be blamed by lesser courtiers for a monarch's whims, as a bad influence) and as persuader-in-chief (to intercede for lesser courtiers). For them, as for parents who heap exorbitant praise on children's rare good behavior, flattery was often spiked with inverted criticism or advice. As one of Elizabeth I's lapdogs was told:

> *Never seem deeply to condemn her frailties, but rather joyfully*
> *to commend such things as should be in her, as though they were*
> *in her indeed.*

Their egos may be more prominent, otherwise absolute monarchs are like you and me. We'll yield to stroking, so long as the flatterer's will to power is veiled, and even perhaps to advice, so long as the person issuing it puts the accent on his own faults.

HOW TO FLATTER

Be appropriate: Obsequiousness is grotesque because out of proportion, exuding surplus oil, making wheels too slippery to turn. Good flattery is weighted to the moment. Medieval historian

Geoffrey of Monmouth recorded approvingly how Julius Caesar placated the rebellious Gauls:

> *He who had once raged like a lion, as he took from them their all, now went about bleating like a gentle lambe, as with muted voice he spoke of the pleasure it caused him to give everything back to them again. This soft caressing behaviour continued until all were won over again and he had recovered his lost power.*

Be unpredictable: The unexpected is both memorable and, because original, seems more authentic. So it is flattering to subvert hierarchical relations—gently—deferring to assistants, cajoling bosses ("managing up"), or smarming to vassals (see Caesar, above).

Glorify in hope, not expectation: Abbasid poet Ibn al-Rumi recognized that flattery is lyrical, not literal—an expression of power, a wish, rather than truth:

> *God has reproached poets for saying what they do not do, but they are not guilty of this alone, for they say what princes do not do.*

Similarly, artful compliments take their recipients on a holiday from drear reality. Why say "Your eyebrows are dark" if you can liken them to dancing calligraphy? Provided you're sincere, the other person will know you mean it. Remember, this grooming exercise attends to the demands of the idealist superego. Indeed, giving a compliment, it is effectively rude not to exaggerate, since you are expressing a feeling, a desire, not a mathematical exactitude.

The one you love is always the most beautiful in the world, because you're asserting the primacy of your world, not Brad and Angelina's. We expect to hear this, even as we understand it isn't factually true. Trust Shakespeare (Sonnet 138):

When my love swears that she is made of truth
I do believe her, though I know she lies,
That she might think me some untutor'd youth,
Unlearned in the world's false subtleties . . .
On both sides thus is simple truth suppress'd.

Forget sunshine: Bring some flattering candlelight into someone's life.

Be indirect: Choosing what to compliment, for subtlety, aim at something allied to a person's prestige or a quality from which you could benefit, as supplicants to irate sultans are wise to trumpet their mercy.

Unpopular trainee geisha Sayo Masuda bought her way out of a reputation for stupidity by cynically playing on it, setting herself up as a compliments broker:

> *When I could see that a customer was important to a particular geisha, I'd watch for a moment when no one else was near and then say something like: "Elder Sister's always talking about you, you know. She must really like you. I like you, too! And Sister likes you even more than I do. I guess that's what it feels like to be in love?" Then I'd flash him a big, innocent smile. Since they all were convinced that I was a bit weak in the head, they'd take me seriously and be really pleased. The customer would tell my Elder Sister. Elder Sister would feel flattered and start taking me with her to parties. And before long, all this effort began to bear fruit. I became popular.*

In the same way, playwright Aphra Behn flattered her king, Charles II, in her dedication to *The Feigned Courtesans*, by bigging up his mistress, ex–orange seller Nell Gwyn:

*Who can doubt the power of that illustrious beauty, the charms
of that tongue, and the greatness of that mind, who has subdued
the most powerful and glorious monarch in the world?*

The better you know someone, the greater the praise: A compliment swells according to intimacy. Equally, not to offer one to a
friend you haven't seen lately might be construed a tacit suggestion
that she's changed, but not for the better. I enjoyed an encounter
with my husband's employer, who gallantly roared I looked no different from a decade ago. Then spoiled it: "Which plastic surgeon?"

HOW TO BE FLATTERED

Compliments present an etiquette puzzle.

Until we hit puberty, it's good manners to say "Thank you" to a
compliment. But after that, at least in Britain, the protocols of politeness demand we say something more elaborate: Simply accepting seems somehow smug. This makes flattery peculiarly helpful to
conversation, especially early on, because the requirement not to
count our laurels compels us to use ingenuity and find something
else to talk about.

We obey what I call the Law of Compliments Disavowal:

Acknowledge the compliment: never simply accept it.

Ideally, this means turning the compliment into an opportunity
to be modest and then give a compliment back. To "That is a lovely
dress" you might say "Oh, I got it in the sales. But yours is *gorgeous.*"
A competitive element can creep into self-deprecation (*"Think this
dress is supposed to resemble an overstuffed sausage?" "No, it's lovely.
But I look like the Bride of Wildenstein's offcuts"*). Nevertheless, at
bottom it's all about showing solidarity and building a comfort

zone. Even if you and your friend end up squabbling about who has the gravelliest skin.

Envy is flattery's handmaiden, so the more truthful a compliment, the wiser you are to acknowledge but not assume it. Gracious composer Franz Schubert thanked Graz Music Society for making him an honorary member, saying he hoped "of being one day really worthy of this distinction." And talk show host Tyra Banks was artfuller still to dismiss "quickly but with a smile" a journalist's suggestion she was "the new Oprah Winfrey, her heroine." Such a response seems only to confirm the merit of her ambition.

Just as no sensible celebrity complains of his isolation, no sage beauty says, "You're right, I am." Professional good-looker Liz Hurley dutifully flicked off an interviewer's suggestion of her gorgeousness by drawing attention to her "ugly" hands. Celluloid-melter Michelle Pfeiffer claimed to another that she looked like a duck. Pure genius, that. Immediately you superimpose a wee duckling over that lovely face, and at once think, gosh, far from unattainable ice maiden, Michelle is cute.

WITH RESERVATIONS . . .

Then again, were Tyra to congratulate Michelle on her unwithered charms, the only polite answer would be "Thank you"; anything else and Tyra might think she was fishing, or weird. In part, because Tyra herself is an infernal radiance, and honesty between equals is more permissible, with no power imbalance to offset. But there is also a cultural difference. Pride in merits remains a keynote in America's meritocratic dream; apart from at high school, there's little terror of tall poppies or being one, and no class war–stained angst about looking down, or up. So stateside, don't match compliment for compliment unless you mean it. As for knocking one back—forsooth, for shame, fuhgeddaboutit.

And tread carefully in Germany, where some take no-nonsense compliments a step further, delivering backhanders with a spin worthy of Boris Becker. A Berlin theater designer found the concept of writing a diary column for a newspaper hard to grasp. Finally we translated.

"Klatsch?"—"Gossip?" (rhymes with *Quatsch*, German for "trash.")

She stared, as if to verify that this being before her was human.

"But you are a serious person!"

TYPOLOGY OF BORES, CHORES, AND OTHER CONVERSATIONAL BEASTS

CREEP *Ickydemus*

Creep arouses similar feelings to a slug: Either you want to stamp on him, or run. But it doesn't end there. These uncharitable sentiments create a negative feedback loop: You feel bad for feeling revolted, then angry at Creep for making you feel bad, and so on, ad infinitum.

What fuels his repulsive force? Speech-act theory explains that statements don't simply communicate ideas, but are themselves actions with social goals. The trouble with Creep is that his noisy aims drown out his words—primarily, with the slurp of sucking up—often lending his speech an undead quality, as if scripted in advance. And since he equates boosting your esteem of him with boosting your self-esteem, he goes in for vertiginous, stack-heeled compliments that only make you shudder, wondering, "What is he after now?"

As Amy Sedaris said, in conversation there's no greater compliment than talking to someone who is really "in the moment"—that is, into you, here, now. Regrettably, Creep never imagines you might like him for himself; fatally, he is too condescending to see his objectives ooze transparently from each overegged word. Many politicians exude the same miasma: We know their smile really says, "I want your vote." Hence we feel like prey. Liked not for ourselves, but as means to their ends.

Tactics: Creep is a vampire, so unless you invite him in, he has no power. Don't feel obliged to be nice. Say stop if he is embarrassing you.

Pluses: Creep reminds us of the importance of sincerity, style, and engaging with others, not trying to get in with them.

12

SHOP TALK
On Conversation as Work

I t was a Sunday in April, but the sun was strong and the sky pressed down like a clammy hand. Nobody in the garden felt like networking, and all seemed in need of refreshment—all except the rosy Irishman, draining the last cool glass of champagne.

"Communication is simple," he said, tapping his head. "All you have to do is get something out of here, and into here," he added, tapping mine.

He knew what he was talking about; he was an ambassador. But rarely does it seem so simple at work. As for the compulsory socializing: business lunches, Christmas dos ... And however pleasant our boss, how many of us haven't felt, as Voltaire did of his sometime patron Frederick the Great, that when he calls you "friend" he means "my slave"?

The social knit of office life is riven with power imbalances and knotty with contradictory demands: to get along and to get ahead; to compete and to cooperate. At worst, fear and loathing make it purgatory, as in Joseph Heller's novel *Something Happened*:

> *In my department, there are six people who are afraid of me and one small secretary who is afraid of all of us. I have one other*

person working for me who is not afraid of anyone, not even me,
and I would fire him quickly, but I'm afraid of him.

At best, it encourages rapport, passion, and imagination—the lifeblood of zestful talk. Nothing can beat conversation for managing the conflict-riveted camaraderie of the workplace. Even when it must be, of necessity, antisocial.

THE CHALLENGE OF SHOPTALK

All communication is hampered by a problem that might be summarized as (*pace* Donald Rumsfeld): "I don't know what you don't know that I don't know you don't know."

Never is this truer than at work, and it is more problematic than in normal conversation, thanks to the social influence we must quietly exert while playing the good professional.

→ Rule one: Never assume that people understand you

Imbalances of power create imbalances of knowledge, and in professional encounters too often we fail to account for the ignorance or otherwise of the person we're talking to. Have you ever staggered away from an accountant, lawyer, or surgeon *not* confused? Had a free and easy exchange with an IT helpline?

Conversely, the less powerful wonder what the powerful are hiding, and tend to second-guess. This compromises the flow of information, sometimes feeding dangerous groupthink, in which a meeting's cyclonic dynamics ensure that leaders hear only what they want to. Think Iraq, or the calamitous Bay of Pigs invasion, which almost tipped cold into nuclear war.

It may be deliberate: Tony Blair unblushingly expected secretaries of state to clear submissions in private before discussing them in Cabinet. Or teams' expertise may be so specialized that managers neither comprehend nor respect it—a risk, foretold by Hannah Arendt, blamed for the woeful communications at NASA that led to the homicidal *Challenger* shuttle disaster.

In business, these issues are further complicated by a basic tension. Each worker, from CEO to envelope stuffer, faces a dual requirement: to be himself and to play his part to get the job done. If the personal and the professional conflict, there can be drama.

→ **Rule two: Artful shoptalk mediates emotion, information, and power**

One solution might be to copy what a best-selling author told me she did to survive speaking engagements: "I put on a rubber head." But nine to five, a smiling mask chafes, and phoniness is repellent. Which isn't to say you shouldn't put up a front. Substituting "if" for an optimistic "when" levers deals. Certainly, without the chutzpah—i.e., fibs—of Tim Smit, cofounder of the Eden Project, regarding other backers' "firm commitments," Cornwall's wildly popular botanical showcase would have remained a fantasy.

Every worker should strive for something beyond balancing personal and professional. To excel means harnessing emotion, severing personal from professional concerns yet building relationships; heating discussion without searing pride or hazing priorities; and communicating clearly, without talking down, or over heads.

Oh, and ideally, all contacts should be personal, as Dee Dee Myers, ex–press secretary to Bill Clinton, advised *West Wing* actress Allison Janney:

> *Your relationships aren't determined by the boundaries of your job. It's by who likes you.*

Face-to-face cements connections that ten thousand emails cannot. Sadly for party-phobes, research has found that newcomers who attend even just one corporate social in their first eight months feel greater attachment to a company than those who don't. Not that they identify paintballing or pub quizzes as the cause: The binding is subliminal.

In the end, said agent Mark McCormack, people buy from a friend. To succeed, treating colleagues and clients like one is the place to start.

What about creative tension? I've worked in companies that set employees at each other in survival contests that rewarded the fittest at politicking (not necessarily those fittest at their tasks). Sure it was chatty, but cost-effective? Backbiting ate time and morale.

This may seem to support the line used by vending-machine salesmen in the 1960s to convince factory owners that canteens carried a hidden cost: camaraderie—staff talking, griping, forming loyal bands able to mobilize and strike. But it can be costlier if employees don't talk.

A business is, in effect, its workers' acts, and the knowledge driving them is a capital asset—and a liability if underdeveloped, or if it leaks. Photocopy company Xerox found this out in the 1970s when engineers and scientists, who saw each other as "toner heads" and arrogant dweebs, stopped talking, and upper echelons failed to appreciate the scientists' ideas. But corporate outsider Steve Jobs spoke the scientists' language, saw a chance, and licensed their innovations. Apple Computer ripened them to bear glorious fruit.

Miscommunication lost Xerox the PC. But just gossip is hugely valuable. So much of twenty-first-century activity is obscure or shrouded in jargon (specialization being one of conversation's arch foes) that sharing with others who get what we're on about is a huge boon. The hardest-hearted manager should appreciate, as Socrates did, that dialogue percolates knowledge, and the stories shared in breaks, handily sorted by cause and effect, dole out user-friendly training on a coffee spoon.

Since Steve Jobs's giant leap, globalization has accelerated competition and adaptive "learning organizations" like Toyota thrive. Smart businesses see employees as their nerves, and seek to unlock the cutting-edge know-how in their fingers and put it to work. But wherever we toil, however unenlightened its communications may be, artful conversation can awaken our own and others' tacit knowledge, make it articulate, wire us into work's quasi-social matrix, and maximize our assets.

MECHANICS AND FLUID DYNAMICS

Productive work conversation means not more meetings, those drains of enthusiasm, but rather making words work harder, coordinating brain and spirit, and saving time.

The instruments are no different from normal conversation, just worth using more stringently than down the pub. And while dialogues—interviews, sales pitches—have different dynamics from group meetings, the same basic principles apply in each. Primarily, that communication is a two-way transaction. Sender and receiver should feel equally responsible for ensuring that messages ring out loud and clear.

→ **Rule three: Make allowances for the blinkers of your position**
The imbalances of power or information in most business exchanges skew perceptions further. For instance, sociologists find that those in charge are biased to perceive unequal outcomes as fair, and less powerful parties strategize far more for encounters, so will be, understandably, correspondingly less satisfied. As if we needed sociologists to tell us that.

Effective communicators compensate for these biases, as golfers account for the slope and swell of the green when they putt. The best go one better and find an advantage. Use these dynamics deftly and you may ensure that others emerge happy from an exchange regardless of whether the outcome is one they wanted.

Tony Blair once had a wizardlike ability, an awed civil servant observed, "to make people walk away feeling taller—having opposed them." Friendliness is less effective, however, if a listening ear doesn't appear to hear. Andy Duncan, formerly of Unilever, then Channel 4, impressed his previous chairman as "open and informal," a great team leader. Yet cynical underlings saw Duncan's "toe-curlingly" pally style as a rubber head, claiming he exploited it to bounce off dissent,

> *maintaining there will always be those who disagree.... His supposed inclusivity was equally disarming: people were invited to talk to him, about anything, to voice their opposition to something, then he did what he set out to do.*

So an enlightened boss should go out of his way to engage staff loyalty, presenting tasks as exclusive to them—i.e., strategize as hard for encounters as underlings. Meanwhile, enlightened employees should appreciate that their boss likes feeling good, and deploy positive presentation to make rewarding them easy. Good news gilds the bearer....

→ Rule four: Every communication is a chance to make business easier

Managing up, down, or sideways, the communication goal is identical: Keep channels open, relationships flexible, feelings positive.

Before anything else, we must manage ourselves, using analysis and planning to compensate for our self-serving inclinations to blame others instead of examining causes and, likewise, to personalize success when surfing a lucky break (like stockbrokers with Master of the Universe complexes, deluded that their success is down to unique investment acuity, rather than prevailing fortunes brought by fair economic winds).

Complaining that a boss is woolly is self-defeating; better to enhance communication, clarify what is asked of you, and be a joy to employ. The pious view is to see it as entrepreneurial conversation, able to catalyze difficulty into a learning opportunity.

The basic recipe for successful shoptalk, like successful relationships, is finding common ground, then stretching it. Its basic ingredients are tact, salesmanship, and a firm grasp of the mechanics of communicating and receiving a message.

DEAR PRUDENCE

By Machiavelli's measure, prudence is analytical and stoical,

> *able to assess the nature of a particular threat and [accept] the*
> *lesser evil.*

When deciding whether to communicate, let cost-benefit analysis be your guide. That is, ask, "So what?"

Say Hayley in sales is taking credit for a deal your contacts secured. Before speaking up, ask, "Is it worth it?" Nobody likes a sneak. So what is there to gain? Is your motive power play, to let off steam, or for mutual benefit? Will speaking out serve either your or the business's long-term interests? So what if you don't?

If it's really the shortest route to meet those interests, plan it.

SALESMANSHIP

We all sell when we communicate, be it an idea, opinion, or joke, just as all workers must flog their skills. Many seem unaware of this, in part, because the idea of selling intimidates. Fools imagine it is all deals, but serious salesmanship forges relationships, using passion and personality as tinder to clients' enthusiasm. Without it there would be no business. Anyone who imagines selling to be beneath them should know it comes garlanded with philosophical plaudits. Aristotle anatomized it in his *Art of Rhetoric* (persuasive speech), identifying three aspects, in ascending importance:

Logos: the virtue and style of the argument
Pathos: the emotions of the audience
Ethos: the credibility of the speaker

As Aristotle discerned, an insight borne out by twenty-first-century research using brain scanners, the best idea matters not a jot if it leaves audiences cold. Even if your words move them to tears, to get a message inside their heads, first they must believe in you—and want to. Smart work communication doesn't focus narrowly on hearing, or saying, yes, but building faith, credit, and the long-term conversation that is a relationship. It:

Shares spoils
Gives credit where due
Expresses admiration and gratitude
Is amusing and amused
Speaks up for the weak
Apologizes frankly and first

A suck-up's charter? It's only human to use rapport to shore up your position. That's how primates do business, with similar networking ploys seen in monkeys. Call it generosity, aloud.

But however casual a work conversation, beware of presuming intimacy. Or humor, that insuperable friendship coagulant—a qualification only time brings. In a 1950s London department store, anthropologists found, incoming workers had to wait three dull weeks to be included in banter, three more before cracking their own jokes.

MECHANICS

Each work conversation is a three-part task, entailing regulating, sending, and receiving messages.

Regulating: For an organized communication, think in advance: when; where; how long; what issues to cover; in what order; what note to strike; what interests and goals are at stake; how to meet or improve them.

At the encounter, greet, introduce (if unfamiliar), and trade pleasantries. This both respects rapport and neatly places it out of harm's way, because the transition into business signals that what follows isn't personal, and it ensures everyone knows who is here and why. (Had he done so, my husband might have avoided the university interview throughout which a don shuffled papers, addressing him "Joanna.")

Preamble small talk also tests and sets the tone, so it may shift the frame of subsequent discussion. Hint you've brought an alternative proposition, for instance, and the other side's conversation strategy is in tatters. Or, off home turf, lead greetings and you may lead the next moves too.

When discussion begins, state purpose and agenda, then explore propositions and decisions, step by step, repeating agreements at the end. Whatever transpires, a friendly farewell helps to restore lost face. And in the absence of minutes, circulate action points afterward to avoid confusion.

Sending: To resonate, present your message as Castiglione's ideal courtier did, never lacking "for eloquence adapted to those with whom he is talking." And be, as director Gurinder Chadha advised wannabe filmmakers,

> *absolutely clear about what you want to say.... What's your vision?*

Don't leave your personality at the door. Karl Marx knew how to package his punches, blending "philosophical seriousness with the most biting wit." Trim vocabulary, pace, and tone to the occasion, aiming at simplicity and concision, using keywords, humor, surprise, and arresting images.

Consider how near listeners to sit; when to look at them to sink a punch, grab their attention; when gestures can add oomph. Draw them on-side with open questions (not answerable by yes or no). And use your voice: volume, pace, and emphasis.

In his 1854 *Rhetoric of Conversation*, George Hervey advised

> *Do not seek a reputation for humility by always daintily avoiding the pronoun* I.

But at work "I think" admits this is your impression, tacitly inviting others to correct it.

Receiving: Judicious listeners adhere, at least on the surface, to the premise of innocent until proven guilty, seeking and sifting clues as to where someone is coming from before deciding where he's going, never mind offering an opinion about whether or not it is a good idea. A methodical approach explores data, then opinions, then propositions, then solutions and decisions. To focus talk, pose questions, repeat, paraphrase. Acknowledge sentiments even if you don't agree with the interpretation ascribed, and if conversation bogs down, step outside it: Observe that it has become sticky, inviting others to explore why.

There is no better means than listening to avoid destructive power games, which fritter away a business relationship's huge asset: the sense of obligation. Indeed, obligation can create a relationship. Benjamin Franklin tamed an ardent political enemy by asking to borrow a book: a small debt that brought a new topic of conversation, then a bond.

TWO-WAY DANCES AND
HYDRA-HEADED MONSTERS

Nice and easy? So it is not always simple. (See Chapters 6 and 13 for nipping and tucking awkward moments.) On the other hand, in most business conversation, whether a dialogue or a many-mouthed meeting, you will have but one motive:

⇢ Rule five: Find the best solution—usually yours

For this, the message to get across is: You want to work with me.

A service ethos can carry you anywhere. Noam Gottesman, megabucked founder of GLG hedge fund, attributed his success to:

> *Paranoia. The secret is about what the clients want. We work in a "what have you done for me lately?" business.*

Don't we all?

Showing what you've done lately, like showing what you can do next, means convincing the other side that your solution fits their needs—and, very often, convincing them of precisely what it is they want. Here is a checklist of tactics for doing so:

Research: Where do interests and advantages meet and diverge?

Align: Map your offer on to their requirements.

Anticipate: Likely questions and objections. Can you build positive answers to potential concerns into a pitch? (A five-year degree? All that charity work ...)

Timing: Think when is most expedient to raise issues or throw in something unexpected.

Lead/follow: In pitch situations, the seller leads—preferable to interviews, where you dance to another's tune, offering a mini product trial. (My nadir? An hour waiting for Liza Minnelli's ex, David Gest; twenty minutes more as he ordered snacks and chatted to someone else. Finally he removed his shades: "Soooo. Talk." I corpsed.)

Soften the dynamics, but don't ignore them. Interviews are voyages of discovery, each side tacking in a different direction: the interviewer pushes for information while the interviewee pulls the interviewer into an avuncular, advisory mode. If either overdoes it, conversation will feel a jumpy failure. So read the signals, match the other's pace.

Wait: If silence is the enemy, rush to fill it and you become your own. Pity Topman clothing brand director David Shepherd, on being asked his target market:

> Hooligans or whatever. Very few of our customers have to wear suits for work. They'll be for his first interview or first court case.

Fear not: Lower emotional stakes to increase confidence. Consider interviews as ways to meet interesting people, and bring your own comfort zone: Memorize five points to convey and you'll feel less like prey (avoiding palpitatory fight-or-flight feelings).

Be easy to look at and hear: Locking eyes announces this is a meeting of equals. When her daughter Floella said she had a job interview, Veronica Benjamin sat her down, beaded her hair, and said, "Do not take your eyes off the interviewer." Floella was soon capering in dungarees on the children's show *Play School*.

Milk the target: Use questions to show off research, expose preferences (what happened to the last employee?) and points from which to link your wares to their needs. Explore objections: Do they stem from misunderstandings, excuses, or material problems?

Mind the gap: Flummoxed? The question is your life raft. Repeat, clarify; show how you think on your feet. (See Chapter 13.)

React: There is a tale of an Oxford University interviewer who removed his shoes and socks to clip his toenails. Demonic strategy? Madness? Who knows. If someone is determined to unsettle you, view it as a test. Joke (my husband could have said, "Only friends call me Joanna"). Reframe a negative positively. Admire the damned clippers.

BEND YOUR WIGGLE ROOM: A NEGOTIATOR'S GUIDE

Negotiating may feel like poker. Trace your negotiating space beforehand to improve the odds. Its coordinates are: what you want, points you can and can't concede, what you'd settle for; and these same parameters for the other side (guess). Where these overlap lies territory for settlement.

Outline concessions, planning points to trade, then step back. Is there wiggle room? Review each side's interests and aspirations. Might something else, not on the table, satisfy both? If so, this is your ace in the hole. Now imagine the consequences if agreement isn't met. Any alternatives? Aim to walk in knowing you can walk away.

At the meeting, explore motives and assumptions behind the other's stance. Clarify and you might shift a position. Don't be shy of stating your criteria or aims either: However shrewd, the other side may not have thought these through. But they should consider them.

If both sides want to do business again, you've won, preserving the long-term deal: your relationship. So never confuse what is fair with what is right; history is strewn with noses cut off to spite owners' faces, as we don't act in our best interests, preferring nothing to a mean deal—just as chimpanzees in tests refuse to perform a task if their reward is a piece of cucumber, but their partner's a succulent grape, even if ordinarily they like cucumber. Why? Fairness isn't logical but psychological: about saving face.

Good negotiators keep deals sweet by keeping them short. Talk too long, positions petrify, and each side thinks the time invested means they deserve more (forgetting the other side has spent just as much, but the pie/grape/cucumber is no larger).

FOLLOW MY LEADER:
MENTAL CARE FOR MEETINGS

"The multitude is wiser and more constant than a prince," averred Machiavelli, after the Medici put him out of a job.

That greatest wisdom dwells not in the greatest minds, but the aggregated views of the crowd, is an insight as old as democracy. All the same, a group thinking aloud isn't necessarily the slickest means of aggregating them.

Analysts find the most successful management teams argue hard, but hold it together because the tone isn't personal: The focus is on gains. Without good governance, however, meetings degenerate into either a brawl or a pack, because dialogue spurs people into increasingly extreme positions. Furthermore, Parkinson's Law of Triviality asserts that the less important an agenda item, the more time is spent on it. Can you doubt it? We speak most freely on matters that won't burn us, or for which any number of solutions is possible and equally desirable.

The net consequence is that all meetings have a natural life span beyond which dementia sets in. A brief biography:

An issue is born.

Slowly, voices are raised, frail heads of opinion sprout.
Some find the light, are watered, grow, others shrivel in the shade,
until one vast opinion takes over, draining resources, until an ax
falls ...

The job of attendees is to represent their positions as best they can, with a keen sense of when and how to back down. The chair is axman. But his duties also encompass those of circus ringmaster.

There's nothing like repetition to persuade people an idea is right (see politicians, advertising, organized religion, etc.). So it's vital to challenge monopolists, reach nuanced decisions not herd opinions, and nip madness in the bud. Stick to the drill:

Agenda: agreed and circulated in advance
Fixed time frame: never too long, never after lunch
Venue: quiet, conducive
The right people: no timewasters

→ Rule six: Keep discussion light and well-ventilated to weigh matters fully

The ideal chair doesn't lay down the law but the shape of discussion, creating rounded decisions by speaking last, listening hard for what is not said, ruling against: rambling, tangents, grandstanders, monopolists, personal attacks, leading questions, debating stunts, dodging, negativity, shillyshallying. And for: mutual interests, uncovering assumptions, testing propositions, exploring alternatives, the devil's advocate.

Wise business leaders would do well to recollect the example commended in Sir Thomas Elyot's 1531 treatise, *The Book Named the Governor:* Belinger Baldasine, "a man of great wit, singular learning, and excellent wisdom," counselor to the king of Aragon, who liked taking "doubtful or weighty" matters home. After dinner he would summon his servants and set a riddle

> *wherein was craftily hid the matter which remained doubtful, would merrily demand of every man his particular opinion, and giving good ear to their judgements, he would confer together every man's sentence.*

In the meantime, savvy communicators will accept social influence for what it is: the engine of communication. They'll do their utmost to wire into the network, to please the powerful, cultivate the weak, and prosecute their cause as persuasively as possible.

NEUROLOGICAL FIREWORKS

Otherwise known as brainstorming. It's an unbecoming image— a cerebella blizzard, or hobnail-booted soldiers stampeding an unyielding cortex. My preferred definition is organized mind-funk: a conversation designed to open minds and bestir synapses and tempests of fresh ideas—not to reach judgments. Although it should liberate participants to say whatever pops into their heads, without structure it will puddle into buffoonery.

Tackling a product or concept, corporate communications expert Linda Conway Correll suggests listing:

1. Facts about it
2. Sensory observations (possible even if the "product" is as abstract as mathematics: think graph paper, protractors, curvy zeroes, fork-like fours, headaches ...)
3. Experiences of it
4. Uses for it

Then do a spot of associative outreach, taking words from these lists to come up with fresh lists: things that share the product's quality; things it isn't like; combinations of elements to describe a new use for that product (for instance, a dog could, conceivably, be renamed a love-alert). Find points of similarity between dissimilar elements, mine these lists for weird new definitions of your product, and soon it'll look very different.

But keep it snappy. Think pinball, not chess.

TYPOLOGY OF BORES, CHORES, AND OTHER CONVERSATIONAL BEASTS

Networking isn't popular. Some sneer it smacks of corruption. But business turns on trust and personal relationships, and few hermits lead corporate takeovers.

Sally Morgan, one-time government fixer turned business adviser, denied exploiting contacts yet conceded, "It's easy for me to pick up the phone." And what is a contact but someone you can touch?

Networking is a posh word for knowing who to talk to and how to make them listen. It's nothing new. Visiting, familiar to costume drama fans, could be a grave social duty. In 1801, decades before becoming Byron's crabby Venetian landlady, Lucia Mocenigo trudged around Vienna on an exhausting mission of social work to restore family fortunes. She

> *diligently wrote down [names], together with their addresses, in a brown leather notebook that was to become her personal social registry. She used those initial introductions to gain access to other illustrious houses, and planned her courtesy visits dividing the city up by areas and neighbourhoods. She called on an average of two to three houses a day, and always wrote down the address and the date. She drew a map and kept a precise tally.*

Facebook seems almost tempting. But ideally, networking brings as much pleasure as profit. I know a delightful couple, great party givers. Numerous threads connect their guests, many of whom might be deemed more powerful than the hosts; but because they meet en masse at the hosts' house, the hosts become the gravitational center, generous spiders in a web of influence. It's a parable of social influence: Be good to get good. No wonder Zeus was often worshipped in the form of the God of Guest-friendship.

Still, networking sometimes feels like dentistry, yourself patient and probe. Sounding out strangers is mined with hazards; touchy subjects like money and professional status. And while being nice, or naughty, or both, to get in with someone lies behind most con-versation, nonetheless we are hypocrites and the tang of an agenda makes us suspicious. Keep yours discreet.

> *In the presence of the king, those who do not speak of what they need will obtain more than those who do.*

(As Casanova misquoted Horace, in the presence of a king, when funds were short.)

A good networker regards everyone as king, himself too. Unlike this nerveball:

> *His voice was quick, anxious, slightly high-pitched, as though he were worried I would leave before he had finished his sentence.*

Enter a room believing the bargain is unequal and awkwardness is guaranteed. What is more, it's unnecessary, because if someone interests you, it's likely you will him. He isn't doing you a favor: You both are, by talking. See this as small-talk plus.

Successful networkers charm widely, aware that the more sparks they kindle, the more they sparkle. To indefatigable *salon-nière* Carole Stone, maladroits are unmistakable:

> *They glide into the room, head straight for the most influential person and hog their attention, before breezing out without a glance at other lesser mortals.*

Think what you might discuss, with whom, but don't buttonhole, and focus away from workaday matters, even if these are what attracts you (that jolly doctor really doesn't want to discuss your sore toe). Showing off homework won't always win gold stars: I was nonplussed when a stranger elaborated my Google CV, a compliment I couldn't return, knowing nothing about him. But I love talking to people who make me see things differently, offer fresh ideas. Trivia, humor, mild provocation . . .

Approaching your agenda, sidelong questions are advisable. But unless the other person volunteers the topic (and you may plant the seed), what need you now but contact details? Win him over, follow up on promises. If he's happy to take your call, you have connected.

13

CHOPPY WATERS

On Navigating Difficult Conversation

So ravishing was the tongue of Madame de Staël that contemporaries rated her one of Europe's three powers (alongside Britain and Russia). Literary titan, political dynamo, and seductress, if not beauty, she encrusted her salon with the great and the good, and helped to gather the forces that toppled Napoleon.

If anyone could twist a conversation to her ends, you might think it she. But no.

Once she had chased the Emperor. She wrote, expressing regret that a "genius" should be saddled with a nonentity "Creole" wife. No reply (he laughed and avoided her). Finally she tracked him down to Talleyrand's and handed him a laurel branch, demanding:

"Who is the woman you most respect?"
Napoleon replied, "The one who runs her house best."
"Yes, I see your point. But who, for you, would be the greatest of women?"
"The one who had the most children, Madame."

No wonder she had it in for him. The moral of her story is, if you have a proposition, tender it sensitively. The moral of his? If you must repel someone, do it nicely. Their ticklish encounter illustrates that every conversation is a negotiation, and bungling one can curdle a relationship. However, the reverse is also true.

→ Rule one: Difficult conversation transforms relationships, for better or worse

Conversation's challenges are as varied as we, but fall into distinct categories. Active: to ingratiate, confront, appease, mediate, seduce, persuade, oppose, rebuke ... And defensive: parrying unwelcome approaches, fielding criticism, diverting attack.

Hardest are conversations with the wounded, whether or not the injury is ours to heal or repeal. What do you say to a person sliding down the razor blade of life? Nothing can feel easier than the wrong thing. You might tell yourself, or him, or her, to let sleeping dogs lie; no use crying over spilled milk. Countless platitudes are on hand to block a messy turn in conversation; arguably, clichés were invented for that very purpose ("shut up" disguised as cockle-warming folk wisdom). All are alibis for engaged sympathy.

What is wrong with skirting sore points? Often it is a shrewd kindness: The shoulder to cry on can get soggy, undesirable by association with past woes, and agony aunts can turn nag, unable to hear when advice is no longer sought. But say nothing, and if a problem is grave, contrary to King Lear's admonition to reticent Cordelia, something will come of nothing, and it won't be nice.

→ Rule two: Assuming conversation is difficult makes it so

Although challenges exist, expecting the worst is what tangles us in knots. Many men are silenced by shame at sharing fear, and neither ovaries nor estrogen make women any less gauche. Mortally ill Sarah Hitchin wrote heartbreakingly of being penalized by friends, unable to believe she still liked "a giggle"; as if she, accessorized by cancer, was no longer she:

Now, if they do ring, they whisper, "How are you feeling in yourself?" One has lost contact after 24 years of friendship.

In the name of openness, unpleasant talk is increasingly out-sourced to paid ears, with the unintended consequence of impoverishing the communication skills and thinning the relationships of the rest of us—as was satirized by mordant teen novelist Nick Mc-Donell in this sterile exchange between a mother and daughter:

> *"Is something wrong? Is something upsetting you?"*
> *"No."*
> *"Because I was thinking if something was, upsetting you that is, then you might want to go and see this doctor I know."*
> *"A shrink? [. . .] I don't know what I would talk about."*
> *"Oh, you'd find things to talk about."*

Then the girl warms to the idea, recalling the bodacious lies her friends tell their shrinks.

↪ Rule three: Avoiding difficult conversation weakens relationships

Today indirect communication is on the up, with so many alternative methods to defer confrontation, fob people off: by email, letter, text.... We might imagine it easier to read bad news, to avoid misunderstanding. As if.

A friend's parents-in-law are great letter-writers, issuing regular bulletins on how he should coddle his kids, cosset their daughter. No doubt they would be shocked to learn these land like a punch in his gut, read not, as written, in calm rumination, but amid the tug-of-war of toddler breakfast. They can't suspect that using a one-way medium inherently renders their message a judgment; that not speaking, abdicating power over their voice's inflection, ensures that it strikes their harassed son-in-law as hectoring, strident, a wee bit mad.

All communication is dialogue, its meaning not its speakers' intentions, but its effect on sender and receiver. Want miscommunication?

How simpler than to bisect the dialogue?

If we ditch the myriad nonverbal cues that help meaning ring out loud and clear, if we lack messages from the other's face, we can't tell how news sinks in, adapt our words to its reception, incorporate new information, correct misperception, or stop before we say too much. And the person at the receiving end can't hear our words' emotional force, tone, let alone counter false impressions or exercise his right of reply.

To say writing obviates difficulty is like saying conversation is clearer wearing a blindfold and earplugs, in separate rooms.

→ Rule four: Tough topics demand flexible conversation

Social scientist Michael Moore has found that face-to-face negotiation conjures a rapport email cannot, a disadvantage that may hamper outcomes. To resolve a problem and preserve relationships, mutual understanding is imperative, and I'd argue no technology supersedes the high-definition, multichannel parallel processing system of two beings' brains, faces, and bodies, talking and listening together.

You can't kiss and make up by phone or fax (although you can dump someone by fax, as the famous actor who allegedly jilted his pregnant lover). Whereas the authentic look of remorse is a priceless addition to the word "sorry."

↪ Rule five: Great conversation is difficult conversation that worked out

Of all the idiocies of dodging tough talk, perhaps worst is the missed joy. What may be lost if we choose, wrongly, silence over risk; laugh instead of listen; say yes, but don't mean it; say nothing for fear of hearing someone doesn't feel the same way?

And how can you tell in advance whether a conversation will be difficult? Act by Crow's law, invented by Second World War intelligence whizz R. V. Jones:

> *Do not believe what you want to believe, until you know what you need to know.*

As the cliché goes, grasp the nettle. First pick a strategy: evasion, mediation, or persuasion? Then, tactics.

EVASION

Good for defensive situations and sloughing off tricky topics.

ABSORB

Don't rise to the bait and you don't give others power. A writer was mesmerized by "unexpectedly likeable" hypnotist Paul McKenna, whom she found "intensely straightforward." Why? He proved "impossible to embarrass," "taking pretty much everything I say as a compliment."

Opportunity: Teflon is proof to minor conflict.
Risk: Becoming impervious to genuine problems, smug, and therefore vulnerable

Quip

At the start of his reign Tony Blair was a gifted hook-wriggler, high on the vapors of Cool Britannia. In July 1997 he hosted a reception for its leading lights and met Oasis rocker Noel Gallagher, a rumored champ of South American energy aids:

> *I told [Blair] that we stayed up till seven o'clock in the morning to watch him arrive at [Labour Party] headquarters and asked him, "How did you stay up all night?" He leant over and said, "Probably not by the same means as you did."*

(How different from the man who, years later, told novelist Ian McEwan he admired his paintings. I'm a writer, McEwan corrected. No, Blair insisted; he really liked his art.)

Opportunity: Deflect or deflate without addressing the central issue.
Risk: Being insufficiently funny or quick

Flirt

Spectacular at disabling reluctant flirtees. Prince, the artist formerly known as squiggle, deployed ruthless coquetry to stall rock critic Mick Brown: batting eyelashes, "touching my knee," sulking, gazing into the distance if he disliked a question, seizing on words as objects of wonder—anything, indeed, but answer.

> *"Hedonist?" He arched an eyebrow and smiled. "For years I didn't even know what the word meant . . ."*

Brown likened the encounter to "fencing with a wraith."

Opportunity: Amusing
Risk: Annoying the wrong person

MEET QUESTION WITH QUESTION

Why not?

My sister-in-law flips questions like pancakes. A stranger demanded: Why did she elope to Finland? Amanda smiled. "Lovely country. You been?"

Opportunity: Fun with the distractible and the persistent
Risk: You might not like the answer.

REFRAME QUESTIONS

Questions are like predictions, framed to shape answers. So use your answer to shift focus and wendy-i-wander from traps.

The wiles of David Linley, Princess Margaret's son, did not escape this scalpel-sharp interviewer, but might pass unnoticed with the unsuspecting:

> *Isn't it a bit scary becoming chairman of Christie's? "Yes, but I've done scary for so long." But then he smoothly revises his answer: "To me, it's less scary, more honour. . . ."*

Other jiggery-pokers include repeating a question, with modifications to encompass whatever you would rather discuss. Or bamboozling: Say, "I'm glad you asked that" or "Yes, that is important, which is why . . ." or "That's an interesting question." This may be followed by a statement that doesn't answer it, without seeming rude, because lip service has been paid to dialogue's to-and-fro.

Sadly, many listeners are so inattentive, they'll accept decoys as explanations if presented as such. I suspect this is why, according to a book called *Yes!*, "because" is often enough to make someone do your bidding: as in, "Please may I jump this queue because I need to buy something"—or, as Mum said, "Because I say so."

Opportunity: Limitless

Risk: Have your wits about you—and hope your interrogator doesn't.

DIFFUSE

Interpretation is up to you. So address an inquiry's theme instead of particulars, as actors do when journalists seek to vivisect their private lives. Cate Blanchett routinely steers "conversation away from the personal to the abstract."

Another journalist met pitiless resistance from Joseph Fiennes:

> *I say, let's try again: do you fall in love easily? "I love travelling. I love cultures." I ask, do you travel to other people's souls easily? [Fiennes] says, not laughing: "You'll have to ask them. I love life. I'm fascinated by human behaviour because that feeds back into my work...."*

Opportunity: Cooperate while turning tables.

Risk: Seeming untrustworthy or maddening

PERSIST

They won't listen? Plow on. Fashion designer Dame Vivienne Westwood

> *has advanced skills in avoiding interruption. When she senses that you are about to jump in, she furrows her brow, breaks eye contact and, without disturbing the deceptively soft rhythm of her voice, hauls on through.*

As Prince showed, looking away makes it harder for someone to pitch in, and helps you concentrate. Or say "Hang on," and counter-interrupt: "Yes, but what I was trying to say ..."; "Maybe I haven't put this well ..." Naturally, you want to hear what the other person has to say—in a minute or ten, once your point has been made.

If a point is extra sticky, talk long enough, and you may substitute another. Memory is so brief, questioners may not recall what was asked, or fear another monologue too much to try again.

Opportunity: Attack disguised as defense, this tactic shows full attention has been given.

Risk: Arrogance. Westwood's frustrated interviewer observed: Those she works with seem to regard her with more respect than warmth.

BLANK

Try forgetful (he claimed) author Douglas Adams's invincible riposte:

> *I refuse to answer that question on the grounds that I don't know the answer.*

Without details, lines of inquiry fizzle. Filmmaker David Cronenberg nuked questions about his childhood with: "Quite ordinary, really."

Opportunity: Skip flimflam

Risk: Credibility. Does the inquirer know more than you suspect?

MEDIATION

For when engagement is unavoidable, indeed desirable. Good in business, negotiation, conflict. As a rule, try to separate issues from personalities to dampen negative emotion.

Go Slow

Singer Diana Krall cannot trill publicists' tune. One writer labeled her "a cow" because her "reserve" and "desire to think about a question before giving a response" led to "disconcertingly long pauses."

Hers may seem a poor example of the virtues of taking time. But in arguments (as opposed to faux-cozy interviews) going slow is a bonus, counteracting the kinetic back-and-forth that may, if heated, accelerate dialogue to insult rally, crisis to drama. Curb that energy: Ruminate, cleave to the point. You won't be sidetracked, and will compel the other side to slow down, think, and listen too.

Opportunity: Stabilizes volatility, helping information to sound out clearer

Risk: Rather than reining yourself in to think constructively, you simply act hoity-toity.

Break Down

Active listening—repetition, agreeing to a précis of a position before moving on—replaces the emotional propulsion of argument with the cooling balm of analysis.

Show respect by inviting the other party to "help me understand"; seek information; check and repeat ("If I'm right, what you're telling me is …"). Gently, without blame, remind others you aren't privy to their thoughts—which may seem obvious, yet is necessary. Think how maddened you are when people don't see how they are impinging on you. But do you tell them?

Opportunity: Dissect difficulty into segmented topics, create an agenda, identify goals, and conversation becomes a process, not combat.

Risk: Apparent condescension

Ten Commandments for Emotional Ventilation

Most conversational difficulty consists of emotion, but explaining that someone should feel differently is the rudest non-advice (trust the old English adage "Proffered service stinks"). Instead, carefully air injuries and you may simultaneously acknowledge their validity while diminishing their emotional power.

1. Explore—don't ignore—feeling ("I see you're upset").
2. Acknowledge the other person must address a problem (even if you don't think it is one).
3. Don't react emotionally or judgmentally.
4. Let the other person talk; don't finish sentences.
5. Only offer opinion or advice if sought.
6. Don't agree or disagree until you must.
7. Limit interruptions to supportive statements.
8. Repeat key words, to show your grasp of issues and to reroute rambling.
9. Display listening: Face the other person square, keep eye contact, an open posture.
10. Question, summarize, and seek opinions on how to proceed.

PERSUASION

You know it is a good idea. Help them to see why.

PREPARE THE GROUND

Breaking hard news, open with a statement that announces, like a sinister puff of dust on the horizon, the character of the words to come: "I'm sorry," "I have to tell you...." Then pause. Often, the other person will complete the sentence.

How you broach a topic can affect reactions, so give it a spin. Say "You know what I'm going to say, don't you?" Even if your news is unexpected, having agreed, your listener will probably persist in the flattering belief that he knew all along.

Opportunity: Diminish impact.
Risk: Overstretch the preamble and you'll wind the other person up.

MAKE IT LOOK EASY

My boyfriend went to lunch with his boss, a journalist who affected the bearing of a parchment-stiff brigadier. Over coffee, lighting a cigar, the boss asked if there was anything else he wished to discuss. Not really, said my boyfriend, then he mentioned our relationship (we worked together). "Oh!" the man cried, spluttering Havana flakes. "Well, you've done nothing wrong, but she'll have to go."

According to a well-placed source, he held that officers oughtn't to consort with foot soldiers. Nevertheless my boyfriend's error was to present the situation as a problem: far better to offer a solution. Castiglione's *Courtier* advises a sage favor-seeker:

> *Skillfully make easy the difficult points so that his lord will always grant it.*

As for my boyfriend, he has had time to rue his mistake. Reader, I married him.

Opportunity: People are lazy.
Risk: Suspending disbelief a bridge too far ...

Play Dumb

Teenager Jellyellie exhorted parents who want to talk about birds, bees, or bongs:

> Start off chatty and informal—never sit your teenager down for a discussion and call them into the room, as they immediately think they've done something wrong and will be nervous for the rest of the conversation.

Similarly, Brendan Duddy, for decades the undercover link between the British government and the IRA, claimed that many breakthroughs took place not seated at tables, but in breaks, "over a cup of tea," when guards were down and people relaxed.

So why let on this is a talk with a capital T? Take an oblique approach—ask for thoughts on a tangential issue. They may lead you to the point.

Overplay the faux-casual card and nobody buys it. (My father quails at "By the way"; my mother quakes at "Incidentally.") Yet the opportune moment may be decisive, and is often unanticipated, when mind or body is otherwise occupied. Aristotle believed lessons were better learned while out walking (his pupil, Alexander the Great, was a fine advertisement). Endorphins boost mood, and in difficult situations, if you are not confined, not confronting the other person's face, you remove dimensions crucial to the drama of antagonism (dimensions that in happier situations deepen engagement).

Why not enlist the optimism inherent in making a journey to suggest changes are not only necessary but easy, desirable?

Opportunity: Act normal and conversation may well be. Serious isn't a synonym for difficult.
Risk: Be unsubtle and the other person may use irritation at your ruse to shunt you off the track—attacking your tactics instead of engaging with the issue.

PLAY GAMES

Broadcaster Evan Davies puzzled over how to come out to his family. Then he turned it into a game, starting with his brother:

"I have something to tell you, can you guess what it is?"

His brother guessed right, then suggested Davies tell their parents in the same way. After Christmas lunch he popped the question. His parents drew a blank, so his brother pretended to guess. Then another brother cracked a joke. No drama, no tears.

Opportunity: Make light of a revelation to dispel an atmosphere of conflict.
Risk: Appropriate?

DIM THE OPPORTUNITY

Why attack a proposition if discreet sabotage can downplay its appeal? Use belittling language, diminutive descriptors (sort of, kind of, stuff); sow each sentence with a negative. Recast the scenario ("You're absolutely sure you want to spend eight hours a day doing nothing on dirt?"—my take on beach holidays). Infuse fantasy with dreary practical considerations ("If we did this, and A, B, and C, then X happened, then Y, then Zzzzzz ..."). For more tips, remember how your parents spoke to you in adolescence.

Or emulate Mark Antony in *Julius Caesar* and use the other side's weapons against them. Caesar's assassins tell the mob they are "honest," then Mark Antony appropriates the word, repeating it in ever-less apposite contexts, making the claim seem progressively ironic, and the assassins, by extension, utterly false.

So take the key word or the emotional tug of a bad argument ("I gambled away our life's savings for you"), hold it up to an unflattering light, and strip it of value and force.

Opportunity: Depersonalize objections.
Risk: The other person is so attached to his crap idea, he takes the attack personally. Perish the thought....

COURTESY CORRAL

How do you tell a girl her ivory gown makes her look like Cling-Wrapped cottage cheese?

Don't. Say the plunging damask one shows off her antelope neck instead.

Anna Valentine, the couturier who attired Camilla Parker Bowles for her wedding to Prince Charles, cajoles brides-to-be by swathing them in attention, ushering them toward comely frocks by focusing on their most flatterable bits. Such schmoozing works on babies, business leaders, and the most tyrannosaurus divas. Swarm over every detail, keep each hint soft-focus, gag potential protest, inducing a diabetic coma from all your sweetness. Few illusions are more intoxicating than that we are captivating. Indeed I watched an otherwise talentless woman propel a meteoric career almost entirely by facelift-obviating smiles, emphatic nods, and resourcefulness at telling people they were fabulous.

Opportunity: Get what you want in the guise of providing a service.
Risk: Exhaustion, sustaining disbelief

PEEL AN ONION

Things aren't going your way? Use emotional levers to jack up your position. Quit the crying and moaning—too near blackmail, as well as liable to make victims fractious. Instead, make feelings instrumental by attaching them to positive arguments for your cause: "I'm so passionate because ..."

Opportunity: Move the other person to sympathy.
Risk: Seeming out of ideas/unreasonable/nutty

MIND YOUR LANGUAGE

In the seventeenth century Thomas Sprat described how Britain's first scientific institution, the Royal Society, enacted a purge to win kudos with rich, influential merchants (hitherto science had been the preserve of highfalutin polymaths like Sir Francis Bacon). Members asset-stripped their vocab in favor of a

> *close, naked, natural way of speaking; positive expressions; clear senses; a native easiness; bringing all things as near the Mathematical plainness as they can.*

The learned members had a thoroughly modern appreciation of how words open the minds that open doors. In persuasion, the task isn't to offer a balanced view, but to win people over. To do this, what matters is how you jigsaw the facts to the picture you wish to present, and frame it to fit listeners' views. But it is a process, and each step should be contrived to bring them with you.

Engage trust and this is tantamount to loyalty, according to hostage negotiation expert Mitchell Hammer:

> *Various studies have shown that when we say we trust someone, we are less critical, we require less information, we share more*

aspects of ourselves, and we give people the benefit of the doubt.

Language can be an incantation to trust, inducing a cooperative frame of mind without advertising to listeners how the mood has been achieved. Social workers talk to clients of "our" strategy to reduce debts. Similarly, police negotiators increase feelings of immediacy, by using present over past tense, and language to imply a cooperative relationship already exists:

"This" not "That"
"These" not "Those"
"Our" not "My"
"Here" not "There"
"We" not "I"

The underlying message—"We're in this together"—resonates subliminally, summoning the sense, delightful in any conversation, of a moment shared.

And the more positive, the better. Mine your situation for opportunities to say yes. Don't browbeat like chef Gordon Ramsay, for whom "Yes?" seems to be a full stop. (Actually, the question mark is debatable: He yaps it like an order.) Rather, find things the other person can nod to and you begin to establish a pattern of agreement.

Start from his needs, and repeat what he says: "So you want a new car?" gets your first yes. Impregnate possibility in every sentence. Say "Let's," "We could," "Would it work if. . . ?" Conversely, to evade responsibility or downplay a situation, use distancing language: "Due to funding problems"; "Collateral damage was sustained"; "An accident has occurred"; "It has come to my attention that your daughter has crashed our car."

To conserve your power of influence, exert it sparingly. The wizard Merlin bewitched the king with his prophecies. But when the king begged Merlin to peer into the future for fun, according to chronicler Geoffrey of Monmouth, he refused:

> *Mysteries of that sort cannot be revealed ... except where there is most urgent need for them. If I were to utter them as an entertainment ... then the spirit which controls me would forsake me in the moment of need.*

Merlin, or rather Geoffrey of Monmouth, was clairvoyant enough to see that scatter wisdom like poppy seed, and the oracle becomes a clown.

The "spirit" that made Merlin's prophecies credible was the king's urgent need to credit them when in dire straits. So whatever your situation, how your listeners feel about you matters more than what you say, because conversation, like poetry, works not by convincing but by stirring. Emotion nixes reason every time. Experiments by psychologist Drew Westen discovered that presented with a bad argument by a politician whom they like, partisans' brains go out of their way to "turn off the spigot of unpleasant emotion":

> *The neural circuits charged with regulation of emotional states seemed to recruit beliefs that eliminated the distress and conflict.... And this all seemed to happen with little involvement of the neural circuits normally involved in reasoning.*

Irrational? Sure. On the other hand, without passion, can we be ethical? Feeling is the ultimate judge of our deeds' merit, not the chopping blade of logic. And since we all feel before we think, of course feelings have the power to drive our thoughts where our beliefs would send them. This is why the most persuasive argument in the world is what we want to hear, from someone we enjoy listening to. Lawyer Clarence Darrow averred:

"The main work of a trial attorney is to make the jury like his client."

So don't try to change someone's mind: use what is there. Learn what he likes. Focus on his face; read his feelings; hear messages in his voice. Smile, even talking on the phone (the muscles alter the tone of voice). Put yourself in the other person's shoes, speak to his interests, and he will range himself alongside you.

Conversare: "to turn around often."

Who needs argument, if you can convert him?

How to Complain

Complaining troubles those for whom it is a confession of weakness (self-censorship at which adherents of the stiff-upper-lip tradition excel). The consumerist ethos is emboldening many. Still, in private life, asking for more, or less, or better, or faster, can be daunting.

Thank Dr. Thomas Gordon for his handy three-part complaint formula:

When you do X I feel Y because Z.

This neat assertion of cause and effect imputes no blame; indeed, it presumes the culprit is unaware of what he is doing. And it is literally undeniable, because only you know how you feel. Whether he feels you should feel that way is another matter.

So if you've bought a pair of dirty shoes, bitten through an elastic band in your salad, or been bumped off your flight and are stranded in Rotterdam at three in the morning, consider how unwelcome orotund rages will be to the person on the other side of the counter—the only person who can help. No need to wheedle; simply assume he wishes to resolve the situation as much as you, and take it by degrees.

Level one: Present your dilemma, but let the other person define it—thereby taking ownership of the problem. As in "I took them home, got them out of the box, and then I noticed"; "Look what I found in my lollo rosso"; "We're stuck."

Level two: Has he upbraided you for sharp teeth? Is he thick? Work-shy? Still assume cooperation, using questions to outline, without dictating, what you think he should do to help: "Can I have the refund direct to my account, or do you have another pair?" "Shame, I was really enjoying the salad. Perhaps you can throw in pudding." "Which hotel do you usually put people up in?"

Level three: No advance? Try a forceful yet positive statement: "In the past this was okay. It would be a huge help if ..." "Please re-mind me of the procedure for claims ..." As you raise the stick, keep the carrot dangling: "It is really kind of you to take the time/lend me your pen ..." He may be doing his job to the barest minimum; nevertheless, help him feel good about helping you, and act as if it's a great personal favor. He may succumb to the undertow of obligation you've implied.

Level four: He is blaming you, suggesting you wore the shoes, arrived too late for your flight, etc. Try mild self-assertion, focused on how he gains from solving your problem, and seek advice: "I'm sorry to inconvenience you. We realize you don't set the policy. How can we get out of your hair?"

Level five: An absurd excuse deserves commemoration. Write it down, asking him to repeat it, to help you "understand" his position. Check spellings and punctuation, ask for the complaints form and his assistance filling it in. The goal is to make it less trouble to satisfy than refuse you, with passive-aggressive attrition. Don't be fobbed off: Grin till your teeth hurt.

Level six: Outright accusation, such as you went break dancing in those sneakers, or ordered that £500 bottle of St. Emilion knowingly (so what if you drank it). This is a gift, breaching the service industry code: The customer is always right.

Show how hurt you are. "Are you calling your customer a liar?" Write his answer down, acting the detective—of the genial, Miss Marple variety.

Level seven: Cry.

TYPOLOGY OF BORES, CHORES, AND OTHER CONVERSATIONAL BEASTS

THE UNIVERSAL EXPERT   *Omniscientus caudex*

No sooner has the Universal Expert asked what you do than he is explaining how to do it better. Fussily furbished minds can lack sensitivity. At a hotel the sotto voce dining room was nightly kebabbed by an amateur food critic's commentary: "This is good," "This is not good," or "Almost good—but not quite," severally repeated, between each bite.

I met a quintessential UE at a dinner. He claimed deep knowledge of each passing shade of a topic and didn't hesitate to illuminate each dim corner. Toward the evening's premature end (no second helpings) he announced proudly, "The most fascinating conversations I've had lately were with complete strangers. Funny, isn't it?"

The host, a relative, smiled wanly. I pictured the man's friends: all strangers, innocent all.

There seem to be growing numbers of UEs; barricaded in industry jargon, gazing down from high pulpits of data, the frail body of their opinion studded with spurious fact. They may not mean to condescend, they may even be clever, but they're too daft to get along. Theirs is an infallible system for avoiding threatening meetings of equals, but as conversation, a cheat. Or worse. After the funeral of a doctor, fellow medics approached the bereaved family and, fishing for something to say, inquired about the sudden illness, then outlined in clinical detail exactly how she would have died.

Tactics: UEs are easily flattered, and easily led by questions. If he means well, you might joshingly suggest your interest in Albanian abattoirs is limited. If not, don't josh.
Pluses: A learning opportunity. Maybe.

14

SHUT-UP SHOP
On How to Wage a Word War

Remember those hopeless insults? Custard pies that boomeranged back, splat, on you?

When sorely tried, letting rip may feel deeply satisfying, but ultimately, like swearing or smacking a child, it's a loser's game. Far smarter is playwright Alan Bennett's policy:

> *I'm all in favour of free expression provided it's kept rigidly under control.*

There is an art to verbal sallies. While the right put-down is glorious, the wrong one is shaming. An ex-colleague once made the office cringe by boasting of her triumph over a youth who had been slow to admit selling her a grubby pair of shoes. "This is why you are a shop assistant," she told him, "and I am a manager." (She worked in publicity.)

If cruelty will show you up, showing you can't take it is little less damaging to prestige. The best policy is to rise above it, like Ivan Vasiliev, a dainty Belarussian ballet dancer known as "the boy who can fly," who confessed to measuring his stature daily,

> *because I have the complex of a small man! In the Bolshoi they have many tall men, so they're always telling me I'm small.*

Did he punch them?

No. I just do something that they could never do.

If flight is beyond you, try a sharp retort—not so much cutting as polished. When words are weapons, counterintelligence spares pain, and it saved lives in ancient Arabia. Before storming into battle, scimitars a-bristle, opposing tribes would send forth their best satirist for a poetic slanging match. This not only dictated morale, but often, if the loser suffered a rout, his tribe would slope off without further ado.

Similarly, the ideal rejoinder muzzles the opposition. I know: I suffered the stiletto of Yorkshire wit, William Hague. I was at Associated Newspapers, waiting for the elevator, when I glanced down into the atrium and spotted the young politician's gleaming pate. It was 1997, Labour had just swept to power, Hague aspired to be Tory party leader, and to that end, I assumed, he had come to woo the influential editor of the *Daily Mail.*

There was something mournful in how Hague sat, alone on the bench, no retinue in tow; like an old codger watching pigeons in the park, or a miscreant schoolboy awaiting a caning. Naturally, I pointed this out to passers-by.

"Look, there's William Hague. Isn't he *sad*?"

Finally the elevator came, stuffed with journalists. My friend Vince walked out.

"Hey," I said. "You see Hague sitting down there, all by himself? Tragic!"

Vince widened his eyes then fled. Puzzled, I entered the elevator.

A familiar voice spoke. "He's not alone anymore."

I, alone, laughed.

I cannot guarantee your sallies will attain Hague's élan, but a little effort can kick-start invective kung fu, and help avert that baleful *esprit d'escalier*, that sense of opportunity lost, which Mark Twain captured in his definition of repartee:

Something we think of twenty-four hours too late.

SHUT-UP SHOP

This is war, and begins with a protocol.

➳ Rule one: Ensure defense is necessary and justified

As the Spanish proverb has it, "Insults should be well avenged or well endured." Or you will end the fool.

If there is no outright aggression, first ignore it. If the offense persists, check that the offender intends to be as rude as he seems. Ask if he meant to say that. You could say he is making you feel uncomfortable. He may shut up.

But with a persistent big mouth or bully, prepare to fight. Your aim is twofold: to silence him and retain moral high ground.

Now consider tactics. Meet slur with slander, take the fight to the lowest verbal skill level, and not only may you cede the high ground, but you may also make it far too easy for your opponent to reply in kind.

➳ Rule two: A smart riposte raises verbal and intellectual stakes

For minimal effort, maximum effect, don't vituperate: cogitate, baffle and confuse, taking the battleground out of an opponent's comfort zone and attacking his mode of attack.

If you can be politer, wittier, or shift the focus from his target—preferably onto him—you will put him off balance. And if he looks foolish, his thrust only injures himself.

Here, in ascending difficulty, follow twenty tactics:

1. Do nothing: As the fourth of China's hallowed *Thirty-Six Strat-agems* has it: "Relax while the enemy exhausts himself." An approach for the supremely confident and powerful (think stoic Mum versus apoplectic toddler). Fold your arms and smile like you're being paid to.

2. Laugh.

3. Challenge: Flip back a challenge, forcing the attacker to defend his attack. Repetition will do: "Idiot!"—"Idiot?"

Elizabeth II walked to a photo shoot at Buckingham Palace with Annie Leibovitz of *Vanity Fair*, sizzling with irritation at having to don her fiddliest ceremonial fig (cumbersome Order of the Garter robes plus tiara).

"I'm not changing anything. I've done enough dressing like this, thank you very much," said the octogenarian to a flunky hefting her train.

Unfortunate then, that at the shoot Leibovitz asked Her Maj to remove the tiara to look "less dressy."

"Less dressy?" demanded the Queen. "What do you think this is?"

She did not need to add that Leibovitz had failed to grasp the import of her robes of state, hardly a casual ensemble one may dress down for a stroll with the corgis....

4. Embrace: Why expend energy on repulsing a strike when you can welcome it: "The pleasure is all mine" or "You're too kind." Can't swallow all their bile? Then share the wealth: "I know, we have much in common."

5. Quibble: Tackle the terms of your attacker's criticism, rather than the central charge: "Sure you wouldn't rather I parboiled my head?"

Another English queen, Elizabeth I, excelled at such parries.

Late into decrepitude, as death drew nigh, she took to lolling in her chamber on heaps of cushions, gawking at nothing, like a baked fish. Anxious courtier Sir Robert Cecil ventured to say: "Your Majesty, to content the people, you must go to bed."

"Little man, little man," she tutted. "The word 'must' is not used to princes."

6. Reject: Put the onus on the other person: "Prove it."

7. Deflect: Feign confusion. Refocus the problem: "Somebody upset you? Let me at them." "Don't put yourself down." "That's no way to talk about your wife." Or be slightly patronizing: "Watch out, someone might take that personally." "Poor you!"

8. Reverse: This might be called "hold up a mirror." I dedicate it to Griff Rhys Jones.

Life is tough for this millionaire comedian, TV host, and producer. He is always being recognized. As somebody else. Culture vulture Melvyn Bragg once introduced him to his daughter (his "biggest fan") as actor "John Sessions." More often he is mistaken for Hugh Laurie or Hugh Grant. And when he met the real Grant, the *Notting Hill* star asked him what he was up to "these days." Hours later Rhys Jones thought of a comeback: "Well, a hell of a lot more than you!"

But I'm glad he didn't use this peevish one-upper. Far mightier, if a mite arch, would have been a straight reversal: "The question, Hugh, is what are *you* up to?"

This tactic is very effective for blunting sly digs ("Well, fancy meeting you here!" "No, fancy meeting *you* here!") My favorite anti-compliment came from a woman who told me, "You look great! Isn't this bar's lighting wonderful. Soooo flattering."

"Yes, it is," I said (in my head, twenty-four hours later). "You look great!"

9. Killing kindness: Spleen feeds on outrage, so starve it: Stifle the abuser with niceness.

Recently I was at a house party, my first all-nighter in years. In the queue for the loo, a mad-eyed man glowered at me. So, in what I thought a cotton-candy, thoroughly amenable manner, I said something along the lines of "Gosh, it's ages since I was at a house party like this, into the small hours. I feel like a teenager!"

"What do you mean?" he demanded.

"Well what I said," I said. "Makes me feel young. Wonderful, isn't it?"

"That is an incredibly arrogant stance," he roared, and strode off.

Later I found myself next to him on the dance floor. He was chewing off a woman's ear. I heard the words "superficial" and "desperate."

"What's up?" I asked sweetly.

"This, all this," he cried. "It's so fake!"

"Oh, that's terrible. Why suffer? Don't do it to yourself. Go home. Now."

"You're absolutely right." He beamed, then asked me to join him.

10. Invert: Can you invert the jibe and find advantage in alleged weakness? An aging politician was attacked by a younger for his ripe years and sparse hairs. In reply, he promised not to exploit the advantage experience and wisdom gave him over the callow youth.

11. Prick the pompous: On the sharp end of a lecture? Dull it with a tease: "I'm afraid you can't reform me." A seventeenth-century lady of leisure ended a suitor's diatribe on the conduct of Philip II by asking:

"Why, sir, will you be wise from morning to night?"

12. Ironic praise: So there he is, face like a psychotic tomato, spitting ire. Take a deep breath and try this trick used by advocates in Ancient Greece: Eulogize a minor and unrelated aspect of the assailant, which should highlight the gravity of his crime, or at least disconcert him. Say: "That color suits you"; "You have wonderful teeth"; "You haven't aged a bit"; "Incredible tan. Gran Canaria?"; "Who told you you're sexy when you're livid?"

If he fulminates long and hard, emulate the Fat Man, Mr. Gutman in *The Maltese Falcon*, who swats off Sam Spade/Humphrey Bogart's cracks as if they were confetti. Say you admire a man who knows his own mind, remark how elegantly he slings his mud . . . or thank him: "It was considerate to let me know you had a problem, and in such detail."

13. Escape the moment: Try an ominous question. Say: "I wonder how you'll remember this conversation" or "Feel good now? Remember, feelings change." This one, overheard by party-talk collector Andrew Barrow, should pull a ranter up short: "Know what I'm thinking? Good job you don't, because it's very rude."

14. Mock the mocker: Conservative politician Ken Clarke once vaporized an opponent's tirade by scoffing, "The Right Honorable Gentleman sounds like a shopping list." (In their laughter, most MPs forgot the charge sheet.)

If someone is crude, you might venture: "I bet you can't say that backwards," "Now spell it," "And words of more than one syllable?", "I'd hate to meet you on a bad day," or "This isn't your first language?" Or offer "Another drink?"

15. Instruction: You might suggest, as Mr. Bennet does to his unmusical daughter Mary at the piano in *Pride and Prejudice*, that your assailant has delighted you long enough. So will he, kindly, shut it.

16. Take him on a journey (a stratagem for the strong): Play consequences, showing what his attitude will cost: flash a Clint Eastwood smile.

David Geffen, then a Warner Bros. exec, went up to Eastwood, after the studio screening of his new film *The Outlaw Josey Wales*. "I only want to suggest one thing. I think it would be better if it was twenty minutes shorter."

Eastwood thanked him. "I'm glad you took the time to see the picture, and I appreciate your comments. But why don't you study the picture some more and see if you have any more thoughts. When you do, give me a call over at Paramount."

"Why over at Paramount?" asked Geffen.

"Because that's where I'll be making my next movie."

"The picture is perfect," said Geffen. "I wouldn't change one frame. Thank you very much."

Eastwood said, "Thank *you*."

17. Distract: Create a sideshow. Mount a demi-attack (implied rather than outright lampoon). Ask, "You always wear your hair like that?", "Did you plan that outfit?", or "Your dentist still in practice?" Or say, "Don't let me keep you, your next drink's waiting" or "Perhaps you'd like to share these thoughts with your mistress. There she is."

18. Back to school: Be childish. Puerile comments are utterly disarming, because they lift calumny to a comic plane—with the happy possibility of fettering an assailant in giggles. And if he reacts badly, he appears worse than childish, humorless. So say: "Unnnh! I'm going to tell on you."

Or try for an absurd aspersion. For instance, the body slam. This stupefyingly infantile compound item pairs an aspect of the aggressor's physiognomy or personality with an unthreatening adjective to form an absurd epithet (alliterative or rhyming for extra impact). Such as: "yogurt-pants," "caterpillar-features," "cheese-brain," "merkin-mouth," "Brillo-brow," "dolcelatte-legs," "sensitive rhino," "subtle clod," "pocket prima donna," "shapely dolt," "spam-head," "parsnip-nose," "spud-u-like," "iguana-face," "Picasso-girl," "leech-lips," "george bush."

Puzzling similes and metaphors are fairly dumbfounding: "When you're emotional you look just like a boiled boot/electrocuted jelly/ wronged flamingo/rhubarb fool." Or label your opponent as some-thing small, dainty, or innately cuddly: "Okay, squirrel/koala/chicken wing/petal/mouse/wee thumb/diddle-diddle-dumpling/champ."

Or personify your assailant's mood: Say, "Sorry, Mr. Depress-ing/Mr. Moan/Professor Crosspatch, what seems to be the prob-lem?" or "Show mercy, Dr. Angry/Mr. Irate." Ask a daft question: "Have you curvature of the brain?" If you're fired up, issue a mock-heroic curse: "May your granny toss salad in Hades" or "May you give birth to humungous hedgehogs." Or a foolish invitation: "Go wild! Smash a grape!" or "Hence, distended dong of a disenfran-chised donkey."

For slurs with staying power, paint a picture. Sixteenth-century literary nitpicker Gabriel Harvey slandered rival Thomas Nashe as the "toadstool of the realm." Alan Bennett neutered a mon-strous uncle with a diminutive "Australian hamster." Popular Brit-ish buffoon-politician Boris Johnson dismissed rumors of adultery with the haunting "inverted pyramid of piffle." A pity the piffle proved true.

19. Bash the basher (not for use on the violent): Take it up a notch with a hecklerism. There are answers for these (in brackets), so handle with care.

"Why don't you take a long walk off a short pier?"   ("Age before beauty.")

"Here's the reason for birth control."   ("Daddy/Mummy!")

"Millions of sperm and they had to pick you!"   ("I'm a good egg.")

"I can recommend a psychiatrist."   (*"Quelle surprise"*; "Keep him busy?")

"Is your personality terminal?"   ("Yours is critical.")

"I bet you're a genius from the knees down."   ("And I have ankles"; "We can't all be heels.")

"I'm sure you're nicer than you look."   ("I'm sure you look nice in the dark.")

"Want to give me a piece of your mind? Can you spare it?"   ("I like giving to the less fortunate.")

20. The most deserved assault in the world: According to Kingsley Amis, Princess Margaret had a "habit of reminding people of her status when they venture to disagree with her in conversation." How sad.

There is no greater conversation-shirking cowardice than pulling rank. If asked "Do you know who I am?" use a boast gag:

"Elvis?"
"Memory trouble?"
"I'd rather not."
"No, who do you think you are?"
"Yes, but I'm prepared to overlook it."

RUDE ART

Excoriation has a riotous history. Here is an inspirational selection:

Putdowns

Beethoven to another composer:

> *I liked your opera. I think I will set it to music.*

Ninon de Lenclos, liberated lover, on toffy-nosed Marquis de Sévigné:

> *He has the heart of a cucumber fried in snow.*

Sydney Smith to garrulous historian Thomas Babington Macaulay:

> *You know, when I am gone, you will be sorry you never heard me speak.*

Woodrow Wilson on Warren Harding:

> *He has a bungalow mind.*

Poet Robert Burns, dissing an anonymous critic:

> *Thou eunuch of language ... thou pimp of gender ... murderous accoucheur of infant learning ... thou pickle-herring in the puppet show of nonsense [etc.]*

Model Jean Shrimpton, on being asked about her relationship with snapper David Bailey:

> *Sex has never been high on my list of priorities.*

Old Lancashire favorite (not for hot pots):

> *A waste of skin.*

Disraeli, converting dour political rival William Gladstone's virtue into a vice:

> *He has not a single redeeming defect.*

Retorts

Lewis Morris, poet: *It is a conspiracy of silence against me, a conspiracy of silence. What should I do?*
Oscar Wilde: *Join it.*

Oscar Wilde to painter James Whistler: *I wish I had said that.*
Whistler: *You will, Oscar, you will.*

Lord Sandwich to libertarian John Wilkes: *Sir, you will die either of the pox or on the gallows.*
Wilkes: *Depending on whether I embrace your mistress or your principles.*

Waiter in Annabel's nightclub to an elderly patron, upon being asked to help find false teeth, which had fallen onto the dance floor: *Certainly, sir. What color are they?*

Winston Churchill's contretemps with fellow politico Nancy Astor are notorious, but worth repeating.

Astor: *Winston, you are drunk, horribly drunk.*
Churchill: *And madam, you are ugly, terribly ugly, but in the morning I shall be sober.*

Astor: *If I were your wife I'd put poison in your coffee.*
Churchill: *If I were your husband, I'd drink it.*

Clare Boothe Luce, letting Dorothy Parker enter a door first: *Age before beauty.*
Parker: *And pearls before swine.*

William Wordsworth to Charles Lamb: *I believe that I could write like Shakespeare, if I had a mind to try it.*
Lamb: *Yes. Nothing wanting but the mind.*

Elizabeth I, greeting jester Pace on his return to court after brief banishment for being rude: *Come now, Pace, let us hear more of our faults.*
Pace: *No, madam, I never talk of what is discoursed by all the world.*

But perhaps the boldest retort, certainly the most learned, came from ninth-century Scottish scholar John Scotus, dining opposite the Emperor Charlemagne.

"What is there," asked the emperor, "between *Sottum* and *Scottum*?" (Meaning, "between a fool and a Scot.")

In a flash, the scholar replied, "The width of this table, sire."

TYPOLOGY OF BORES, CHORES, AND OTHER CONVERSATIONAL BEASTS

SAYING SORRY   *Coprophagy*

Jaded representatives of the world's press gathered in Vancouver for an up-close-and-personal at the dress rehearsal for the first show on the Spice Girls' comeback tour. Only, no girls. Then:

> *Suddenly, the five appeared in a flurry, like a flock of goldfinches alighting. They had come to offer their apologies for the delay, explain the frazzled condition of their nerves, promise that none of their costumes would fall apart, and hope we enjoyed our-selves. In a long lifetime of attending large concerts, I have never witnessed anything remotely as charming. Some might say this was the work of conniving minxes, but then they weren't there.*

Stunt or not, this keep 'em waiting, treat 'em nice maneuver is highly effective, building expectation, then earning honesty credits from an inconvenience of your own making. Not that I'm suggest-ing you contrive any such thing. My point is: What is lovelier than humility?

When you cause offense, how you acknowledge it, or don't, can deepen the injury. "Never apologize, never explain," said to be Elizabeth II's motto, might work for monarchs, but reticence is a cat's scratch from rudeness. So say sorry instead.

Or should we? The word is under attack. Novelist Sandra How-ard argued that it has become so devalued as to be meaningless. Certainly, often it prefaces self-justification or refusals to compro-mise: "Sorry, you had it coming," "Sorry, but it was your idea," "Sorry you feel that way, but we will go ahead." However, as these examples show, the word isn't at fault; the problem is tagging others onto it, demoting "sorry" to the prelude to a squabble over responsibility.

Apologizing is a finely balanced art, of judgment more than self-expression. Far from a negotiating point, "sorry" should be a final concession, and every self-exculpatory word you add puts more blame on you. If the story is complicated, explain what you think happened, showing your regret without accepting full responsibility. If the fault is yours, say so.

Yielding should steer dispute to an end. And bear in mind that rolling over too soon may be damaging. Charles I advised Lord Wentworth,

Never make a defence or an apology before you be accused.

But then, as history relates, had Charles bowed to his people, he might have kept his head.

15

ARE YOU RECEIVING ME?

On Stitching Conversation into Your Life

Why did ex-supermodel Christy Turlington cast her Black-Berry in bronze?

To save her marriage.

Adultery with an elfin communication console has yet to enter the statutes, but how many of us have not felt, like this lady, harassed by

> *the sudden violent irruptions of unnecessary possibilities into our daily lives, the incessant wrenching of the mind away from one subject and bringing it to bear upon another, the constant need of making decisions, albeit of the most trivial and unimportant kind. How is it possible under these conditions to think to any purpose? How can our rolling minds gather any moss?*

Lady Florence Bell, to give her full title—she of the absurd small-talk book—was bemoaning the invention of her namesake, Alexander Graham Bell, the telephone. She was writing in 1907. One century on, her objections have a sinisterly modern ring.

But unless you're a multimillionaire yogini or aristocratic aesthete, junking technology and retreating to the tranquillity of an eco-friendly yurt, while assistants take care of business, probably isn't an option. And would you wish it?

Modern conveniences free time to talk. Julie Burchill defended superstores for

> *the buzz of* getting things done quickly *so one can then move on and do something one loves, be it sex, conversation or lazing away the day on the sofa or the beach.*

All the same, what if home is a high-rise, or you don't own a car, or you live alone?

Conversation need not have a purpose to have a point. Unfortunately, the price of many of our conveniences is the loose change of socializing, with inconvenient long-term costs that sociologists, teachers, and psychologists are only beginning to count. Points of contact that once sewed the day together are being unpicked: The rise of electronic banking, the demise of post offices and corner shops, condemn many, especially the old and poor, to stay at home.

I don't deny technology makes life more kaleidoscopic. On the upside, with communication technology, fresh opportunities to make connections abound. I love that I can twitter to a guy in Albuquerque about Gorgonzola cheese. On the downside, it rarely encourages us to prize unalloyed moments together, and I would point out to Professor Martin Jones, author of *Feast: Why Humans Share Food,* that TV dinners bring families no nearer the conviviality of our grizzled ancestors, gawking at crackling fires, than the Victorian dining room did—at least, not in promoting talk; not unless there is only one TV set and no phone, stereo, Xbox, or computer to compete. However, in 2007, 40 percent of British under-fours had a TV in their bedroom....

Our gizmos make great diagnostic tools for measuring other people's crapness—even as they exacerbate or even invent it. "Why doesn't he pick up the phone?" we ask—without asking, "Why should he?" Who hasn't complained of the unanswered email, or wasted time waiting, checking, interpreting, speculating? How much likelier are we to screw up or offend if we've so many messages to process that they receive only cursory attention? How much worse if we lose traction with our most sophisticated communication medium, conversation?

Something must be done. Luckily, it need not be much. With a little effort, you can tame the attention eaters and draw conversation into the center of your life.

→ Rule one: Say hello
And good-bye, to everyone you have dealings with. In shops, queues, on buses, customer helplines ...

→ Rule two: Ration your attention
I applaud the sign at my liquor store:

> *Customers talking into mobile phones will not be served: it is rude!*

Ignore the phone, better still turn it off. The voice mail is there to be used.

Train people not to expect instant feedback. Only deal with emails and so on at a set time, and don't answer colleagues outside paid hours except in emergencies; even if they work abroad, they should respect your time zone. Otherwise your day will become 24/7, and you'll be so fried that soon everything will be an emergency—giving employers a more worth less.

→ Rule three: Think before text
According to a survey in 2008, seven out of ten Britons text or email when a face-to-face conversation is possible, believing this saves time. But does it? The average employee spends one-and-a-half to two hours a day panhandling streams of verbiage, and a

friend in industry is tormented by confusions that stem from trig-
ger-fingered coworkers' harebrained emails. Even email etiquette
gurus Will Schwalbe and David Shipley are susceptible:

> *By the time we had sorted out our timetable, three weeks had
> passed, lots of emails had been exchanged, and a question that
> should have taken one minute to answer had eaten up hours.
> We had come face to face with one of email's stealthiest charac-
> teristics: its ability to simulate forward motion. As Bob Geldof,
> the humanitarian rock musician, said, email is dangerous be-
> cause it gives us "a feeling of action"—even when nothing is
> happening.*

Before tapping the keys, ask: Is this the best way? Why agonize over
an annoying email if you can see your colleague?

Just for a week, use email and text solely to send documents
or schedule phone or face-to-face chat. How much time do you
free up?

↪ Rule four: Appreciate the voice

Computers screen a great deal, as a Ready4Life etiquette course
teacher told students:

> *You're losing so many of your social tools on email. We can't see
> the other person. Are they smiling? Are they angry? We just can't
> see it.*

Text is weak at expressing tone, the emotional dimension that
gives words much of their meaning. For this reason, the expressive
typography popular in the last communication revolution, the eigh-
teenth century—a Ballyhoo of Capital Letters, Zany—Punctuation,
and *emphatic italics*—is reborn in dastardly emoticons. :-(

But as Pebbles, seventeen, a Ready4Life student pointed out:

Everyone perceives them differently—like that sarcastic eye-rolling one.

Similarly, columnist Sophia Money-Coutts endured paroxysms over text message politesse: She asked me whether I signed off with a big kiss (X) or a little one (x). "Is there a distinction?" I asked, aghast that I might have committed romantic hari-kiri by sending big ones. "I'm not sure," she replied, "but isn't it all just so unclear?"

Indeed. There is the phone, in your hand. So, as David Gest would say, talk.

→ Rule five: Question your definition of problems

Things once central and convenient—family dinners were cheaper, playing with kids kept them quiet—have come to be seen as optional, or obnoxious. Far from pleasure, play is a problem to Scott Huskinson, vendor of Tadpole (rubber cases that turn iPods into toys):

> *I thought how parents all over the world use in-car DVD players, but there's no solution for entertaining kids once you leave the car.*

The concept of "quality time" (invented in 1970s corporate America, gaining general currency in the cash-and-grab culture of the 1980s) implies that we sense much of it is impoverished. But such language is also a license to dole it out grudgingly, as if to convince us it is proper that most hours should be distracted, second best, or negligible; a warrant to neglect that we like to imagine is benign. Why else are TVs in toddlers' bedrooms, DVD screens in backs of car seats, and teddies with computer games in their bellies? Today's kids not only play with toys but expect them to interact. Does this help them interact with one another? I lost a year to a

Donkey Kong game, in the playground, with a similarly fixated Mario Bros. fan. Her name? No idea. But I remember the girls at dance club.

Does your attention-seeking teenager have a point? Is that chore a joy in disguise—something satisfying to do while catching up with someone you like? I was never convinced by invitations to "Come paint my flat—we'll have beers, it'll be fun!" or "Build dry-stone walls in beautiful Cumbria—only £699!" But I'm prepared to rethink.

↪ Rule six: Spring-clean routines

Anyone can clear space in routines for conversation. Mealtimes, bathtimes, relaxation, hobbies—all potential shared times. Coordinate timetables; be in the same room. Turn off the central heating. If you can, leave the car, walk and, yes, shop together. Want to spare the other person the trouble? If you're trogging around the supermarket while she watches TV, you're depriving her of quality interaction. The best way to unwind, and create distance from stresses and strains, is to talk and put them into perspective.

And be hospitable. Invite someone to tea, coffee. These rituals once paced out the day, but have been downgraded to snacks grazed on the hoof, depleting their soul food: talk. As writer Bee Wilson points out, they're kinder to host and guest:

> *"We must have you round to dinner" seems to slip inevitably out of one's mouth as soon as a friendship reaches a certain stage. But how much more fun life would be, for lots of reasons, if we had people round for afternoon tea instead.*
>
> *The bliss of tea is that it brings no expectations.*

A slice of toast will do. Less fuss, less outlay, more fun for you.

→ Rule seven: Make plans

Why fix to meet if we can improvise on the hoof?

Because you might not get around to it. Flexibility makes us flaky, and many city friends see each other less than out-of-towners because they feel less urgency about keeping in contact. Don't settle for catch-ups by phone or email, which can deceive us that we're in touch at the same time as they displace direct encounters. Be a stickler, buy a pocket calendar, fill it with indelible arrangements.

→ Rule eight: Make it matter

Once you're with them, leave the phone alone.

→ Rule nine: Relish silence

Inevitably time feels impoverished, experience intangible, if we don't notice spending it. Fast for a day: no TV, computer, music, PlayStation, film. Unplug the toys, plug in, be a tourist in your world, and you'll find there is no silence: too much is going on.

What will you see? Whom will you meet? Perhaps you'll have a conversation.

→ Rule ten: You tell me

www.catherineblyth.com

CONVERSATION SURVIVAL KIT

Nervous? Prepare and travel light. Remember five points:

1. **Attention:** It's not about you: Prepare to listen. Watch others' faces, the clock by which to measure turns on the floor.

2. *Imagination:* Every utterance contains the seeds for further discussion (except, possibly, "Fine").
3. *Enthusiasm:* The fount of inspiration.
4. *Focus pull:* Direct conversation to the other person's interests: You'll soon find what interests you about him.
5. *Ingredients:* Review topics as you might before a news quiz. One headline issue, one trivial, one gossipy.

There is no shortage of communication, but is it not telling that globalization has created Globish, a nuance-stunted Anglo-lingo spreading like ivy across the globe, which contains only fifteen hundred words? Its codifier Jean-Paul Nerriere, once of IBM, hymns its limits:

> *It is designed for trivial efficiency, always, everywhere, with everyone. . . . One thing you never do in Globish is tell a joke.*

Guidelines include: Repeat yourself, avoid metaphors and colorful expressions, and keep sentences short. However, with so few words to play with, this isn't always possible (rather than "siblings" you must say "the other children of my mother and father"). Conversation friendly it is not.

So much of communication transcends language that conversation's telepathy—seeing behind screens; hearing what is told, not what is said—is invaluable. Friendships flower from such tiny prompts; the twitch of a mouth, a shared glance—all the unsaid, perhaps unsayable things. Henry James wrote:

> *Small children have many more perceptions than they have terms to translate them; their vision is at any moment much richer, their apprehension even constantly stronger, than their prompt, their at all producible, vocabulary.*

It's true of us all. But even remote encounters make life better.

One day I called my bank to check a credit. A singsong voice said it had arrived, then perhaps she asked what the money was for; anyway, somehow we began talking about books and exchanged recommendations. I asked where she was based and she said Wales.

"Out of the window I can only see green. Nothing else. We're surrounded by trees," she said. "Where are you?"

I described my London street, said how lucky she was.

"Yes, it's beautiful." She sighed. "But it's blooming boring. That's why I read."

And we laughed.

In 1956, Dorothy Parker said: "Civilization is coming to an end, you understand."

But ever since it was thought of, civilization has been failing: that is why we work at it.

Conversation's finer points may be lost without our world tottering. Still, as communication, it is unimprovable. Of all arts the oldest and most captivating, it is also the easiest, free to all. As prices soar, and time shrinks, and space compacts, it is one luxury that costs nothing. Protect it, prioritize it, and reap the wealth of a companionable, convivial life.

Let conversation bring you the world.

P.S.

Are you fond of farewells? Is the person with you rather less so?

Shoving to the exit, or dawdling, a hint of other business hanging like a bad smell, is awkward. But there are gentle ways to usher conversation to its close.

First, choose a line or topic that will suggest this is the end, my friend:

Arrangements: Talk of the Next rings the knell for Now.
Any statement starting "Finally," "Lastly": Suggests an agenda is nigh complete.
Troubles: Having plumbed the depths, re-ascending to froth is somehow psychologically impossible.
Satisfied customer: A labeling comment to convey a job has been ticked off the list: "Well, I just wanted to check everything was okay."
Farewell by implication: Pre-goodbye goodbyes: passing regards to the wife, etc. (Further reason to remember the personal details of time-guzzling clients and employees.)
Past tense: To kill the Now without committing to future encounters, say "It was great seeing you again," "This was fun." Or ask,

"Was there anything else?" "Now what did I mean to tell you? No, no, it's gone."

Time's wingèd chariot hurrying near: That oh-so-pressing world you must be getting on with, or the missus will kill you, or the shops will have run out of Christmas trees, or the kids will be starving ...

Rescue remedy: Is a loved one being mumbled in the maw of a bore? Are you tired? Be direct without offending the third party by implying that your loved one is reluctant to go, but is inadvertently imposing on you.

"Dear one, we must leave now"; "I'm sorry, but I'm going to have to drag you off—early start"; "The babysitter?"; or this treat, overheard: "David, you're liable to capsize any moment!"

Mustn't keep you: To suggest that you're halting the other person's day is polite, but be warned, use repeatedly and it gains a tinct of condescension (so you're busy: so say so).

Now an exchange of verbal bows to ensure both parties agree our work is done.

ME: Well?
YOU: Well.
ME: So!
YOU: So.
ME: Okay then!
YOU: Okay.
ME: Bye.
YOU: By the way ...

Can you hear the questioning uplift in the first speaker, the downbeat of the second? In effect, you are engineers, running through final items before clearing the plane for takeoff ("Check?" asks Engineer One; "Check," confirms Engineer Two).

Similar exchanges occur to tread water when a conversation stalls. They're all opportunities: to raise another subject or prize open an exit. Just wait for a "So ...," introduce a turning-point word—"well," "listen," or "now"—then say it's been great talking, but, sadly, you must go. . . .

If ever you wonder "Why are we still talking?" it is time to say how much you have enjoyed it, then good-bye. A little thing, like hello, it joins the dots of our increasingly dotty lives.

Knowing when to leave, wrote salon moralist, La Bruyère, is "an art that vain men rarely acquire."

Like the art of conversation, you cannot attain it in vain.

Goodbye.

ACKNOWLEDGMENTS

This book has enjoyed indecent amounts of luck. Here are some of the reasons why.

First thanks must go to my magnificent agent, Eugenie Furniss, out of whose conversation the idea sprang, and to my inspiring editors, Eleanor Birne, Erin Moore, and Helen Hawksfield. I'm grateful to all at John Murray, especially Nikki Barrow, Sara Marafini, Roland Phillips, James Spackman, and the other unseen hands who helped usher this book to the shelves; to Bill Shinker, Jessica Sindler, Amanda Walker, Lisa Johnson, Carrie Swetonic, and the rest of the Gotham team; to William Morris, in particular Shana Kelly, Rowan Lawton, and Jay Mandel; and to Henryk Hetflaisz and Remy Blumenfeld, who live in the realm of the possible and make it contagious.

Many individuals provided help and guidance, including: Emily Anderson, Jessica Axe, the late Shereen Baig, Nicola Barr, Andrew Barrow, Vick Beasley, Chris Blackhurst, Heidi Blyth, Jenny Blyth, Stephen Blyth, Vivian Blyth, Caroline Bondy, the staff of the British Library, Helen Burdock, Jackie Burdock, Emily Charkin, Kay Chung, Pete Clark, Vin De Silva, Andrea di Robilant, John Elliott, Theo Fairley, Max Gadney, the late Frances Gillam, Jane Gillam, the late Michael Gillam, Vince Graff, Clare Grafik, Louise Haines, Louise Harding, Carolyn Hart, Robin Harvie, Emily Hayward, Alice Horton, James Hughes-Onslow, Virginia Ironside,

Gillian Johnson, Alex Key, Irma Kurtz, Leonard Lewis, James Lewisohn, Michael Mack, Oliver Mack, Helen Marshall, Francesca Maurice-Williams, Harriet Maurice-Williams (a fine classicist whose help I corrupted), Walter Meierjohan, the staff of the North Kensington Library, Emma Parry, David Patterson, Chrystalla Peleties, Harry Phibbs, Gerrie Pitt, Dominic Prince, Rose Prince, Robert Procopé, James Ribbans, Andrea Rossini, Laetitia Rutherford, Professor Sophie Scott, Amanda Shakespeare, Christopher Shakespeare, Francesca Shakespeare, John Shakespeare, Lalage Shakespeare, Nicholas Shakespeare, Matthew Sturgis, Ben Summerskill, Petra Tauscher, Anne Turner, Dominic Turner, Susan Urquhart, Edward Venning, Sarah Venning, Marilyn Warnick, John Williams, Hywel Williams, Andrew Wilson, Bee Wilson, Katie Wood, Beverly Yong, Toby Young.

Not forgetting what is owed to some wonderful teachers: Brenda Atkinson, Dick Clarke, Gary French, John Glover, Dr. Paul Hartle, Hazel Hill, Dr. and Dr. Holding, Neil Jarvis, Tom Morris, Dr. Jonathan Smith, and most of all, Professor Germaine Greer.

Studying conversation can feel like chasing butterflies, but some ace netters eased my task. Thanks to the interviewers, reporters, and analysts who catch idiosyncrasies on the wing.

And lastly, to my husband, Sebastian Shakespeare, who has had enough conversations about conversation to be forgiven for wishing no more, but is still talking to me.

SELECT BIBLIOGRAPHY

Aitchison, Jean. *The Articulate Mammal.* London: Routledge, 1998.

Andreae, Simon. *Anatomy of Desire.* London: Little, Brown, 1998.

Arendt, Hannah. *The Human Condition.* Chicago: University of Chicago Press, 1998.

Aristotle. *The Art of Rhetoric.* London: Penguin, 1991.

Bacon, Francis. *The Essays.* London: Penguin, 1985.

Belot, Michèle, and Marco Francesconi. *Can Anyone Be "The One"?* London: Centre for Economic Policy Research, 2006.

Brown, John Seely, and Paul Duguid. *The Social Life of Information.* Boston: Harvard University Press, 2000.

Brownell, Judi. *Building Active Listening Skills.* New Jersey: Prentice Hall, 1986.

Buss, David M. *The Evolution of Desire.* New York: Basic Books, 2003.

C., S. *The Art of Complaisance.* London: John Starkey, 1673.

Casanova, Giacomo. *The Story of My Life.* London: Penguin, 2001.

Casey, Neil. *Social Organisation of Topic in Natural Conversation.* Plymouth: Plymouth Polytechnic, 1981.

Castiglione, Baldesar. *The Book of the Courtier.* London: Penguin, 2003.

Cicero, Marcus Tullius. *On Obligations.* Oxford: Oxford University Press, 2000.

Collier, Jane. *An Essay on the Art of Ingeniously Tormenting.* Oxford: Oxford World's Classics, 2006.

Correll, Conway Linda. *Brainstorming Reinvented.* London: Response Books, 2004.

Craveri, Benedetta. *The Age of Conversation.* New York: New York Review of Books, 2005.

Dean, Greg. *Step by Step to Stand-up Comedy.* Portsmouth: Heinemann, 2000.

Elyot, Sir Thomas. *The Book of the Governor.* London: J. M. Dent, 1962.

Fisher, Roger, William Ury, and Bruce Patton. *Getting to Yes.* London: Arrow Books, 1987.

Goldstein, Noah J., Steve J. Martin, and Robert B. Cialdini. *Yes!* London: Profile Books, 2007.

Gourevitch, Philip, ed. *The Paris Review Interviews, I.* Edinburgh: Canongate, 2006.

Gristwood, Sarah. *Elizabeth and Leicester.* London: Bantam Press, 2007.

Guazzo, Stefano. *Civile Conversation.* London: Constable, 1925.

Hickman, Katie. *Courtesans.* London: Harper Perennial, 2004.

Hirstein, William. *Brain Fiction.* Cambridge: MIT Press, 2005.

Humphrey, Nicholas. *Seeing Red.* Cambridge: Harvard University Press, 2006.

Hunt, Leigh. *Table-Talk.* London: Smith, Elder, & Co, 1902.

Irwin, Robert, ed. *The Penguin Anthology of Classical Arabic Literature.* London: Penguin Classics, 2006.

Karpf, Anne. *The Human Voice.* London: Bloomsbury, 2006.

Leech, Geoffrey N. *Principles of Pragmatics.* London: Longman, 1983.

Levinson, Dr. Stephen C. *Pragmatics*. Cambridge: Cambridge University Press, 1983.

Levinson, Dr. Stephen C., and Dr. M. L. Owen. "Topic Organisation in Conversation," 6810/2. London: Social Science Research Council, 1981.

Macdonald, Scot. *Propaganda and Information Warfare in the Twenty-First Century*. London: Routledge, 2007.

Malloch, Stephen N. "Mothers and infants and communicative musicality." *Musicae Scientiae* (Liège: ESCOM, 2000).

Masuda, Sayo. *Autobiography of a Geisha*. London: Vintage, 2004.

Mercer, Neil. *Words and Minds*. London: Routledge, 2000.

Miller, Stephen. *Conversation*. New Haven: Yale University Press, 2006.

Monaghan, Leila, and Jane E. Goodman, eds. *A Cultural Approach to Interpersonal Communication*. Oxford: Blackwell Publishing, 2007.

Monmouth, Geoffrey of. *The History of the Kings of Britain*. London: Penguin, 1966.

Morgan, John. *Debrett's New Guide to Etiquette & Modern Manners*. London: Headline, 1999.

Nilsen, Don L. F. *Humor Scholarship*. London: Greenwood Press, 1993.

O'Connell, Sanjida. *Mindreading*. London: Heinemann, 1997.

Pinker, Steven. *The Language Instinct*. London: Penguin, 1995.

Poole, Steven. *Unspeak*. London: Abacus, 2007.

Provine, Robert R. *Laughter*. London: Faber and Faber, 2000.

Ridley, Matt. *The Origins of Virtue*. London: Penguin, 1996.

Romaine, Suzanne. *Language in Society*. Oxford: Oxford University Press, 1994.

Rovine, Harvey. *Silence in Shakespeare*. Michigan: UMI Research Press, 1987.

Runciman, W. G. *The Social Animal.* London: HarperCollins, 1998.

Schwabe, Kerstin, and Susanne Winkler, eds. *On Information Structure, Meaning and Form.* Amsterdam: John Benjamins, 2007.

Shapiro, James. *1599.* London: Faber and Faber, 2005.

Shepherd, Margaret. *The Art of Civilized Conversation.* New York: Broadway Books, 2006.

Shōnagon, Sei. *The Pillow Book.* London: Penguin, 2006.

Stevenson, Robert Louis. *Memories and Portraits.* London: Chatto and Windus, 1900.

Stewart, Rory. *The Places in Between.* London: Picador, 2005.

Tannen, Deborah. *Conversational Style.* Oxford: Oxford University Press, 2005.

Tannen, Deborah, and Muriel Saville-Troike, ed. *Perspectives on Silence.* New Jersey: Ablex Publishing, 1985.

Van der Molen, Henk T., and Yvonne H.Gramsbergen-Hoogland. *Communication in Organizations.* Hove: Psychology Press, 2005.

Vasari, Giorgio. *The Lives of the Artists.* Oxford: Oxford World's Classics, 1998.

Westen, Drew. *The Political Brain.* New York: PublicAffairs, 2007.

Williams, Justin H. G. "Copying strategies by people with autistic spectrum disorder," in *Imitation and Social Learning in Robots, Humans and Animals.* Cambridge: Cambridge University Press, 2007.